*The French Revolution
in Global Perspective*

The French Revolution in global Perspective

Edited by

SUZANNE DESAN, LYNN HUNT,

and WILLIAM MAX NELSON

CORNELL UNIVERSITY PRESS   *Ithaca & London*

An abridged version of chapter 11, "Every Revolution Is a War of Independence," by Pierre Serna, trans. Alexis Pernsteiner, was published as "Toute révolution est guerre d'indépendance," in Jean-Luc Chappey et al., *Pour quoi faire la revolution?* (Marseille: Editiones Agone, 2012), 19–49.

First published 2013 by Cornell University Press
First printing, Cornell Paperbacks, 2013
Printed in the United States of America

Library of Congress Cataloging-in-Publication Data

The French Revolution in global perspective / edited by Suzanne Desan, Lynn Hunt, and William Max Nelson.
    p. cm.
    Includes bibliographical references and index.
    ISBN 978-0-8014-5096-9 (cloth: alk. paper) — ISBN 978-0-8014-7868-0 (pbk.: alk. paper)
    1. France—History—Revolution, 1789–1799—Congresses. 2. France—Foreign relations—1789–1815—Congresses. 3. Globalization—Political aspects—France—History—18th century—Congresses. I. Desan, Suzanne, 1957– II. Hunt, Lynn, 1945– III. Nelson, William Max, 1976–
    DC157.F74 2013
    944.04—dc23   2012033632

Cornell University Press strives to use environmentally responsible suppliers and materials to the fullest extent possible in the publishing of its books. Such materials include vegetable-based, low-VOC inks and acid-free papers that are recycled, totally chlorine-free, or partly composed of nonwood fibers. For further information, visit our website at www.cornellpress.cornell.edu.

Cloth printing   10 9 8 7 6 5 4 3 2 1
Paperback printing   10 9 8 7 6 5 4 3 2 1

Contents

Acknowledgments

Most of the chapters in this volume were first presented as conference papers at the 2011 meeting of the Consortium on the Revolutionary Era in Tallahassee, Florida. We would like to thank Rafe Blaufarb and the organizers of the meeting for accepting our panel proposal and providing us an ideal venue to discuss and develop the project. We would also like to thank John Ackerman and Cornell University Press for being so supportive of this project from the beginning and helping us turn the conference papers into an edited volume. We had the good fortune of receiving exceptionally good feedback, criticism, and advice from the Press's anonymous readers. William Nelson would like to thank the Institute for Historical Studies at the University of Texas at Austin where he was a fellow during the development of this volume.

The French Revolution
in Global Perspective

Introduction

SUZANNE DESAN,
LYNN HUNT, AND
WILLIAM MAX NELSON

The French Revolution had an undeniable global impact. As the early nineteenth-century German philosopher G. W. F. Hegel wrote, it was "World-Historical," meaning that it changed the history of the entire world.[1] The French Revolution galvanized and divided populations across Europe and the Americas, transformed the map of Europe through the creation of "sister republics," and led to slave revolution in Saint-Domingue (Haiti) and the first abolition of slavery in 1793–94. Its continuing wars upset the status quo in Egypt and other parts of Africa, India, and ultimately even places as distant as Java. Yet, despite the recent interest in global or transnational history, the Revolution in France itself has been analyzed in largely national terms. It might have reshaped the world outside France, but its own causes and processes have been explained by reference to French factors. This volume aims to show how global factors shaped the French Revolution in France and helped make it "world-historical."

We begin, then, with a paradox. From 1789 onward, participants, observers, and commentators alike considered the French Revolution a global event, yet they almost never sought global causes for it. In 1790, for example, the Anglo-Irish politician and writer Edmund Burke claimed: "All circumstances taken together, the French Revolution is the most astonishing that has hitherto happened in the world."[2] The most influential interpreters of the French Revolution in the nineteenth century, Karl Marx and Alexis de Tocqueville, likewise recognized the global significance of the French Revolution. For Marx, the Revolution of 1789 marked a decisive shift in the class struggles that shaped every society: the capitalist bourgeoisie overthrew the aristocracy and with it feudal society, inaugurating the conflicts between manufacturers and workers that would characterize modern society.[3] Tocqueville considered the French

Revolution a pivotal moment in the modern destruction of aristocracy and its replacement with unstable and potentially despotic forms of democracy.[4] Yet all of its interpreters sought the causes of the French Revolution itself in developments within France. This was particularly surprising of Tocqueville, since he was deeply involved in the colonial politics of his day and believed that "the physiognomy of governments can be best detected in their colonies." In *The Old Régime and the French Revolution*, he claimed that "the administrative centralization of the old régime can be best judged in Canada," and while his interpretation of the French Revolution revolved around the issue of administrative centralization, he relegated this observation to a note at the end of the book.[5]

More recently, historians have focused in new ways on the international dimensions of the French Revolution. Many scholars have asked how the French Revolution had an impact abroad and how various peoples—in the Caribbean, in the Americas, in Europe—interacted with the French Revolution to forge their own revolutionary traditions.[6] For example, rebel slaves in the Caribbean fused revolutionary ideology with West African military expertise and Caribbean cultural practices to demand emancipation. Already in 1789, local officials in Martinique received an anonymous threat signed "we the Negroes [nous, Nègres]" that declared: "We know that we are free and that you accept that rebellious people resist the orders of the King. . . . We will die for this liberty; we want it and we mean to gain it at whatever price."[7] Analysis of the diffusion, appropriation, and transformation of French revolutionary culture has contributed powerfully to our understanding of the revolutionary era, but it has only just begun to provoke questions about the impact of these international movements in France.

Two different models have been used in recent years to connect the French Revolution to broader developments: the Atlantic world and the global imperial crisis of the eighteenth century. Historians who emphasize shared developments in the Atlantic world have drawn attention to the circulation of ideas, goods, and people around the Atlantic Ocean. It is no exaggeration to say that scholarship on the French colonies, especially Saint-Domingue, the richest slave colony in the Caribbean, has reframed the field of French revolutionary studies.[8] The Caribbean colonies provided an important source of revenue for France, exports from them (sugar, coffee, cotton, indigo, tobacco) stimulated new consumer demands in France, and the great slave revolt of 1791 in Saint-Domingue not only led to the abolition of slavery and the eventual establishment of the first state founded by former slaves (Haiti) but also transformed France's foreign policy and imperial designs. The slave trade, the slave economy, and slave rebellions during the French Revolution had hardly figured in accounts of the French Revolution in the past. Now they cannot be ignored. France's economy, social structure, culture, and politics were shaped by its participation in the wider Atlantic world.

The emphasis on the colonies, slavery, and circulation within the Atlantic world expanded in transformative ways on the notion of "Atlantic Revolutions," which was first developed in the 1950s by R. R. Palmer and Jacques Godechot. Palmer and Godechot argued that the French Revolution should be seen as part of a broader Atlantic movement that included the American Revolution, British radicalism, and the Dutch, Belgian, Swiss, and even Polish revolts as well as the French Revolution.[9] Many historians in France rejected this "Atlantic thesis"; some denounced what they saw as an effort to use history in an ideological way to prop up the Atlantic Alliance of the Cold War (a charge Palmer and Godechot vehemently denied), while others disliked the very idea that other, lesser revolts could be compared to the French Revolution.[10] Current scholars of the Atlantic world target a different weakness in Palmer and Godechot's Atlantic framework: its failure to address slavery or the colonies in the Caribbean.

However, even this new, expanded Atlantic model is too constrained for understanding the revolutionary dynamics of this era. In the eighteenth century commerce, finance, and colonization took place in a global, and not just Atlantic, realm. The preconditions of revolution in France must therefore be sought on that more expansive scale. During the Revolution itself, France's cultural dialogue and colonial ambitions encompassed areas, notably places such as Italy, India, and Egypt, that do not fit in the Atlantic framework. Finally, since the French revolutionaries conceived their own project as "universal," they necessarily thought of themselves as painting on a worldwide canvas. Admittedly, they turned first to Europe and then to the Americas before including other parts of the globe, but their vision of global significance is nonetheless crucial to the Revolution's claim to legitimacy, its crusading mentality, and the ties between ideology and empire building.

The second major model of explanation—the global imperial crisis of the eighteenth century—embraces a wider geographic frame. In this model, expensive warfare and competition caused all the European colonizing nations, Britain and Spain as well as France, to organize, tax, and reform in ways that stirred up social and political opposition. Metropole nations facing revolution often reinvented and revitalized empire in new ways.[11] For example, Britain may have lost the American colonies, but in this same era the British Empire emerged as a more flexible and aggressive power in other parts of the world, such as India, Egypt, Java, and southern Africa. And, no longer a colony, the new United States pursued aggressive imperial expansion of its own.[12] This interpretive framework sees the period of 1760–1840 more as an era of "imperial revolutions" than as the "age of democratic revolution."[13] In this model, warfare frequently played a larger role than did revolutionary ideas in producing key changes, such as slave emancipation.[14]

Using the global crisis approach, Christopher Bayly in particular has broadened our understanding of the revolutionary age beyond Europe and the Atlantic world by examining "conjunctural revolutions" that grew out of imperial crisis, warfare, and diverse universalizing ideologies, such as the Buddhist millenarian movement against the Qing in China, or the Islamic purist revolt of the Wahhabis in Saudi Arabia against the Ottomans. Bayly also underlines the complex interactions across the globe between local practices and transnational ideologies of rights and sovereignty. In the "fragile 'age of equipoise'" after the revolutionary era, in many cases, the state—especially the colonial state—emerged strengthened and invigorated.[15]

This volume suggests a third model that emphasizes France's participation in early modern globalization. Rather than underlining the similarities in France's response to a more general crisis of empire, our approach draws attention to the specifically French responses to the processes of globalization. It does so in the hopes of explaining why the French Revolution, among all the other political upheavals of the time, had such far-reaching effects, not only in France but around the world. Globalization is a notoriously loose term, and scholars disagree vehemently about its definition and its chronology.[16] Indeed, most of the contributors to this volume avoid using the term because its mere mention seems to require long digressions on definitions and possible pitfalls. Nonetheless, taken together, the chapters in this volume show that the causes, internal dynamics, and consequences of the French Revolution all grew out of France's increasing participation in processes of globalization. In particular, they demonstrate that republican political innovations emerged from international processes. The volume builds on the recent explosion of work on colonization, the international circulation of ideas, and the burgeoning global economy to explore how these factors shaped the revolutionary dynamic in France, and in turn, how the French Revolution left its stamp on colonial practices and local experiments in politics far beyond the hexagon.

Globalization is the process of increasing interconnections across the globe. Hardly confined to economic and colonial connections, it can also take place in the realms of migration, disease, communications, war, political culture, and ideas. While some commentators want to limit globalization as a concept to developments since the middle of the nineteenth century, we favor a longer history in which events in France in 1789–1815 play a special role. The Seven Years' War of the mid-eighteenth century (1756–63) was the first European war to take place on a worldwide stage, as fighting raged in Europe, North America, the Caribbean, West Africa, India, and the Philippines. From then on, no European imperial power could deny that military and naval might, colonial implantation, and trade were intertwined. The tensions created by the need to protect the colonial empire, increase trade, borrow more money, and build up the navy helped cause the French Revolution, and as the Revolution took political, cultural, and economic forms never previously seen, it transformed the Atlantic world, the nature of imperial rivalries, and political expectations in central and southern Europe, Egypt, Latin America, and parts of Asia.

The chapters in part 1 of this volume show that the French Revolution cannot be explained without reference to French participation in increasingly globalized circuits of economic exchange and worldwide geopolitical competition, in particular with Great Britain, France's leading colonial rival. These early modern forms of global economic circulation and geopolitical competition opened the door to new conceptions of commerce, such as free trade, and to the intensified circulation of political ideas, such as republicanism.[17] During the Revolution itself, events continued to be informed by France's insertion in global economic, political, and intellectual networks. As the chapters in part 2 demonstrate, cosmopolitanism, the belief in regeneration, abolitionism, and feminism all had roots in the transnational and usually trans-Atlantic exchange of ideas and practices. As these ideas fed into the French republican aspiration to enunciate universal claims about all humankind, they inevitably had an even broader and increasingly global resonance that continues in many ways right down to the present. The chapters in part 3 show how the new global geopolitics of republicanism and empire actually worked on the ground in three very different sites. Thus, even when not named as such, globalization features prominently in all the chapters.

This global approach offers the opportunity to overcome the current impasse in interpretations of the French Revolution. In the 1950s, 1960s, and 1970s many historians, especially those influenced by Marxism, sought to explain the French Revolution in social and economic terms (dissatisfaction of the peasantry, middle-class resentment of nobles, etc.). In the 1980s and 1990s, critics insisted that a social or socioeconomic interpretation, and especially a Marxist one, could not explain the most important developments, such as the emergence of the Terror or the failure to establish an enduring republic. Under the influence of this criticism, historians focused more attention on short-term politics, ideology, and cultural factors. Without abandoning the political and cultural emphasis, a global framework brings back social and economic factors from a new angle. Building on recent work on the globalizing economy, several of the chapters in this volume ask how international commercial dynamics—the influx of foreign products such as tobacco and textiles, the speculation in money and debt instruments, and Anglo-French competition over trade and empire—interacted with French state building and the fiscal choices of the crown to bring about the Revolution and shape its dynamics. With a global approach, it is not necessary to choose between culture, ideology, and politics on the one side and social structures and economic trends on the other. In fact, the promise of a global approach is the same as its challenge: to see the connections between seemingly disparate historical elements and forces, bringing them together in a way that brings their features into better focus and provides us with a clearer picture of their interactive influence.

The influence of globalization is especially evident in the chapters in part 1 on the origins of the Revolution. In chapter 1, Michael Kwass shows how the regime's efforts to regulate products of global trade—New World tobacco and Indian calicos—inadvertently stimulated the development of a huge underground economy of smuggling, complete with armed gangs. The government's attempts to repress these gangs created resentment not only in the popular classes but also among elites, who were repulsed by the heavy-handedness of royal officials. In reaction the elites pushed for far-reaching reforms. In this way, global trade translated directly into armed resistance and political opposition.

Underlining the links between Indian Ocean commerce, African slave trading, colonial trade in the Caribbean, and French participation in the Spanish carrying trade, Lynn Hunt argues in chapter 2 that the French monarchy confronted a fiscal crisis not because it faced high deficits but rather because it lost control of its finances during a period of increasing globalization. Interconnections were intensifying in world trade, in the international market for capital, and in the banking sector more generally. Foreign bankers offered the French crown access to foreign capital and a reprieve from necessary fiscal reforms, but in the end the result was revolution instead of reform.

Charles Walton focuses his analysis in chapter 3 on one important sector of France's global trade, commercial relations with France's main colonial rival, Great Britain. In a stunning reversal of its usual embrace of protectionism, the French government signed a free trade treaty with Great Britain in 1786. Called the Eden Treaty after the British negotiator William Eden, its results turned out to be anything but Edenic. Many indigenous French industries lost out to British competition, creating yet another group of disgruntled subjects, from textile workers to wholesale merchants. Free trade had revolutionary effects, but not those intended by the treaty's negotiators.

Kwass, Hunt, and Walton all tie their analysis of economic matters to the cultural criticism of politics on the eve of the Revolution. If the economic results of the Eden Treaty spurred merchants and manufacturers to demand political representation and participation in policymaking, the state monopoly on consumer goods provoked Enlightenment thinkers to castigate royal repression and call for the overhaul of fiscal and economic policies at the heart of the Old Regime state. Likewise, Hunt argues that pamphlet warfare over speculation and the crown's participation in this frenzy played a key role in bringing down the government in 1789. As an observer of popular resistance commented in 1788, people should "stop accusing an 'ignorant' public of getting worked up without knowing why."[18] On the eve of Revolution, France's global policies, finances, and commercial interactions hatched multiple reasons for voicing discontent and contributed directly to a sea change in public political culture.

Focusing more directly on the intellectual origins of Revolution in chapter 4, Andrew Jainchill demonstrates how republicanism—a significant strand within the growing political ferment—was given new life by the transnational circulation of ideas and people. The revocation of the Edict of Nantes in 1685 engendered a Huguenot diaspora with far-reaching consequences. The very presence of Huguenots, scattered across Protestant Europe and its colonies, offered a visible reminder that it was difficult, if not impossible, to root the sacred legitimacy of the French monarchy in a single religion. More directly, Huguenot authors, many living in the Dutch Republic, took the lead in introducing English republican ideas to the French through translations and political commentary. Their exegesis of a mixed and balanced constitution offered a potent alternative to France's absolutist monarchy.

Jainchill contributes to the broader attempt of this volume to carve out a more global approach to revolutionary political culture. In focusing on the international Enlightenment, this volume proposes that France's engagement in a global colonial and commercial project informed the Revolution not just in material ways but also in the very genesis of revolutionary ideas and culture. The French revolutionaries drew on concepts and practices developed in the colonies, and the act of attempting to create an international movement and spread revolution abroad—whether by dialogue, propaganda, or force—influenced how the revolutionaries crafted their own political culture. The French imagined their project as a global one. By articulating a series of claims to universalism, they simultaneously built legitimacy for their own revolution at home, positioned France on the frontlines of international revolution, and generated a powerful, global ideology in favor of republicanism, rights, and popular sovereignty. At times, the revolutionaries used their new ideology in turn to justify expansionism, but they had also created a language and set of practices that underpinned resistance.

This universalist ideology drew on ideas and practices that had emerged in the transnational Enlightenment. That movement, itself often engaged in theorizing and critiquing the emerging global dynamics, helped supply the revolutionaries with crucial concepts, such as progress, rights, and cultural comparison.[19] In chapter 5 William Nelson weaves together analysis of colonial and Enlightenment influences: when the revolutionaries debated how to reform people and "regenerate" them as citizens within the new nation, they drew directly on the "science of man" that had developed out of the long history of colonization.[20] European notions of moral "perfectibility" emerged from an intellectual arsenal created via diverse colonial writings on medicine, travel and ethnography, linguistic theory, political economy, and above all, natural history. Colonial practices also informed the revolutionary attempt to fuse France's diversity into a universal whole, such as Nicolas-Louis François de Neufchâteau's ambitious statistical survey of commerce, agriculture, politics, and religion across France.

To explore the construction of republican universalism, in chapter 6 Suzanne Desan analyzes a revealing incident: the revolutionaries' decision to grant citizenship on 26 August 1792 to a select group of foreign thinkers and activists. The surrounding debate brings to light how the revolutionaries built universalism not solely out of rights ideology but also by incorporating foreign peoples and projects into the republic and by politicizing Enlightenment cosmopolitanism. In addition, the 26 August event offers insight into how contradictions emerged within universalism: seeking to construct the republic against the aggressive geopolitics of monarchies, the revolutionaries appropriated the cosmopolitan renunciation of conquest and crafted an ideology supporting each people's sovereignty, but they also transformed cosmopolitanism into an international crusade to regenerate, liberate, and colonize neighboring territories.

The relationship between universal rights ideology and France's status as a global power is examined by Denise Davidson in chapter 7 from the angle of the classic question of the rights of women and slaves during the revolutionary era. She explores various interconnections between feminism and abolitionism: numerous reformers, such as Olympe de Gouges, Condorcet, and Mary Wollstonecraft, took on both causes. Davidson especially asks how and why the quest for women's rights used analogies to slavery, especially before its abolition in 1794. Stretching well beyond the revolutionary era, she argues for the persistent power of rights talk into the nineteenth century and provides a compelling illustration of how France's colonial practices informed political activism within France, which in turn helped shape global discussions of feminism and abolitionism.

As Nelson and Desan show, however, the ideals of Enlightenment, regeneration, cosmopolitanism, and rights also had a darker side, which became apparent when the French tried to export their ideals to other places. There may have been a universal "instinct for liberty," to use the phrase of Anacharsis Cloots cited by Desan, but the universal republic that was to be built on it was basically French. The French had seen the light of reason first and soon proved all too willing to bring it to others, even those who resisted their influence. This link between the democratic and republican aspirations of the revolutionaries on one side and the conquering, colonizing effects of French arms on the other helps explain not only the rise of Napoleon Bonaparte but also the conflicting responses of other peoples to the French republic.

Because of their global range and ideological inflection, the French revolutionary wars had effects that no one could foresee. In part 3, the authors look at three very different arenas of conflict: Egypt, where the French had only a small presence through a community of French traders before the French invasion led by Napoleon; the French colonies of the Atlantic world, which were legally and politically distinct from metropolitan France in a way that the revolutionaries would attempt to eliminate; and North America, where the French had lost their colonial presence more than a quarter century earlier.

Egypt lay just across the Mediterranean and was viewed by the French as a kind of global gateway, in particular to British-controlled India. The French invasion and occupation of Egypt by Napoleon Bonaparte in 1798 offers one of the most striking examples of how revolutionary republicanism interacted with empire and broke apart the previous frame of European geopolitics. While the Egyptian expedition has been represented as a quixotic adventure resulting in little more than the twenty-four-volume *Description de l'Égypte*, in chapter 8 Ian Coller situates this event more broadly within Egyptian politics and French geopolitical ambitions. Originally favoring a network of geographically linked "sister republics," the government of the Directory turned toward building the "Grande Nation," an expanded territory united and dominated by the French. As part of the Grande Nation, the Egyptian expedition became France's final failure to combine republican freedom and equality with territorial expansion, and Napoleon's miscarriage there played a key role in his shift toward "imperial *machtpolitik*" within Europe. Paradoxically, as Coller illustrates through his analysis of Egyptian responses, just as Napoleon turned away from republicanism at home and abroad, the Egyptian experiment provoked republican aspirations among a diverse group of Egyptians. Coller provides both a global context to understand the "expedition" to Egypt and a perspective from which to understand the momentous effects of this episode on the history of French republicanism and imperial expansion within Europe.

Using the prism of slavery and the case of Guiana, the small and sparsely populated French colony on the northeastern coast of South America, in chapter 9 Miranda Spieler investigates how revolutionary law and political culture reached the outer edges of the French empire. More than just demonstrating the effects of the Revolution on slave regimes in the Atlantic colonies, Spieler shows that core revolutionary principles and laws look dramatically different when the full expanse of the French empire is taken into consideration. While there were important acts like the 1794 emancipation and the 1795 constitution, which purportedly brought legal unity to metropolitan

France and the colonies, Spieler insists that a true unity was never achieved. In fact, on the edges of the French empire, even the implementation of core republican principles and revolutionary laws (such as universal emancipation) was often ambiguous, inconsistent, and contradictory.

Although the French lost hold of their colonies in North America in the Seven Years' War, Rafe Blaufarb argues in chapter 10 that the French Revolutionary Wars had a significant impact on the development of North America.[21] By draining British and Spanish resources, the wars of the 1790s with France helped bring about the "first rapprochement" between the United States, the British, the Spanish, and various groups of Native Americans. In turn, the new terms of the relationships eliminated the primary obstacles to American westward expansion and created the circumstances for American continental hegemony. The Revolutionary Wars thus weakened the New World presence of the British and Spanish empires while helping to lay the foundation for the rise of another.

Chapter 11, by Pierre Serna, functions as a coda to the collection. It builds on the global perspective of the preceding chapters while provocatively challenging almost the entire existing historiography of the French Revolution. Serna inquires into how the Revolution would appear if it were placed in a long tradition of revolutions that share their origin in peripheral places far from the centers of power. This would include colonies struggling against metropolitan centers, just as it would include provinces resisting capital cities. These revolutions would be united in their character as wars of independence from central authority. They could all be seen, in essence, as anticolonial struggles, and they would stretch from the revolt of the United Provinces against the Spanish in the sixteenth century to the wars of decolonization in the twentieth century, even possibly including the revolutions in North Africa in the early twenty-first century. In his global recasting, Serna challenges some of the traditional claims to French exceptionalism, in effect suggesting that the French Revolution can be provincialized while at the same time being elevated to a place in "an infinite spiral" of revolution that never ends and never repeats.[22]

Despite the common emphasis on a global perspective, the chapters in this volume do not add up to a single, monolithic new interpretation of the French Revolution. Even Serna, who comes closest among the contributors to such an overarching view, does not claim to explain everything about the French Revolution in the anticolonial terms that he proposes. In any case, we do not aim to demolish previous interpretations but rather to find ways of integrating them into a more capacious view. The French Revolution was a democratic revolution in Palmer's and Tocqueville's sense, albeit with an even broader significance than they attributed to it. Popular mobilization for wider political participation, for limiting the power of royal and aristocratic government, and for republicanism grew out of global and not just domestic sources. Moreover, democratic revolution took place not only in France, Europe, and North America but also all around the Caribbean.

This volume links the democratic revolution to an imperial one. The French Revolution did not just participate in a global realignment of empires, as recent scholars have argued; it may have grown out of a more general global crisis of empire, but it then dramatically accelerated the realignment of empires, including the French empire, the British, the new United States, and especially the Spanish and Portuguese empires, which ended up losing almost all their New World colonies by the 1820s. Imperial competition and momentous national upheavals came together in repeatedly explosive interactions that generated both centrifugal and centripetal forces: clamoring demands for independence from the peripheries, both national and imperial, reacted against and sometimes helped propel an astonishing centralization of state power. Revolutionary republicanism—in conjunction with potent geopolitics—both undercut and reinvented empire. As the French strove to spread revolution abroad and accomplish their own territorial ambitions, they injected new political practices and ideas into local dynamics from Egypt to Italy and simultaneously precipitated imperial experimentation within Europe and across the globe. Violence in both old (war) and new (reenslavement) forms accompanied these endeavors.

In short, a global approach to the French Revolution highlights the ways in which the revolutionaries generated controversial new forms of politics, at once democratic and imperial as well as anticolonial and centralizing, in continual dialogue with multiple international forces, including the diaspora of people and ideas, the clash of warfare, the development of colonial practices, and the internationalization of trade and finance. This volume thus puts an older approach that emphasized how French revolutionary ideology emerged out of the European Enlightenment in dialogue with the more recent attention to colonization and empire. This method should make it possible to trace continuities from the Revolution's origins in global competition and transnational Enlightenment ideas to the emergence of a revolutionary political culture that fused immense idealism with territorial ambition and combined the drive for human rights with various forms of exclusion. The chapters in this volume point toward these links, but much more remains to be done in explaining how they worked. The French Revolution does not have to be about just one big thing: democracy, centralization, violence, protototalitarianism, human rights, or imperialism. Nor need it be studied with just one approach taken from economic, social, political, cultural, or intellectual history. It was, after all, "world-historical" precisely because it changed so many things in so many, often contradictory directions.

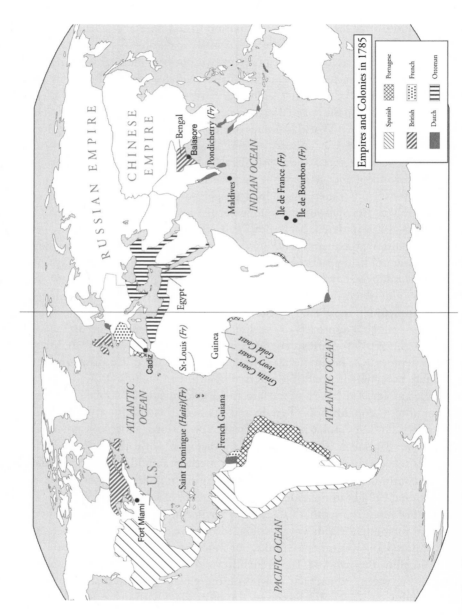

Map 1. Empires and Colonies in 1785

PART I

Origins

1 The global Underground

SMUGGLING, REBELLION, AND THE ORIGINS
OF THE FRENCH REVOLUTION

MICHAEL KWASS

In recent years, historians have globalized the origins of the Industrial Revolution. It is no longer possible to explain how a new system of production emerged in Britain at the end of the eighteenth century without discussing that nation's prior expansion into the New World, Africa, and Asia.[1] Can a similar case be made for that other monumental turning point in modern history, the French Revolution? Did globalization cause the French Revolution? It is a difficult question, not least because globalization is often understood to be an economic phenomenon, while the French Revolution was above all a political event. Any satisfying answer would have to show how the effects of economic globalization penetrated the metropolitan political sphere to generate prerevolutionary tensions, ideas, and debates. However daunting, such a project is of utmost importance, for it holds the promise not only of globalizing the origins of the French Revolution but of integrating a field marked by ever-widening divisions between economic and political-cultural history.[2] Introducing globalization into revolutionary studies may help to reverse this process of historiographical fragmentation by drawing together various strands of economic, political, and cultural history. The stakes could not be higher.

The most serious obstacle to globalizing the origins of the Revolution is, ironically, the term "globalization" itself. In common parlance, globalization alludes to an ill-defined, self-propelling process by which world markets inexorably integrate and nation-states inevitably decline as goods, people, and information zip across once-formidable borders. Not surprisingly, historians are skeptical of applying such a simplistic and inherently neoliberal conception of globalization to the past. Dissatisfied with vernacular uses of the term, scholars are formulating more sophisticated theories that take into account the "specificity, contingency, and contestation" at work in long-term historical processes.[3]

A more rigorously historical understanding of globalization is particularly important for the study of the early modern period. In the seventeenth and eighteenth centuries, when oceanic trade linkages between Asia, Africa, Europe, and the Americas proliferated to create worldwide commercial circuits, government policies were anything but liberal, and trade was anything but free. Indeed, the growth of early modern world trade was bound up inextricably with the rise of powerful European states. As rival European rulers competed for military, diplomatic, and economic hegemony, they intervened in a fast-rising global economy to gain access to, and control over, transcontinental flows of goods. Projecting their dynastic and national rivalries onto the wider world, they built formidable navies, chartered overseas trading companies, founded and fought over colonies, subsidized the transatlantic slave trade and the New World plantation complex, instituted all manner of national prohibitions, monopolies, tariffs, and navigation laws, ran up enormous public debts, and taxed just about anything that moved. It was this bewildering jumble of state policies that Adam Smith rejected as the "mercantile system."[4] Yet, contrary to Smith's claim that mercantilism was less productive than free trade, recent research suggests that aggressive and exploitative imperial policies deeply enriched early modern metropolitan Europe.[5]

To acknowledge that world trade emerged in a profoundly illiberal environment is to begin to construct a useful theory of globalization. It may also help us to rethink the origins of the French Revolution, as is underscored by recent studies on the destabilizing effects of global military conflict and rising tensions between colonists and metropolitans.[6] Building on such work, this chapter contends that the monarchical state's engagement with world trade helped to undermine the legitimacy of key institutions, opening the way to revolution. In particular, I will argue that the crown's interventions in expanding global markets for New World tobacco and Asian cloth inadvertently stimulated the growth of a rebellious underground economy. Not only did the illicit economy give rise to new forms of popular revolt, as legions of smugglers clashed with customs agents while whisking contraband into France, but it provoked an outpouring of politically charged discourse on the need to reform fundamental state institutions.

Among the myriad policies by which Louis XIV engaged world trade, two particularly bold interventions inflamed French politics down to the Revolution. First, in 1674, seeking to harness the fiscal power of domestic consumption, the Sun King turned west to the Atlantic world and established a state tobacco monopoly.[7] One of a handful of tropical psychoactive products to inundate Europe in the seventeenth century, tobacco was widely regarded as a potent medicinal remedy and miraculous catalyst of social interaction. It was also addictive. Capitalizing on soaring home demand—and exploiting a new system of slave labor in the New World—the French monarchy banned all private trade in the leaf and marketed millions of pounds of slave-produced American tobacco to its subjects. The tobacco monopoly went well beyond the geographic confines of its elder sibling, the salt monopoly, drawing the French monarchy into a sprawling Atlantic economy that connected peoples from four continents and several empires.

To manage such a large-scale operation and to police the domestic ban on nonstate tobacco, the crown leased the monopoly to the General Farm, a private financial company that contracted the right to collect indirect taxes while advancing enormous loans to the king. Initially adhering to the basic mercantilist principle that mother countries should, whenever possible, import raw goods from their own colonies, the Farm procured tobacco from the French Caribbean colony of Saint-Domingue and from Louisiana. But the Farmers General, the wealthy financiers who ran the Farm, soon spurned the French colonies and turned to British merchants, who could deliver cheaper, better-quality leaf from Chesapeake Bay in North America.[8] By the middle of the eighteenth century, the Farm was purchasing millions of pounds of Virginian tobacco a year, processing it in colossal manufactories, and shipping the final product to some ten thousand tobacconists across France. State tobacconists peddled the herb to local consumers, who smoked, chewed, and, above all, snorted it at their leisure, filling the royal coffers annually to the tune of 30 million livres (henceforth l.).

Next, to protect French textile producers from global competition, Louis XIV turned east to erect a shield against the influx of inexpensive, high-quality cloth from Asia, in particular Indian calico.[9] Long before and well after the arrival of the first European vessels, India was the greatest textile producer in the world, its renowned cloth gracing markets from the islands of Southeast Asia to Islamic Persia to the Swahili ports of East Africa. When European traders first approached Indian textile merchants in the early seventeenth century, they did not dream of reorganizing the region's system of labor and production, as their counterparts would do in the New World. Rather, they established fortified trading settlements on the coast and, with an occasional military assist, tapped into existing commercial structures. In 1664, jealous of the commercial success of his rivals, especially the Dutch Republic, Jean-Baptiste Colbert established the French East India Company.[10] With a large injection of state funds, this "Versailles of commerce" joined the fray in the Indian Ocean, shipping cloth from the subcontinent around the Cape of Good Hope to Lorient, in Brittany. Printed with vivid designs whose colorfast brilliance far surpassed anything European producers could fabricate, Indian calico became so popular among French consumers that traditional textile manufacturers, panicked by the overseas competition, vigorously lobbied the government for protection. In 1686, the monarchy responded by banning all importation of the cloth. Policed by the guards of the General Farm—and hence intertwined with the monarchy's fiscal apparatus—the prohibition lasted seventy-three years, only to be replaced with a heavy tariff in 1759.

The tobacco monopoly and the calico ban met with resounding success. The monopoly gave a much-needed boost to royal finances, while the ban helped protect a critical sector of the domestic industrial economy. But the two interventions in world trade had the unintended consequence of spawning a massive underground economy. Although the principal commodity of the French black market had long been salt, a local French product whose sale in many parts of the kingdom had for centuries been monopolized by the monarchy, the tobacco monopoly and calico prohibition provoked a surge in contraband, in effect globalizing the metropolitan parallel economy in the final century of the Old Regime.[11]

The scale of this illicit trade was immense. Easier to transport and, pound for pound, far more valuable than salt, contraband tobacco flooded all quarters of the French monopoly zone, from the coast of Languedoc in the south to the littoral of Brittany and Normandy in the west. Supply ships hovered off the mainland as small craft ran tobacco ashore, where locals picked it up and hauled it inland for distribution. The most heavily trafficked routes into the territory of the monopoly, however, lay to the north and east, where precious Virginian tobacco entered the Continent by way of Dunkirk and the ports of the Netherlands to pool just beyond the French fiscal border. From there, the leaf flowed in an arc that stretched across Alsace (a privileged French province not subject to the monopoly) down through the Swiss pays de Vaud to Savoy. All along this trajectory, the Virginian was mixed with cheap, homegrown European weed to create an inexpensive yet good-quality blend that was perfect for smuggling. Traffickers purchased blends for as little as 12 sols a pound and sold them in the monopoly zone for as much as 36 sols in the provinces and up to 50 sols in Paris, tripling their money and helping to put tobacco within reach of poor consumers, who could ill afford the 62 sols charged by the Farm.[12] By the middle of the eighteenth century, an estimated one-third of the tobacco consumed in France was illicit.[13]

Just as the tobacco monopoly failed to prevent contraband leaf from entering France, the 1686 calico ban did not stop the influx of calicos from India. Smugglers secreted the cloth into France from the Netherlands, which had not banned its import, while employees of the French East India Company slipped what they could through customs. Permitted to import the fabric for the exclusive purpose of reexportation, company officials and sailors nonetheless siphoned off portions of their cargo into the domestic shadow economy. Most of the "Indian" cloth that was smuggled into France, however, was not produced in India at all. Whereas today we associate Asia with the mass production of counterfeit Western goods (think Nike sneakers), in the eighteenth century it was the Europeans who manufactured imitations of high-quality Asian products. Producers in free ports like Marseille and enclaves like the Comtat Venaisson joined counterparts east of the French customs border in Switzerland and Alsace to manufacture prodigious supplies of low-quality knockoffs. Between genuine Indian calico that seeped in from the reexport market and European-produced facsimiles that were smuggled into France, there was plenty of cloth to be had on the black market. One contemporary economist estimated that 16 million l. of calico was illegally consumed in France every year during the ban.[14] After the prohibition was lifted in 1759, the domestic calico industry boomed as Swiss firms transplanted themselves onto French soil, but the 25 percent tariff still made it worthwhile for foreign producers to circumvent customs.[15]

Countless men, women, and children trafficked in tobacco and calico to supplement their household income. While the underground salt trade remained a largely artisanal affair in which indigent laborers eked out an existence in a punishing economy, the extraordinarily high profits to be had in tobacco and calico trafficking attracted professional types as well.[16] Noble and merchant investors wheeled and dealed behind the scenes; mobile professionals (peddlers, coachmen, cart drivers, soldiers, and bargemen) built false compartments in their vehicles or buried contraband beneath heaps of legitimate cargo; innkeepers offered weary smugglers everything from credit and storage space to food and shelter; and domestic servants stored wholesale supplies in their masters' residences, passing them on to dense networks of urban retailers, the capillaries of the distribution system. Paris was positively crawling with petty tobacco dealers who, operating out of cramped apartments, neighborhood bars and cafés, and secluded cemeteries, hawked half ounces of snuff wrapped in paper cones.[17]

One measure of the increasingly organized underground market was the rise of gangs. Salt gangs had existed since the chaotic final years of Louis XIV's reign. They were soon joined by sophisticated tobacco and calico bands that plied a high-volume trade along the eastern border. In northeastern France, authorities were aware of at least thirty-eight large bands operating in the second half of the eighteenth century.[18] In the southeast, the intendant of Dauphiné estimated in the 1730s that around four hundred smugglers were active in twenty-five to thirty different bands, the largest of which, the band d'Orange, was composed of seventy men, all "armed to the teeth."[19] The most famous band of the century was that of Louis Mandrin, who in the mid-1750s smuggled tobacco and calico from Switzerland and Savoy into southeastern France.

In economic terms, the expansion of the underground helped to fuel a remarkable rise in eighteenth-century consumption by bringing prohibited colonial goods to market, whether such goods were overseas imports, European imitations, or a mixture of both (as in the case of blended Euro-American tobacco). But the growing illicit economy also had profound *political* implications. To begin with, it prompted significant institutional changes in the monarchical state. During the final century of the Old Regime, the monarchy attempted to roll back the global underground by expanding the Farm police to some twenty thousand guards, the largest paramilitary force in Europe, and investing the corps with extensive powers of search and seizure. It also strengthened the criminal justice system, hardening the penal code against smuggling and creating extraordinary law courts called commissions, which, funded by the Farm, judged all contraband cases involving gangs, arms, and rebellion. Over the century, the new commissions executed hundreds of smugglers and, along with numerous lower-level financial courts, dispatched tens of thousands more to galleys and labor camps. Perhaps half of the more than 100,000 men who entered the galleys between 1685 and 1791 were incarcerated for their participation in the underground economy. Indeed, the birth of the modern French prison owes much to the Farm's crackdown on smuggling, a fact Michel Foucault overlooked in his celebrated work on the genesis of Western incarceration.[20]

The other political consequence of growing illicit trade was rebellion. Although well-publicized and highly ritualistic executions and galleys sentences were designed to stigmatize the practice of smuggling, traffickers refused to internalize the criminal status imposed on them. Rather than folding under the weight of repression, many smugglers struck back, engaging Farm officials and guards in violent conflict. In fact, violent conflict engendered by illicit commerce became so widespread in the eighteenth century that it has fundamentally changed our understanding of the history of popular revolt in early modern France. Historians long assumed that revolt took the form of anti-tax and anti-military uprisings in the crisis-ridden seventeenth century, giving way to protorevolutionary bread and seigneurial riots in the more stable eighteenth century.[21] But a pathbreaking work by Jean Nicolas exposes deep flaws in this narrative. Compiling evidence from across the kingdom, Nicolas demonstrates that from 1660 to 1789 tax rebellion remained the single most common form of French revolt, far outpacing other collective actions, such as bread riots, seigneurial disputes, workplace disturbances, and religious conflicts. Within that predominant category of tax rebellion, the vast majority of incidents were provoked by the repression of contraband.[22] Salt smugglers who continued to clash with Farm police were now joined by calico and tobacco traffickers, the latter constituting the most rebellious group of all.[23] Far from petering out during and after the splendid reign of Louis XIV, rebellion remained vigorous down to the French Revolution, thanks in large part to the globalization of underground trade.

Revolt did change form, however. In the middle third of the seventeenth century, during the "turning of the fiscal screw" under Richelieu and Mazarin, a period when direct taxes soared and indirect taxes were extended, France experienced twenty or thirty huge, province-wide uprisings. These massive revolts posed serious territorial challenges to an embattled monarchy. In the eighteenth century, by contrast, as taxes and prohibitions became regularized and large-scale uprisings subsided, resistance manifested itself through the black market as small-scale attacks by smugglers and their allies became increasingly prevalent. If the crown succeeded in relegating the furious tax uprisings of the Grand Siècle to the past, it never firmly established what German sociologist Norbert Elias claimed was a double monopoly on taxation and violence.[24] Behind the veneer of post–Louis Quatorzian stability raged an ongoing guerilla war between the elephantine Farm and legions of highly mobile traffickers.

In this war—and "war" was precisely the term contemporaries used to describe the conflict between Farm and smuggler—three kinds of rebellion predominated. One was resistance to arrest, classified as "rebellion" by the criminal justice system. When caught red-handed with contraband, many smugglers resorted to violence to escape the clutches of Farm guards, whose intrusions into their affairs they considered wholly illegitimate. Take the case of Jean-Claude Loviat, a domestic servant who hawked illicit tobacco from his Paris apartment. When Farm agents showed up at his door in 1773, he shouted, "Get the hell out of here!" and began throwing punches as his wife bolted with the contraband. After pummeling an agent with his door keys, he chased the bloodied man through the elegant Place Royale (now known as the Place des Vosges) and triumphantly made his escape.[25]

A second type of contraband rebellion involved crowds of local residents who protected smugglers in their midst from Farm agents, in the belief that they were defending the larger community's norms, customs, and rights. Consider the rebellion that erupted in the Norman parish of Saint-Victor-de-Chrétienville in 1710, when six officials arrived to investigate a tip that a man named Vivien was openly selling contraband tobacco. As soon as villagers identified the outsiders as agents of the Farm, they cried: "Seize your weapons, the dog-buggers are here. . . . Let's kill them and cut them in pieces." The local priest sounded the tocsin, summoned a crowd "armed with muskets, pitchforks, halberds, billhooks, axes, and metal-tipped staffs," and, rifle at his side, delivered a tirade against the Farm in which he invoked the name of God. After a tense scuffle with the crowd, the agents beat a quick retreat.[26]

Less common yet still more aggressive, a third type of rebellion consisted of premeditated assaults on ambulatory Farm guards, customs posts, and prisons in which alleged smugglers awaited trial. Legendary smuggler Louis Mandrin staged precisely these sorts of brazen attacks during his midcentury expeditions. Not content to conduct trade in the shadowy depths of the underground, Mandrin appeared in the full light of day to pry open the tobacco monopoly. In the fall and winter of 1754, with a force of over a hundred men, he occupied towns and raided state tobacco warehouses, compelling Farm agents to purchase his contraband tobacco. Such forced sales became Mandrin's signature method of doing business. Although he could easily have plundered the coffers of the Farm without leaving anything in return, he deliberately sustained the pretext of engaging in reciprocal commercial exchanges, which, while coercive, were considered morally sound by band members, local spectators, newspaper correspondents, and even certain royal officials. Contrasting the rank illegitimacy of the Farm's monopoly with the moral validity of the parallel economy, Mandrin's political theater drew widespread public attention. Although he was eventually captured and executed, his subversive legend lived on in popular songs, almanacs, chapbooks, and engravings (like fig. 1).

Pervasive, violent, and intractable, contraband rebellion contributed to a spike in revolt during the last decades of the Old Regime. "It is clear," John Markoff affirmed more than a decade ago while assessing Nicolas's preliminary data, "that the term 'prerevolution,' widely used for the elite conflicts and crises of the last years of the Old Regime, had a plebeian counterpart, largely neglected in current accounts of revolutionary origins."[27] If the plebeian prerevolution has been overlooked, so too has its global dimensions, for the smuggling of New World tobacco and Asian calico helped to fuel this dramatic rise in contraband rebellion. The most common form of revolt on the eve of the Revolution, such rebellion destabilized the kingdom, especially its border provinces, and directly contested the power of the Farm, a pillar of the absolute monarchy and arguably the single most important financial institution in the kingdom.

The full political impact of the war between Farm and smuggler, however, cannot be measured by the number of rebellions alone, for the conflict had far-reaching cultural ramifications. Unfolding during the Enlightenment, when writers subjected state institutions to widening public scrutiny, the spiraling cycle of contraband revolt and repression drew the attention of elites, who briskly incorporated the problem of illicit trade into a broader and rapidly

Figure 1. "Mandrain Capitaine des Contrebandiers." Reproduced by kind permission of the Bibliothèque Nationale de France. Estampes N2 Mandrin.

developing rhetoric of reform. It was this dual thrust, of popular revolt and elite reformist discourse, that fully politicized the global underground. From the 1750s to the Revolution, as literature on political economy and criminal justice soared, Enlightenment thinkers identified the violence attendant on smuggling and its suppression as one of several major problems with the existing fiscal and regulatory apparatus of the state. Although writers had long ridiculed tax farmers as vulgar social climbers, after the middle of the eighteenth century they reached beyond indictments of personal character to lay siege to the entire institutional complex of the Farm, especially the prohibitions and monopolies it was in the business of enforcing. Writers did not merely transpose popular rebellion into print; they appropriated it to forge a powerful critique of the state.

The first wave of printed literature to address the underground economy emanated from a small group of thinkers around Jacques-Claude-Marie Vincent de Gournay, a member of the royal council of commerce from 1751 to 1759.[28] Attempting to cultivate in France the kind of commercial culture that had catapulted England to great-power status, the Gournay circle espoused a philosophy of economic liberalism that advocated unregulated industry, open competition, and free trade. Gournay and his associates came to the issue of smuggling through the controversy over the prohibition of calico. Although the importation and production of Indian cloth had been banned in France since 1686, the royal council of commerce began to soften the law in the 1750s, granting privileges to a handful of domestic manufacturers to produce the forbidden cotton cloth. When traditional textile manufacturers got wind of this, they flooded the council with petitions against the permissions and published appeals to the reading public. Opponents of the ban responded in kind, disseminating blistering criticisms of the prohibition and the logic of protectionism that sustained it. In this way, the calico controversy was born, and with it the first modern debate on trafficking and its repression.

Gournay's contribution to the polemic centered on what economists today call "consumer sovereignty," the notion that it is the consumer, rather than the state or the producer, who ultimately decides which goods are produced and in what quantity. It was pure folly to deny consumers what they wanted, Gournay reasoned, for any attempt to cut them off from the goods they desired produced illicit markets, which in turn generated wasteful and inhumane struggles between smugglers and the state. "The contraband of calicos gives rise to the daily loss of a great number of men from both sides of the conflict; there is a continuous war on all our borders in which an infinite number of people perish arms in hand, in prisons, in the galleys, & on the scaffold, & this only to force 20 million men to act against their inclinations, instead of adapting to these inclinations and profiting from them." "For anyone born with human sentiments," the loss of so many otherwise useful men was "so palpable . . . that it is not possible to consider its full dimensions without shuddering."[29]

Philosopher and economist André Morellet elaborated on Gournay's ideas by insisting that just as consumers had a "natural right" to dress as they wanted, traders mistakenly condemned as criminals by the state had a right to answer the call of consumer demand. Brutally punishing the poor for profiting from a perfectly legitimate but illegal commerce flew in the face of Enlightenment notions of progress: "Will our descendants be able to believe that our nation was truly as enlightened and civilized as we pride ourselves on it being when they read that in the middle of the [eighteenth] century a man in France was still hanged for having bought in Geneva at 22 sols what he could sell in Grenoble for 58? Will they be able to believe that men in often dire poverty were presented with such a strong temptation as profit & were punished so severely when they succumbed to it?"[30]

In 1759 the prohibition was finally lifted, although its replacement by a heavy tariff continued to encourage smuggling. By then, a new group of economists, the physiocrats, was in the ascendant. The physiocrats were liberals too, but far more rigid in their advocacy of free trade and more dogmatic in their insistence on the primacy of the agricultural sector. They believed that French agriculture was in an abysmal state of decline because French policy had deviated from natural economic laws created by God. All was not lost, however. By aligning state policy with the natural economic order, France could recover from its slump and enter a new age of prosperity. Such an alignment would require major policy reversals, including an overhaul of the fiscal system in which all taxes on consumption would be replaced by a single levy on income from land. As the debate over smuggling shifted from the Gournay group to the physiocrats, the target of economic criticism moved from the calico prohibition, which purportedly violated principles of free trade and consumption, to the Farm's fiscal monopolies, which purportedly violated something much larger: the laws of nature itself. To claim that Farm monopolies contravened natural law was to radically challenge the legitimacy of an institution at the very center of the French fiscal state.[31]

In a vivid sketch of the new physiocratic program, cofounder marquis de Mirabeau tapped into popular hostility by advancing that the "vampires" who ran the Farm were violating the natural rights of underground traders and sapping the economy. If there was a moral villain in this conflict, it was the Farm, not the smuggler:

> [The Farm] seizes the opportunity to raise armies to guard the borders of regions prohibited from enjoying the gifts of nature, portending the coming of slavery on the whole territory. Prisons, galleys, gallows, and sinister tribunals are established at the cruel whim of financiers to punish inhumanely the wretch who exercises his natural right. . . . Although the Farm feigns to draw blood from the capillaries, it bleeds the people at the throat. . . . The more heated the civil war that results from a regime insulting to natural law, the more the Farmer profits and becomes important, & the more public order and decency is annihilated.[32]

Not all physiocrats were so melodramatic. Employing a more scientific tone, Guillaume-François Le Trosne suggested that smugglers were simply poor men and women rationally pursuing profit in a challenging economic climate. They were acting in accordance with "the laws of the natural order," which recognized the liberty "to buy and sell in a condition of full competition." It was only indirect taxation that turned otherwise innocent merchants into "guilty parties," multiplying "crimes and misdemeanors." "Public opinion doggedly insists on absolving" this crime, Le Trosne observed, but the crown "persists in condemning" it.[33] This would all change as soon as physiocratic reforms were instituted and the Farm's consumption taxes were abolished. Taxes "will no longer require victims, the guilty parties will disappear, every subject will be submissive and faithful, their obedience to the law no longer compromised," and courts "will prosecute only real crimes whose punishment will be applauded by all because it will be inflicted only to assure and avenge collective security." The "crime" of smuggling was in fact no crime at all, Le Trosne concluded. It was an unfortunate by-product of a deeply flawed fiscal regime in which positive law had deviated from natural law. Le Trosne and his fellow physiocrats were, in theory at least, rescuing smugglers from criminal infamy by bringing them into the legal fold of legitimate trade.[34]

In the 1760s, amid the financial conflicts occasioned by the costly Seven Years' War, magistrates and legal reformers widened the criticism beyond economic theory to formulate a judicial critique of royal repression. Chief among the magistrates' objections was the creation of extraordinary commissions that encroached on the jurisdiction of venerable tribunals to sentence smugglers to the galleys or even death. Such harsh punishment drew fire from economists, as we have seen, but it particularly irked magistrates in the *parlements* and *cours des aides*, who viewed the commissioners as illegitimate and tyrannical rivals. The magistrates of the parlement of Grenoble, some of whom had ties to the underground, lambasted the "hydra" of the Farm for arbitrarily hauling suspects before its "sinister tribunals where the blood of liberty runs at the whim and furor of the Traitant [a pejorative term for financiers]."[35]

Repression also drew attention from liberal legal thinkers, who, more attuned to Enlightenment currents than most practicing magistrates, crafted an entirely new philosophy of criminal justice. Montesquieu had made an appeal for penal leniency in his 1748 *L'esprit des lois*, warning specifically against the transfer of judicial power to financiers. But it was a young Italian named Cesare Beccaria who would galvanize the French movement for reform. Beccaria's *On Crimes and Punishments*, translated into French in 1764 by Morellet (the same *philosophe* who had objected to the calico prohibition) at the behest of Guillaume-Chrétien de Lamoignon de Malesherbes, president of the most powerful tax court in France, assailed the entire edifice of Old Regime criminal justice: the presumption of guilt over innocence, the cloak of secrecy that shrouded trials, the use of torture to elicit confessions, the arcane methods by which judges reached verdicts, and, above all, the cruel disproportionality between crime and punishment. For Beccaria, no offense better illustrated such rank disproportionality than smuggling. A violation that stemmed from "the law itself" rather than a broadly based moral code, smuggling was a victimless crime, or was at least perceived as such, and yet the punishment for it was equal to or more severe than that inflicted on criminals commonly regarded as scoundrels, such as thieves and forgers. It was time to bring the punishment for smuggling in line with popular moral codes.

It would be difficult to overstate Beccaria's influence on the movement for French legal reform. *On Crimes and Punishments* deepened the thinking of a long line of liberal magistrates, lawyers, and philosophers, from Voltaire and Michel Antoine Servan to Jacques Pierre Brissot and Marquis de Condorcet.[36] Nowhere did the influence of Beccaria make such a profound impact on political thought as in the writings of Malesherbes, president of the Paris *cour des aides*. With Malesherbes's elegant remonstrances, theory and practice came together in a cogent and highly publicized call for reform. It is worth noting that the president, having long objected to the severity of antismuggling laws, was utterly radicalized in 1770 by a case before his own court, the Monnerat affair. Guillaume Monnerat was an unlucky tradesman whom Farm officials suspected of dealing illicit tobacco. Tossed in the Bicêtre, the notorious prison-hospital that housed Paris's undesirables, for more than a year, Monnerat was finally freed when the Farm failed to dig up enough evidence against him to initiate a trial. An apparent victim of mistaken identity, he was released into the streets of Paris and immediately filed suit in the *cour des aides*.

Shocked by the charges, Malesherbes investigated the circumstances of the arrest and was horrified by what he found, especially the rampant use of *lettres de cachet* (special warrants) to imprison suspected traffickers. The president ruled in favor of the plaintiff, slapping the Farm with a weighty fine, and from that moment forward incorporated searing critiques of Farm repression into his political theory. One of the century's most important expressions of French political thought, his celebrated remonstrances of 1775 distinguished between royal absolutism, whereby the king legitimately held unlimited authority over his realm, and outright "despotism," under which "each executor of [the king's] orders also employs a power without limits." Malesherbes systematically applied this theory of despotism to every level of Farm administration, excoriating the Farmers General for forcing cash-starved monarchs to issue brutal penal legislation, Farm guards for riding roughshod over defenseless peasants, and Farm courts for handing down sentences that were "repugnant to humanity." Echoing Beccaria, he observed that the punishment for smuggling was tragically out of proportion to the crime. How had it come to pass, he courageously demanded of Louis XVI, "that the death penalty was pronounced against citizens out of a financial interest?" Like growing numbers of magistrates, the president of the *cour des aides* believed that there was only one way to defeat this and other forms of despotism: the king would have to call the Estates General, the national representative body that had lain dormant for almost two centuries. Only an institution as powerful as the Estates General could expunge the toxic Farm from the body politic, reform the fiscal state, and save the monarchy.[37]

Over the course of the eighteenth century, royal efforts to control the trade in, and consumption of, global commodities from the Atlantic and Indian oceans (namely, American tobacco and Indian calico) generated antistate movements at two levels. At the level of popular politics, smugglers and their allies engaged the Farm in a protracted "war" from below, fueling unrest in the border provinces, challenging the authority of the Farm, and limiting revenues the crown desperately needed to plug gaping financial deficits. Meanwhile, Enlightenment economists and legal reformers delegitimized the Farm from above, widely publicizing the need to abolish a "despotic" institution that had somehow become a cornerstone of the absolute monarchy. Demanding the eradication of tax farming, commercial prohibitions, fiscal monopolies, and extraordinary justice—demanding, in other words, a root-and-branch reform of entrenched institutions—such protest coalesced with other prerevolutionary movements to undermine the legitimacy of the Old Regime state, which finally collapsed in 1789.

The full implications of popular and elite opposition to the Farm became clear only once the Revolution commenced.[38] At the popular level, the Revolution began *not* with the storming of the Bastille, as is commonly thought, but with the sacking of the customs gates that encircled the city of Paris. From 11 to 14 July, professional and part-time smugglers joined merchants, petty traders, artisans, laborers, and the unemployed to destroy no fewer than forty customs posts, erected just a few years earlier to stem the flow of illicit tobacco and wine into the capital.[39] For three days, with axes and hammers in hand, the men and women of Paris chased Farm agents from their posts and demolished the newly constructed pavilions. They ripped down the iron railings that closed off streets, burned auxiliary stables and sheds, vandalized statues, and gutted the neoclassical stone buildings of scales, registers, beds, benches, tables, and doors—anything that could be thrown out the window and set aflame in the street. As news of the sacking of the Paris gates radiated outward from the capital, peasants and artisans in the provinces, many of whom smuggled on the side or regularly consumed illicit goods, took their cue and rebelled against the Farm as well. The dramatic culmination of more than a century of contraband rebellion, the fiscal uprisings of 1789 took on a distinctly revolutionary air as rioters went beyond contesting the authority of the Farm to demand its complete abolition, explicitly linking their acts of protest to the national rise to power of the third estate.[40]

From 1789 to 1791, such pressure from below had a profound impact on high legislative politics. The grievance lists commoners composed to inform deputies to the Estates General of their constituents' wishes had already made a sharp distinction between direct and indirect taxation. Although direct taxation was in dire need of reform, it was considered legitimate and even crucial to revolutionary constitutionalism and citizenship. Indirect taxation, by contrast, was associated with tyrannical prohibitions, abusive monopolies, and the perversion of justice; it was perceived as fundamentally illegitimate and would have to go.[41] In the year following the convocation of the Estates General, widespread rebellion against the Farm, coupled with an aggressive black market that no longer took the trouble to hide itself, reinforced the language of the *cahiers de doléances* to send legislators the unequivocal message that high consumption taxes and strict consumer prohibitions would not be tolerated in the new regime. Although deputies to the National Assembly, like most propertied men of the day, abhorred popular violence, many were steeped in the literature of economic, fiscal, and legal reform and therefore proved surprisingly receptive to this popular message. In the spring of 1791, after months of legislative debate and wrangling, the Assembly finally unveiled the Revolution's new fiscal system. Reversing a trend that had been developing since the seventeenth century, the new system shifted the fiscal weight of the state from indirect taxes on consumer goods to direct taxes on property. Administered locally by elected municipal governments and distributed equally (in theory) among property owners, the new direct "contributions" enacted the revolutionary principles of liberty and equality that had been enshrined in the Declaration of the Rights of Man and Citizen.

As legislators established new direct taxes with one hand, they demolished what one deputy described as the "gothic edifice" of indirect taxation with the other.[42] In an early first step, taken on 23 September 1789, the Assembly dismantled the judicial machinery that had criminalized trafficking, not only abolishing the infamous commissions that had condemned so many illicit traders to death and the galleys but forbidding any court from inflicting corporal punishment on nonviolent smugglers. Then, between the fall of 1789 and spring of 1791, the legislature abolished the *gabelle* (salt tax), erased internal fiscal borders, trimmed customs duties, and restricted the police powers of customs officers. The final and most contentious question deputies faced was what to do with the tobacco monopoly. From the floor of the Assembly, its opponents insisted that "the people" had already declared its will on this matter when it sacked customs checkpoints throughout France in 1789. In a speech that unreservedly appropriated the popular movement by portraying anti-Farm rebels as leaders of a sovereign people throwing off the shackles of despotism, the Alsatian Jacobin Charles-Louis-Victor de Broglie thundered: "If any doubts lingered about the people's profound aversion to this dreadful regime [of tobacco], recall what happened during that remarkable moment when the Revolution began. All the customs barriers that the General Farm had erected against the circulation of tobacco in the kingdom were overthrown at once . . . [and] the fiscal chains under which the people moaned" were finally broken. Only when "all the henchmen and inventions of the fisc" are banished will "France be able to believe in its liberty."[43] On 20 March 1791, the Assembly shuttered the tobacco monopoly and nullified the contract between Farmers General and king. The fiscal-judicial complex that had become such an integral part of the French monarchy since the reign of Louis XIV was now officially destroyed to make way for a new revolutionary order.[44]

An examination of the underground economy of the Old Regime reveals heretofore hidden links between globalization and the origins of the French Revolution. Fractious from the outset, globalization proved anything but a smooth and autonomous historical process. France's engagement with the wider world, tied inextricably to the rise of the absolutist state, produced political contestation at almost every level of metropolitan society. Although that contestation was manifold, I have chosen to focus on the political ramifications of two major interventions in world trade: the creation of a tobacco monopoly designed to harness the fiscal power of Atlantic production and consumption; and the imposition of a prohibition on calico intended to protect metropolitan producers from Asian competition. The monopoly and prohibition differed in their goals—the former sought to exploit home demand for a global commodity, while the latter attempted to stifle it—but their effect was the same. They stimulated the growth of a massive, transcontinental shadow economy. Historians have long known that interimperial smuggling was rampant in the colonies of the New World, but such illicit trade was part of a larger global underground that penetrated metropolitan Europe as well.[45]

In France, the emergent global underground produced significant political conflict, galvanizing prerevolutionary social and intellectual movements.[46] As contraband rebellion destabilized border provinces and contested the fiscal, commercial, legal, and moral claims of the crown, its harsh repression captured the attention of Enlightenment reformers—economists, men of law, philosophers—who transposed the "war" against the Farm into print, simultaneously publicizing the conflict and shifting blame for the "crime" of smuggling from traffickers to an allegedly illegitimate complex of institutions at the very heart of the monarchical state. The dual force of popular rebellion and public discourse exerted tremendous pressure on a state that could be fully reformed only through the act of revolution.

We know that the French Revolution had multiple origins: economic, social, political, intellectual, and cultural. Historians have spent the last half century debating which was most important, often treating one causal factor in isolation from the others. If we widen our field of inquiry to the global, it is possible see how different dimensions of the Old Regime were fundamentally related to one another. Globalizing eighteenth-century France illuminates how several vectors of development—overseas trade, state formation, popular politics, and Enlightenment culture—intersected to produce some of the principal preconditions of the Revolution.

2 *The global financial Origins of 1789*

LYNN HUNT

Although debate still rages about the long-term causes of the French Revolution, almost everyone agrees that the immediate precipitating cause was the fiscal crisis of 1787–88. The threat of bankruptcy forced the crown to seek new sources of revenue, and when it could not get them from a specially convened Assembly of Notables or the Parlement of Paris, it reluctantly agreed to call the Estates General to consider new taxation. Since the Estates General had not met for 175 years, its convocation in May 1789 opened the door to a constitutional and social revolution.

Less certain are the causes of the fiscal crisis itself. Was it due to the size of the deficit, an inability to pay the interest on the debt, the failure of efforts to rationalize and equalize taxation, the limitations of the financial administration, or the reluctance of the king's government to develop accountability to the public? All of these factors are essentially internal causes of the fiscal crisis.[1] While it would be foolish to downplay their significance, especially when taken together, a global perspective casts them in a different light and offers a more convincing explanation of the origins of the French Revolution.

Two intersecting global processes were transforming government finances: France was extending its global commercial empire in order to increase its resources; and like many other great powers, it found itself increasingly dependent on an international capital market to bankroll its ambitions and even its everyday operations.[2] In the 1780s France had to pay more and more to protect and administer its overseas empire, and it borrowed more and more from international creditors to do so. Foreign bankers located in Paris facilitated French access to international credit by buying French bonds for foreign investors. While the two global processes were intersecting, they effectively pulled France in different directions: on the one hand, the French government believed that pursuit of a global empire would increase its power; on the other hand, despite the country's growing wealth, the government was losing control of its finances.

The deficit ballooned when France supported the colonies during the American War of Independence. France took the side of the colonists in 1778 in order to counter Britain's increasing naval and commercial power. Armed intervention cost the French between 1 and 1.3 billion livres, almost all of it borrowed.[3] Debt and deficits are always relative, however. The French had spent even more to fight the Seven Years' War (1756–63) and lost, whereas they fought on the winning side in the American war and gained a measure of commercial and even naval parity in its aftermath. Comparative studies of the British and French debts have shown that the French monarchy was no worse off than its British counterpart in 1788: while the proportion of debt service to tax revenues was slightly higher in France, the ratio of debt to GNP was much lower, as was the ratio of taxes to GNP.[4] Neither the size of the deficit nor the debt ratio can explain the fiscal crisis.

After the peace of 1783 victorious France found itself in a paradoxical, even contradictory, situation. With the end of war, international commerce took off, and the French gained a greater share of the expanding wealth. At the same time, the French government had to pay for both the war and the protection and administration of its growing global commerce. In the eighteenth century, the British government spent twice as much on the navy as on the army.[5] The French proportions were reversed because France needed a large standing army to confront its potential challengers on the Continent. As a result, France was always playing catch-up by building new ships of the line, which invariably prompted Britain to build more of its own. This naval arms race, especially intense after 1783, put additional pressure on French finances.[6] Moreover, the British and Dutch governments could borrow at a lower rate than the French: 2.5–3 percent for the Dutch, 3–3.5 percent for the British, and 4.8–6.5 percent for the French.[7] Yet even though the French had to pay more to borrow, the higher yields made investment in French debt attractive to Italian, Swiss, and especially Dutch investors who could not get as good a return at home. The convergence of growing wealth, growing needs, and growing supplies of international capital made it possible for the French to borrow themselves into bankruptcy.

The Dutch and British governments could borrow at lower rates because they had more transparent forms of managing public debt. The Dutch led the way by establishing public bonds in the sixteenth century whose sale was controlled by the tax receivers themselves, but as a consequence the public debt was largely held on the provincial, not the national, level. The British ran their debt through the Bank of England, which was chartered in 1694:

investors bought stock in the bank, and the bank in turn arranged loans to the government. In 1751 the government converted the stock into consols or consolidated annuities (essentially perpetual bonds). Since rates of interest were so low in Holland, Dutch investors bought into the higher yields on the British debt and from the 1760s onward also invested in Swedish, Danish, Austrian, Russian, and eventually French and United States debt as well.[8]

The French government had a publicly funded debt too, but it was not consolidated or guaranteed through the operation of a national bank. Because the French monarchy had a long history of partial defaults, either through suspensions of payment or absorption of higher interest annuities into new issues at lower rates (not to mention the practice in previous times of arresting creditors and confiscating their goods), the government had to pay a risk premium, an interest rate higher than the market rate. The sheer variety of debt instruments contributed to those high rates, in part because it aggravated the systemic difficulty faced by those attempting to draw up state budgets or make sense of them as investors. Among the elements of the monarchy's public debt were rentes sur l'Hôtel de Ville de Paris (the most secure annuities because interest was paid directly out of tax receipts, but also difficult to buy and sell on the market), bonds and shares in the French East India Company, which became government obligations with liquidation of the company in 1770, the twenty different government loans offered for subscription between 1763 and 1787 (most of them either life annuities or loans with supposed set terms), and the Caisse d'Escompte (whose establishment as a discount bank in 1776 constituted in itself a government loan from investors because the government required as a condition of its establishment that 10 million l. of its initial capitalization of 15 million l. be deposited in the royal treasury).[9] In addition, in order to circumvent higher rates of interest the crown regularly borrowed through the intermediaries of provincial estates, cities, companies of tax farmers, and venal officeholders.[10]

The crown's budget proved so difficult to pin down that the two most prominent finance ministers of the 1780s, Jacques Necker (in office 1776–81 and 1788–89) and Charles-Alexandre de Calonne (1783–87), carried on a pamphlet war about the balance sheet, each accusing the other of deliberately distorting the truth about the deficit.[11] Necker claimed he left office in 1781 with a budgetary surplus; Calonne insisted that Necker had manipulated the figures to obscure the existence of a deficit that continued to grow. Both argued for reforms; neither succeeded in achieving them. Still, they each proved all too successful at raising loans. The Swiss Protestant Necker became minister, after all, because he offered direct access to Genevan funds, being a rich foreign banker himself. It was the success of French borrowing in the 1780s that helped bring on the fatal crisis in 1788–89.

European banking had been crossing national frontiers since the fifteenth century, and it traversed them ever more frequently as international trade intensified. Global trade networks in the eighteenth century relied on bankers to provide financing of ships, insurance, and especially, bills of exchange (*lettres de change*), the paper equivalents of silver and gold. Bankers themselves began to cross national frontiers. French banking houses installed branches in Spain, where they had more immediate access to the Spanish gold and silver needed in the East India trade. Swiss bankers played an increasingly prominent role inside France. Of the seven original administrators of the Caisse d'Escompte, for example, five were Swiss in origin.[12] In the 1780s political upheavals in Geneva, Amsterdam, and Brussels prompted a new influx of foreign financiers into Paris. They bought and sold French government bonds for foreign investors, arranged investment in private French companies and those with government privileges, and, in some cases, played the currency markets.[13]

The globalization of the banking sector went hand in hand with the rising volume of international trade. Silver production in the Spanish colonies increased over the course of the eighteenth century, and when war ended in 1783, Spanish imports of silver and therefore French access to it dramatically increased.[14] After 1783 the French share in both the slave trade and Indian Ocean commerce increased dramatically. During the war years from 1778 to 1783, the British controlled 52 percent of the slave trade to the Americas, while the French carried only 13 percent (see fig. 2). The French lost no time in recovering their position; in fact, the French slave trade culminated between 1787 and 1791 (just as abolitionism got going) when the French transported

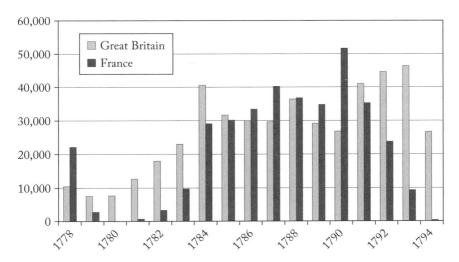

Figure 2. Slaves Transported, 1778–1794. Data from http://www.slavevoyages.org.

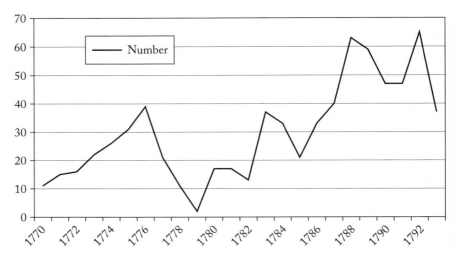

Figure 3. French Ships Going to Indian Ocean, 1770–1793. Data from Philippe Haudrère, *La compagnie française des Indes au XVIIIe siècle 1719–1795* (Paris: Librairie de l'Inde, 1989), 4:1, 215.

40 percent of the slaves compared to 23 percent for the British.[15] The East India trade reached its height at the same time (see fig. 3); the French sent the greatest number of vessels past the Cape of Good Hope between 1787 and 1792.[16] The French finally surpassed both the Dutch and the British in the number of vessels traveling to the Indian Ocean.[17]

Although companies usually specialized in one region of the global trading networks, the carrying trade in the Americas, commerce in the Indian Ocean, and the Atlantic slave trade were linked together by silver, bills of exchange, and ultimately therefore bankers, who guaranteed the equivalence of silver and bills of exchange.[18] Banking thus helped knit the American, Indian Ocean, and African networks into a unified French commercial empire, not to mention tying it to merchants and bankers in a host of other countries.[19] The French had long had a major share in the Spanish trade with the Americas, whether through direct sales of goods, indirect participation in Spanish shipping, or credit supplied by French bankers.[20] Involvement in the Spanish carrying trade with the Americas was critical because it offered access to silver. The biggest French commercial houses, such as Lecouteulx, had branches in Spain, especially in Cadiz, which was the main transhipment point for silver to the Indies. In the eighteenth century the French had twice as many international trading houses in Cadiz as any other nation, and the French often did more business than their more numerous Spanish counterparts.[21] In 1782 transplanted French bankers helped form the new Banco Nacional de

San Carlos (Banque de Saint Charles) in Madrid, which had a royal privilege to control the export of precious metals. Lecouteulx in Paris was charged with drumming up investors in the new bank, and by May 1785 the Lecouteulx family was the largest investor in the Spanish bank.[22]

The French global empire depended on Spanish silver.[23] In his *Manuel du commerce des Indes orientales et de la Chine* of 1806, Pierre Blancard called on his thirty years of experience in the Indian Ocean trade to describe a typical cargo of a 600-ton vessel. Going to the Coromandel coast and Bengal, it would carry 795,000 francs (the franc was the equivalent of the prerevolutionary livre) worth of silver, twice the value of all the rest of its cargo, which would include, by contrast, only 40,000 francs worth of gold.[24] The silver shipped to Bengal bought a variety of goods, among them the textiles and cowries (shells) used to purchase slaves in Africa.[25]

The cowry-silver exchange is a fascinating subject in itself. The cowries of the slave trade came from the Maldive Islands, off the coast of India; cowries grew elsewhere, but those of the Maldives were more desirable to West Africans. They were fished by women who waded into the sea and detached the shells clinging to stones underwater. The shells were buried in pits on the beach until the mollusks inside decayed and could be washed out. In Balasore, a town just south of Bengal, or Ceylon, the Maldive traders sold cowries to local merchants for rice, and Europeans in turn bought the cowries with silver. The cowry price of slaves in West Africa rose steadily during the eighteenth century, from 40,000–50,000 cowries per slave in the 1710s to 160,000–176,000 cowries in the 1770s. As a consequence, the proportion of cowries used in the purchase of slaves steadily declined from about one-half to one-third or less, yet it remained a critical element in the slave trade. Between 1700 and 1790 the Dutch imported to West Africa on average 74 metric tons per year, which translated to 60 million individual shells per year. The English average for the eighteenth century was 50 metric tons per year. A French comparison is impossible, as there is no similar statistical series available, in part because of the up-and-down fortunes of the French East India Company.[26] The available evidence indicates that cowries played the same role in the French slave trade as they played in that of their competitors.[27] Without Spanish silver, then, there would have been no trade with India, no cowries or Indian textiles, no slaves, no slave economy, no sugar, no coffee, and so on.

Silver did not do this all on its own. Bills of exchange stood in for silver at many stops in the trading networks.[28] Ships took the cowries, textiles, and other goods bought in the East Indies back to Europe where they were sold for specie (gold and silver) or bills of exchange and used to outfit slave ships; once purchased with cowries, cloth, and other manufactured items in West Africa, the slaves were then sold either on credit or for specie in the Americas;

the slavers then bought sugar, coffee, or other goods to take back to Europe. The goal at every stage was to make a profit, but to arrive at that end, silver had to be illegally or legally obtained from the Spanish and sent to India. Many scholars have described the slave trade pattern as triangular, linking Europe, Africa, and the American colonies. As this brief review suggests, it consisted, rather, of two huge loops that extended in one direction from Europe to Africa and the Americas and in the other from Europe to India and China. The circulation of goods, specie, and credit was global, not merely transatlantic.[29]

Although its share of this global commerce grew dramatically after 1783, France confronted international developments that potentially threatened its continuing access to silver and credit. The longest-lasting of these problems was the loss of position in India at the conclusion of the Seven Years' War in 1763. Even after 1783, when the French regained some of their commercial outposts in India, French merchants increasingly relied on local British agents (and even British pilots) to carry out their local transactions. When Calonne reestablished the French East India Company in 1785, he planned to link the revived French company directly to its British counterpart. The French foreign minister Vergennes rejected this arrangement for political reasons, so the new company had to rely on financing from bankers in Paris (including the Caisse d'Escompte) and on insurance and financing of ships provided by private banks in London.[30]

The position in India mattered even though many more ships went to the Caribbean than to the Indian Ocean. The revived French East India Company sent 63 vessels to ports on the Indian Ocean and China in 1788, for example, while slave merchants in the French Atlantic ports were sending 783 ships to the Caribbean, 465 of them to Saint-Domingue.[31] Yet India's goods were essential for trade in Europe and Africa, and the profits in India could be high. A study of the British balance of payments at the end of the eighteenth century has shown that net transfers from India were equal or even superior to profits made from the British slave trade.[32] The French balance of trade with India was much less positive, however. The British East India Company was bringing home goods valued at more than three times the amount of specie shipped to India and China between 1785 and 1791, whereas the comparable French ratio was only one to one. The French company made good profits for its directors, ranging from 5–60 percent per voyage, and offered regular dividends of 6 percent to shareholders, but it did nothing for the balance of payments of the country.[33]

The French also faced a realignment of trade with Spain, one that would foreshadow Spain's break with France and alliance with Britain after 1793. In the 1780s the Spanish not only established a new national bank to control currency exports but also began to withdraw France's long-standing status as most favored nation in trade.[34] French textiles faced higher import duties, and European competitors began taking a larger share of the internal Spanish market. French bankers might still make large profits off their dealings in Spanish finances, but French manufacturers were crying foul.[35] In both cases—France's position in India and in Spanish trade—developments in the 1780s favored finance over trade and manufacturing.[36] Underlying structural degradation of France's position in international commerce thus encouraged the tendency of investors, both French and foreign, to make money off of French financial instruments rather than investing in productive enterprises.

The abundant supply of capital generated by the increase in production of silver, the international growth in trade, and the expansion of the international capital market proved too great a temptation to a French crown that continued to resist the establishment of a consolidated national debt based on accountability to the public. Necker's *Compte rendu* (Account of Finances) of 1781 had broken the habitual secrecy of French government finances, but its publication provoked a furious barrage of hostile pamphlets by other high-ranking officials (including, later, Calonne).[37] Necker was fired a few months later. In his account, published in the midst of the American war, he explicitly drew attention to the link between British credit and the public availability of government accounts and in particular the submission of government accounts for approval to Parliament, precisely the issues that would return with such vehemence in France in 1787–88.[38] Rather than go that route, the French government seized on the new availability of capital and encouraged increasingly speculative investment in its credit instruments.[39] A surplus of capital made it possible for Necker's successors to put off the day of reckoning, but when the day came, the result was revolution, not fiscal reform.

When Calonne became finance minister a few weeks after the conclusion of the peace settlement in September 1783, conditions were ripe for a speculative frenzy. The reestablishment of the East India Company in 1785 provides a telling example. Rather than simply invest in the revived company and through it in Indian Ocean trade, individuals (and families) with capital began to speculate on the value of the company's shares. Despite the government's efforts to limit speculation by requiring brokers to declare all shares that had been bought on time contracts (some bet on a decline, others on a rise in share prices), opportunists began snapping up shares not only in the East India Company but also in the Caisse d'Escompte, the new water company, and three new insurance companies.[40] Share values rose precipitously in late 1785 and 1786. In an attempt to stave off a collapse that was widely feared at the end of 1786, Calonne funneled 11.5 million l. in treasury funds to a syndicate instructed to buy up East India Company and water company shares in order to shore up the prices. One of Calonne's chosen agents took the occasion to corner the market (get control of all the shares in order to drive up prices) in league with a clergyman from a noble family and major shareholder in the East India Company, Marc-René Sahuguet d'Espagnac. When the market manipulation was revealed in a pamphlet published by Mirabeau in March 1787 (*Dénonciation de l'agiotage* [Denunciation of Speculation]), Calonne ended up losing nearly 25 million l. for the government.[41] Just when he was trying to convince the Assembly of Notables to reform government finances, Calonne had to order liquidation of the corner and absorb the losses of speculators. Two leading Parisian bankers, the Swiss-born Rodolphe-Emmanuel Haller (son of the famous Swiss writer Albrecht von Haller) and Barthelemy Lecoulteulx de la Noraye (also involved with the Banco de San Carlos), were charged with selling the cornered shares, which promptly declined in value. Calonne was fired in April because he had lost his credibility.

The speculative boom had more than one source, but contributing to it was the influx of foreign financiers who were coming to Paris in response to political upheavals in surrounding countries. Étienne Clavière came to Paris in 1784 after finding himself on the losing side of the Genevan revolution of 1782. The Dutch bankers Balthazar-Élie Abbema and Jean-Conrad de Kock fled to Paris to escape the repression of the Dutch patriots in 1787. Others, like the Belgian comte de Seneffe, one of those originally working for Calonne to buy up shares, or the British banker Walter Boyd, a financial agent for the French East India Company, came because a "get rich quick" atmosphere prevailed after Calonne came to power in November 1783.[42]

Clavière never established a big bank like Haller, Lecouteulx, Seneffe, or Boyd, yet because he was arrested and his papers were confiscated during the Terror, his activities provide the most insight into the financial machinations occurring at this critical time. Among his papers was a register with entries dating from April 1786 until July 1789.[43] For April 1786, when he started the register, he listed holdings of 4,668,117 l., which included investments of 104,750 l. in shares of the Caisse d'Escompte (with which he did regular business), 1,269,582 l. in shares of the revived East India Company, and 16,000 l. in the water company. He also held 135,000 l. in English consols and 2,296,160 l. in various French government bonds and annuities. Clavière's debts outstripped his assets, however. He listed outstanding obligations of 6,549,284 l. Clavière was a *baissier*, a short seller. He owed 393,090 l. on East India Company shares, 318,996 l. on water company shares, 108,350 l. on shares in the Caisse d'Escompte, and 380,911 l. on shares in the Banco Nacional de San Carlos, which had also become the subject of French speculation.[44] Clavière undertook more than one kind of maneuver. His multimillion l. gamble on shares included speculation on the share price (borrowing shares, selling them at a high price, then repurchasing them later at a much lower value and returning them to the borrower and pocketing the difference) or betting, in the case of the Caisse d'Escompte, on the dividend that would be paid, hoping again that the rate would fall over time.[45]

Clavière did not trust the market to achieve his aims, so he fed information and probably even pages of prose to Mirabeau, who wrote pamphlets against speculation in shares of the Banco Nacional and the water company, and later to Brissot, who published pamphlets against the water company and a proposed fire insurance company.[46] Clavière hoped to benefit from a resulting decline in share values, and he also wanted to set up his own water and insurance companies. He played a leading role in the formation of two new insurance companies, one against fire (1786) and one for life insurance (1787). Having lived in Great Britain after his exile from Geneva, he had learned about actuarial tables and saw an occasion to profit from his new knowledge. He and his allies had the right contacts at court to get the projects approved, but the schemes hardly got off the ground before 1789 (needless to say, his mouthpieces did not attack these two companies in print). For all his efforts, Clavière could not always correctly time the market for company shares, and in the end he preferred investing in French government debt, for "the high rates of interest make up for the risk."[47] Clavière wrote those words to one of his biggest creditors, Pieter Stadnitski, an Amsterdam banker, who had loaned him 521,429 l. (Stadnitski was one of the chief funders of the debt of the new United States).[48]

Most striking about Clavière is the suddenness with which he entered the speculative scene. His *livre de caisse* (account book) runs from January 1781 until October 1787 with some unfortunate gaps. From January 1781 until March 1784, the sums involved are not immense, ranging from a starting credit of 15,443 l. in mid-January 1781 to a reconciliation of accounts at the end of 1781 at 53,297 l (not exactly a trivial increase, however).[49] In December 1782 he reconciles his accounts at only 6,130 l. (folio 24), and in March 1784 at 3,150 l. (folio 34). Suddenly, eighteen months later, in August 1785, he opens with 136,945 l., most of it commercial paper from various bankers (folio 35).[50] The numbers rise vertiginously thereafter: by mid-November 1785 the amount is 198,682 l. (folio 38), and three weeks later 279,116 l. (folio 40), all of which he has paid out. Having once again restarted his accounts, by mid-January 1786 he has 437,581 l. (folio 42), and by mid-March 1,017,253 l. (folio 44, all paid out). He restarts his account again in April 1786, and by the end of September he has 2,516,836 l. (folio 55), by the end of November 4,963,840 l. (folio 57), by early January 1787 7,185,970 l. (folio 59), and by the beginning of April 1787 10,044,991 l. (folio 62).[51] At the end of June 1787 he stops putting in figures, and the account ends altogether in October. Clavière pays out even more than he brings in, but under paying out he includes paying for shares in various companies, which constitute his investments. Although it is impossible to determine the precise size of Clavière's own fortune from this account book, it is clear that in a very short period of time and in a newly speculative setting, he parlayed substantial loans from bankers into major holdings of his own. Clavière made his fortune entirely from speculative investments.

Mirabeau, Brissot, and Clavière all gained reputations as righteous denouncers of market speculation, whereas Calonne lost his job, and the rates on government loans increased to ruinous levels (7–10 percent).[52] Yet insiders knew that investors were mounting pamphlet wars for something other than high-minded ends. When Mirabeau's *Dénonciation de l'agiotage* appeared in March 1787, just as the Assembly of Notables was beginning its deliberations, a widely read underground newsletter seized on its significance: "What renders his zeal even more suspect is the adroitness with which he only unleashes his lightning bolts of eloquence against those who are playing for a rise in the market. . . . Such a pronounced partiality has not failed to make people suspect those betting on decline, Clavière, Panchaud and others, of having once again solicited this latest production at the same price for which they obtained previous ones."[53] The editors of the newsletter nonetheless worried that the damage was done; Mirabeau's vitriolic denunciation of Calonne and his prediction that the finances of the country would be ruined and bankruptcy was therefore inevitable had provoked public indignation and undermined the financial credibility of the government. In the end, then, the combination of speculative excesses and the linking of them to the government through pamphlet wars played a greater role than the deficit itself in bringing down the government. Calonne's successors could not stanch the blood, and the door opened to revolution and the promise of massive fiscal reorganization.

The machinations of bankers, foreign and French, and the pamphlet wars that sapped the government's credibility were not the only factors bringing on the upheaval of 1789. Massive unemployment in the textile sector, which followed the free trade treaty signed with Great Britain in 1786 and poor harvests in 1788 and 1789, inflamed both urban workers and peasants who could not afford to feed themselves. When the constitutional crisis began, the popular classes were ready to make their voices heard, whether in riots or meetings held to assemble their grievances in preparation for the Estates General. The intervention of the popular classes radicalized the revolution that unfolded, but there would have been no revolution if the nation's creditors, both foreign and domestic, had not lost confidence in the government.

After the Revolution began, the issues of the government's debt and the international bankers' role in it did not disappear. In 1789 Clavière argued strongly against the repudiation of the crown's debt, and in 1792 he became finance minister.[54] Arrested as one of the Girondins on 2 June 1793, he committed suicide before he could be tried.[55] By the end of 1793, many foreign bankers had fled, been arrested, or executed. Global finances would be as crucial to the unfolding of the French Revolution as they had been in causing it.

Confidence is not an entirely rational calculation, as any investor in stock markets knows all too well. Investors in France in the 1780s had many reasons to feel confident. France's global trade was soaring, and the supply of silver as well as credit was increasing. True, France had had to join a war against Britain in order to protect its global commerce and imperial ambitions, and that war was expensive, but no more so than it was for Britain. Peace opened a period of prosperity and profits, but exaggerated expectations among those with access to capital led to a crisis that could no longer be solved by the usual methods. Central to that crisis in France were the operations of an ever more-globalized commercial empire and an increasingly international market for capital.

9 *The fall from Eden*

THE FREE-TRADE ORIGINS OF THE FRENCH REVOLUTION

CHARLES WALTON

Is free trade revolutionary? If so, what kind of revolution does it tend to bring about? Does it foster peace, democracy, and human rights? Or can it trigger economic crisis, social dislocation, and political unrest? These questions remain as pressing and contentious today as they were in the late eighteenth century, when democratic revolution and theories of commerce swept through the Atlantic world. Some optimists at that time, like some today, saw free trade and democracy marching triumphantly together: "The liberality of principle," a British commenter observed in 1787, "in the commercial as in the political world, [is] gradually diffusing itself over the opinions of mankind at present."[1] In late eighteenth-century France, the relationship between free trade and democracy—between economic and political liberalizations— was far from harmonious. Tensions between the two owed much to the Anglo-French commercial treaty of 1786, the "Eden Treaty," named after the British negotiator William Eden. Largely ignored in recent overviews of the period, the Eden Treaty was considered by several late nineteenth- and early twentieth-century historians to be a key cause of the socioeconomic crisis of 1788 and 1789. This view was rejected by several midcentury historians, who argued that the treaty had neither harmed the French economy nor provoked as much outcry as previously claimed. The older literature, this chapter suggests, was closer to the mark, but the historical significance of the treaty goes beyond its devastating economic consequences for France. The Eden Treaty, I argue, marked a diplomatic and economic revolution, one that involved a rethinking of France's global influence and approach to foreign policy. Its impact, however, prompted grievances that were expressed in the political revolution of 1789.

The 1780s saw a "rage for commercial treaties" in the Atlantic world.[2] The trend took off during the Peace of Paris negotiations of 1783, which brought an end to the American War of Independence. The belief that expanded commercial relations would secure peace owed much to the century-long development of ideas about the reciprocal benefits and the civilizing potential of trade. Many Enlightenment writers posited *le doux commerce* as an alternative to brutal mercantile warfare.[3] Montesquieu's claim that "the natural effect of commerce is to bring about peace" was echoed by British, French, and American leaders and diplomats as they sought to end hostilities. In his speech to the House of Lords in February 1783, the British prime minister, William Petty, 2nd Earl of Shelburne, tried to make free trade with the United States and other countries the touchstone of the peace settlement: "All that we ought to covet upon the earth [is] free trade and fair equality."[4] Benjamin Franklin, negotiating for the Americans, welcomed Shelburne's position. In a dispatch to the foreign secretary in London, Britain's plenipotentiary, David Hartley, noted: "Be assured, Sir, that [the Americans] have no sentiments of hostility nor any desire to injure or to affront any part of the British nation, nor has the Court of France in the least degree any influence over them. They declare themselves in the most explicit terms ready to concur in every measure of reciprocity with Great Britain."[5] The commercial coziness of Britain and the United States, not to mention the evident friendship forming between Franklin and Hartley, was making the French foreign minister jealous. Charles Gravier, comte de Vergennes, already had reasons to be disappointed with the United States. The Franco-American Treaty of Amity and Commerce of 1778 had been designed to undermine Britain's commercial empire, but by 1781, U.S. trade with its enemy, Britain, was nearly twice that with its ally, France.[6]

Ultimately, Parliament refused to sanction free trade with its colonial rebels, but all the talk of commercial treaties at Versailles in 1783 made France risk appearing foolish, winning the war but losing the peace, which was being measured in commercial terms. Determined not to be left out of the commercial potlatch, Vergennes persuaded Britain to accept article 18 in the Treaty of Paris, which called for subsequent negotiations to conclude a bilateral commercial treaty. Despite intense Francophobia in England, Shelburne concurred, and the two powers agreed to draft a commercial treaty before 1 January 1786.[7]

Trade talks between France and Britain stalled until the winter of 1786, largely because Shelburne's successor, William Pitt, had more pressing matters on his agenda, including efforts to establish free trade with Ireland. (Parliament rejected his Irish Propositions in 1785.) Meanwhile, the French administration sought to whet the appetite of British merchants and manufacturers and test the leverage they had with the British government by dropping wartime trade barriers. Commerce between the two countries immediately increased, but in 1785 the French ministers became impatient and reversed policy, placing prohibitions on a wide range of British goods.[8] Alarmed, British merchants drafted petitions, and Pitt swung into action, replacing his negotiator in Paris with William Eden.[9] The deadline was extended, and serious talks got under way in the spring of 1786.

A mix of idealism, pragmatism, and realpolitik appears in the reports and diplomatic correspondence during the trade negotiations, as does a rethinking of imperial strategies. In a letter to his brother-in-law, Eden confided his imperial vision of what a free-trade agreement with France would mean: "This is certainly a great country, though I try not to look here as if I thought it so. . . . The utmost I admit . . . is that if she has the good fortune to make a cordial friend of England, we may jointly give Law to the world; I believe it."[10] What did Eden mean by "giv[ing] Law to the world"? Vergennes offered a fuller explanation. In a note to the controller general of finances, Charles Alexandre de Calonne, he wrote: "When the two most powerful and enlightened nations—those that all others want to imitate—give the example of friendly relations involving honest and mutually beneficial communication, other nations will but have to follow this example. . . . The wisdom of the King will have reformed the world; it will have established a universal exchange of benefits."[11] He continued: "Nothing appears more desirable, and more conformable to [His Majesty's] principles, than a general freedom that would remove all obstacles to the circulation of products and merchandise of all different countries . . . making all nations one in commerce."

Global peace and prosperity through trade, with Britain and France setting the terms—these were utopian liberal-economic imaginings, with distinct imperialist overtones. Yet, the two nations' desire to conclude a commercial treaty involved pragmatic objectives as well, especially revenue. By lowering tariffs, which were often prohibitory, to levels that would compete with insurance rates for contraband, the two states would transform smuggling into legitimate trade and gain revenue. But the French administration had still other, shrewdly calculated reasons for concluding a commercial treaty with Britain. Vergennes's reasons were geopolitical. Already in the mid-1770s, he had been contemplating a radical change in policy toward Britain, France's longtime enemy and commercial rival. As an alternative to hostilities (privateering, colonial wars), he considered opening up trade with Britain and, by wooing its merchants, exerting indirect influence on the British government.[12] Once the British were hooked on French markets, he thought, France would have leverage to pursue its geopolitical agenda. The plan was put

on the back burner during the American War of Independence but brought
forward and implemented in 1783.

Vergennes knew that Parliament would never agree to a commercial treaty
unless it saw Britain securing the greater advantage, as he admitted to his
agent in London, François, marquis de Barthélemy: "I much prefer . . . that
the British believe [they] have made the better bargain than if they thought
we had entrapped them."[13] Mission accomplished: Britain got the better deal,
as Barthélemy readily concluded upon seeing the treaty's final terms.[14] The
treaty's economic shortcomings for France aside, it is worth noting the
revolutionary aspect of this diplomacy. Vergennes sought not only to turn
Britain, France's "natural enemy," into a friend, but also to use liberal trade as
a means to neutralize and manipulate it. This was realpolitik, but it was *liberal*
realpolitik, quite different from mercantilist strategies of the seventeenth and
eighteenth centuries.

Calonne's motivations for pursuing liberal commercial relations with
Britain were more cosmopolitan, if more controversial, than Vergennes's. In
light of provisions in the Treaty of Versailles, by which Britain allowed France
to conduct trade in certain parts of India, the administration considered
reviving the Compagnie des Indes, which had been shut down in 1769.[15] With
national interests foremost in mind, Vergennes imagined the company trading
directly with the natives in the areas permitted by the treaty. Calonne and the
minister of the navy, the maréchal de Castries, devised a different scheme.
They began secret negotiations with financiers in Paris and London to form
an international cartel.[16] According to their plan, the new French company,
reestablished in 1784 and financed through public stocks, would conclude a
treaty with the British East India Company to purchase goods from it (the
British company), rather than directly from the natives in India, as was
permitted by the treaty. The establishment of a privileged trading company
was hardly revolutionary, but binding that company to a foreign one, thereby
forming an international cartel with state backing, was.[17]

Vergennes was furious when he learned about Calonne's scheme through
his agent in London, Barthélemy. The foreign minister bided his time until the
treaty terms between the British and French trading companies were brought
before the *Conseil du roi* for approval in December 1785. Vergennes's assistant,
Conrad Alexandre Gérard de Rayneval, submitted a memoir blasting the
arrangement: "What interest has the state in enriching a small number of
individuals at the expense of the other citizens [who would be banned from
trading with India], of the revenues of the state [because of the company's
fiscal privileges], of liberty itself, which a wise administration does not restrain
except for the good of the state and not for the purpose of making anyone
rich?"[18] The treaty between the French and British trading companies was

now a dead letter, and the value of the French company's stock plummeted. Embarrassed, Calonne issued a new round of shares to keep the company afloat and secretly drew 11.5 million livres from the royal coffers to buy them through front agents. His efforts became mired in the financial havoc so well described by Lynn Hunt in her contribution to this volume. Despite the successes of the Compagnie des Indes's early ventures, the agents engaged those funds in the speculation war between the bulls and the bears on the Paris stock market, losing 9 million.[19]

Vergennes and Calonne were thus driven primarily by geopolitical and financial objectives. They knew that the commercial treaty might inflict harm on French industries, but they surrounded themselves with experts, such as Rayneval, Pierre-Samuel Dupont de Nemours, and Edouard Boyetet, who insisted on the inherent benefits of free trade. In a joint memoir promoting the treaty, Dupont and Boyetet anticipated the complaints of French manufactures but insisted that the treaty was "the most advantageous one for France ever concluded," that it was "based upon wise, incontestable principles," and that even if there were initial hardship, "the natural course of things" would eventually lead to prosperity for all French industries. Since the British would not want their ships to return from France empty, they would fill them with French goods.[20]

Neither country heeded warnings that a too-abrupt shift toward liberal trade relations might produce socioeconomic shock. The author of a report found among Eden's papers urged implementing the treaty slowly and in a limited manner, offering both sides time to assess the results before expanding it. "Otherwise the one may overstock the other with certain articles of manufacture and thereby deprive a great Body of People of Bread, before they have an opportunity of converting their industry to other pursuits."[21] It is not surprising that the British did not heed this advice, since it had little to lose, but France rejected it as well. A memoir addressed to Calonne counseled prudence in negotiating with England, a nation that was "extremely Enlightened about its interests," knew those interests "in the greatest detail," and "would never entertain any view that called for sacrificing them."[22] Anticipating great losses for French manufactures, the author urged the ministers to consider more than the monetary value of exchanged goods. It was also important to appreciate the value of an industry for "furnishing people the means to live, [which is] the only true way for a state to assess the value of each one of its industries." Calonne dismissed these concerns. In the margin, he commented: "[England's] advantage will diminish as a result of the care we take to perfect and encourage our national industries."

But the administration failed to "perfect and encourage" French industries. In the fall of 1787, Rouen's chamber of commerce conducted an investigation of the treaty's impact. Although its findings confirmed widespread impressions, the authors did not demand the treaty's revocation. They admired England's economic ingenuity and hoped that Rouen, "France's Manchester," would catch up.[23] The problem, in their view, was the lack of state support. In his response to the chamber's report, Dupont assured that every one of its recommendations had already been proposed within the administration before the treaty's signing.[24] Although many physiocrats opposed state subventions for industry (they thought profits from agriculture were sufficient to finance industrial growth), he agreed that such support was needed to help French industries weather the initial effects of the treaty. Bureaucratic logjams, he explained, partially accounted for the failure to deliver aid, but fraud and incompetence at customs offices compounded the problem, depriving the state of revenue. As if to strengthen the chamber's case, he provided the example of imported razors, which were being declared at one-fifteenth their true value.[25] Dupont expressed exasperation that between the signing of the treaty in September 1786 and its implementation in May 1787 "the most important measures [to encourage industry] . . . did not take place."[26]

Industrial encouragements in France were indeed feeble, but the scale of the negligence should be stressed. Between 1740 and 1789, the administration accorded 5.5 million livres in subsidies and incentives.[27] Calonne's ministry alone accorded 550,000 livres, or roughly 110,000 livres per year. Thus, the annual sums invested by the French state to help make its industries competitive with the largest manufacturing country in Europe amounted to less than half of what Marie-Antoinette spent on her wardrobe in 1785. They amounted to 1 percent of the sum Calonne was willing to spend on propping up speculation on the Compagnie des Indes. They equaled what the administration spent on getting balance of trade statistics in 1788.[28] Worse, these meager subsidies were often suppressed or diverted to pay protégés or the salaries of regulators.[29]

Shortly after the implementation of the treaty, French manufactures underwent shock. Despite Dupont's claim (repeated by some historians) that the treaty's negative impact concerned only two or three provinces, the pain produced by the sudden influx of British goods and exports of raw materials was felt widely.[30] France's northern regions were, to be sure, the hardest hit. In areas stretching from Normandy to Champagne, between half and two-thirds of industrial workers became unemployed.[31] And as British retailers set up shops in Rouen and advertised their goods in the local newspapers, the city saw its earthenware industry wiped out, permanently, and its citizens emigrate in record numbers. Bankruptcies abounded.[32] Manufactures in Lille and Roubaix saw production drop 25 to 50 percent in the late 1780s.[33] By 1791, when cotton spinners around Lille begged the National Assembly for subventions, they reminded deputies that "this is the only industry remaining [in the area], the only one that has not yet been wiped out by the treaty with England."[34]

Was contemporary outcry against the treaty exaggerated? Some historians believe so, but their arguments are based more on assertions than evidence. They point out that the French economy was already in decline before the implementation of the treaty in May 1787.[35] This view overlooks the fact that liberalized trade with Britain had already gotten under way before then. As we have seen, Vergennes's strategy since 1783 had been to entice British merchants to avail themselves of French markets in order to bring the British government to the negotiating table and to neutralize it as France pursued its own interests elsewhere. Aside from the brief period of prohibitions in 1785, France turned a blind eye to smuggling.[36] Rayneval, Vergennes's assistant, admitted as much. He explained to Eden that the administration's toleration of smuggling was a "connivance" and that "it is in the power of the French government at any moment and with little exertion to put a stop to it."[37] This was an overstatement, but there was some truth to it, since even sporadic seizures of contraband—and Britain did worry about them—drove up insurance rates for illegal trade, making British goods less competitive.[38]

Historians seeking to rehabilitate the Eden Treaty sometimes concede that it was harmful for French industry but claim it was a boon for French agriculture.[39] This assertion needs to be qualified. Liquor (wine, eau-de-vie) was France's most important export to Britain and the one on which the administration placed its highest hopes. Exports of Bordeaux reds, "claret," did increase in the mid-1780s, especially in the year spanning the signing and implementation of the treaty, but they dropped soon thereafter, reaching their second lowest level in twenty years in 1789.[40] In part, the failure of French wines to catch on had to do with English machismo at the time: "Men drink port, boys drink claret."[41] It also had to do with the fact that France quickly lost its trade advantage over Portugal. Although Britain agreed to lower tariffs on French wine, it reserved the right to honor its prior treaty obligations with Portugal (the Methuen Treaty of 1703), which stipulated that tariffs on Portuguese wines would always be one-third lower than those of the lowest other trading partner. Unsurprisingly, and despite assurances to the contrary before the treaty's signing, in 1787, England set tariffs on Portuguese wines below those on French ones.[42] Thus, the advantage for France was short-lived. Meanwhile, Bordeaux's glassworks suffered from the sudden arrival of cheap British bottles.[43]

Nor were French exports of agricultural products without negative domestic effects. Arguably, they aggravated France's socioeconomic crisis on the eve of the Revolution. In June 1787, the government authorized grain exports, an extremely unpopular measure.[44] As Jean-François de Tolozan, intendant of commerce, noted in 1789, France's grain production was so close to its level of consumption that exporting the staple was forcing the French state to repurchase it from abroad at higher prices.[45] While merchants profited, many starved, and the state dug itself deeper into debt. Although a ban on grain exports was issued in 1788 in the wake of bad harvests, the mixed signals the government was sending about market freedom led to uneven and contentious implementation of the ban.[46] Meanwhile, increased wool exports to Britain via Marseille had the effect of raising the product's price within France, making it increasingly difficult for France's already fragile wool industry to manufacture it.[47] And as unemployment increased, so, too, did indigence. Local officials complained that they could not distribute enough charity to keep up with rising destitution. Many desperate people took to the road, thereby raising rural fears about brigands. Some emigrated; others surged into Paris, making the city more of a social powder keg by 1789.[48]

Alarmed by public outcry against the treaty, Lomenie de Brienne, the new controller general of finances, instructed the administration's Bureau of Commerce in February 1788 to investigate the situation.[49] The government soon received reports about the crises unfolding in Amiens, Reims, Troyes, Alais, Marseille, Saint-Yrieix, and several towns in Vienne and Dauphiné.[50] An inspector of manufactures and future minister of the interior during the Revolution, Jean-Marie Roland, summed up the situation in the *Encyclopédie méthodique* like this: "We have just concluded a commercial treaty with the English which may well enrich our great grandchildren but has deprived 500,000 workers of bread and ruined 10,000 commercial houses."[51] Provincial complaints were expressed in many *cahiers de doléances*, the formal grievances drafted by all three estates on the eve of the meeting of the Estates General of May 1789. The third estate of Varages, in Provence, described the suffering of its earthenware workers, many of whom "were taking their talents and industry to foreign countries, where they receive the aid that their own country refuses them."[52] The third estate of Montpellier said that its cotton industry had been hammered by foreign competition, especially the influx of calicoes from India; it asked for protections to be raised on imports. Bordeaux, which was supposed to reap great benefits from the treaty, complained as well. Its third estate demanded "a revision of the treaty of commerce with England," with special attention to the articles harmful to Bordeaux and national industries.[53] The third estate of Quimper, on the western edge of Brittany, demanded the revocation of the treaty, the "shock" of which was "ruining many manufactures" and reducing "an immense quantity of workers to the most dreadful misery."[54]

By 1788 and 1789, government officials began acknowledging the scale of the catastrophe. Tolozan, intendant of commerce, concluded that the Eden Treaty had all but destroyed France's glass and earthenware sectors, and he lamented that the French government had put "political priorities" before "the general interest of commerce" in drafting it. He also noted the aggravating failure of customs offices to collect revenues, which might have been used to mitigate those hardships.[55] Boyetet, former codirector of commerce (with Dupont), expressed his regrets. In a letter to a deputy to the Estates General in 1789, he wrote: "No one more than I senses better the need to inform the Nation about the consequences of the treaty of commerce, which is crushing and destroying [us]; not even the Administration now doubts this."[56] The administration's Balance of Trade Office documented the damage. In its report on the treaty's first eight months (May through December 1787), it calculated France's trade deficit with Britain to be 9 million livres, but it offered hope that the trend might soon be reversed. In a later report, however, the director of the Balance of Trade Office, Jean Potier, estimated that the trade deficit had spiked to 16 million in the first six months of 1788.[57] Moreover, he accused Dupont of distorting the bureau's data to show, misleadingly, that France had had a favorable trade balance in 1787. Potier's impressions were confirmed by his successor, Ambroise-Marie Arnould, in 1791. Reviewing the data and taking into consideration contraband and fraudulent declarations at customs, Arnould concluded that "France had an unfavorable balance [of trade with Britain]." He criticized the treaty for satisfying the whims of wealthy consumers at the expense of workers' livelihoods: "[When] the hands of the most numerous class and the indigent lack work, they are deprived of the means of subsistence."[58]

The devastating socioeconomic impact of the Eden Treaty in France spilled over into politics, spurring demands for representation.[59] What the French architects of the treaty had failed to take seriously was its effect on an increasingly self-conscious and politically powerful public opinion. Their correspondence and reports show them to have been quite willing to sacrifice industries in the pursuit of other goals, such as geopolitical leverage (Vergennes) or financial gain (Calonne), with little concern for how the public might respond. In an early internal memo of 1784, Dupont predicted that France would run an annual 2-million-livres deficit with Britain (it turned out to be closer to 26 million), but he believed that the economic pain would be temporary and even redemptive, since it would force industries to modernize.[60] The administration saw itself as a doctor applying curative pain: "We must consider this treaty as a surgical operation," Rayneval explained, "which is painful at first but necessary to oblige our manufactures to improve their products."[61] From this perspective, it was pointless to listen to the cries of patients. Thus, when a deputation of manufactures from Louviers arrived in Versailles in 1784 to present their concerns about the treaty negotiations, the ministers refused to see them. The manufactures later complained: "Each article of the treaty was analyzed, discussed, and weighed in London by those who had a stake in the treaty; in France, to the contrary, discussion was secret, limited to a small number of individuals."[62]

Public outcry against the Eden Treaty was widespread and, in some places, seethed with hostility. Arthur Young, a British agriculturalist and promoter of free trade, heard the beating of war drums in Lille in 1787: "The cry here for a war with England amazed me. . . . It is easy enough to discover that the origin of all this violence is the commercial treaty, which is execrated here, as the most fatal stroke to their manufactures." Young did not deny the bleak situation but bemoaned the locals' ignorance: "These people . . . would involve four-and-twenty millions of people in the certain miseries of a war, rather than see the interest of those who consume fabrics preferred to the interest of those who make them."[63] When popular violence erupted in 1788 and 1789, some observers identified the Eden Treaty as a contributing factor. Commenting on the explosion of violence in Paris in August 1788, the author of one pamphlet wrote: "Oh, that people would stop accusing an 'ignorant' public of getting worked up without knowing why; . . . there are many powerful reasons besides the [government's] suspension of the Parlements, and they concern all classes; . . . [one reason] is the treaty of commerce."[64] The following year, the author of a pamphlet published shortly after the storming of the Bastille alluded to the Eden Treaty in enumerating the sources of popular grievances: "A weak and corrupt government, which instead of preparing triumphs for the nation, bought peace through the most dishonorable sacrifices, wasting what was left of our political and military consideration on obscure negotiations. . . . The most important transactions, the most decisive treaties, were concluded before us, without us, despite us."[65]

The high-handed manner in which the French administration concluded the Eden Treaty, foreclosing public debate and consultation with interested parties, fueled demands for political representation and participation in policymaking. In its report on the impact of the treaty, Rouen's chamber of commerce requested that the state "consult the chambers of commerce and wholesale merchants in circumstances where decisions must be made concerning the nation's commerce."[66] The demand was repeated in many *cahiers de doléances*. The third estate of Alençon insisted "that all potential treaties of commerce be sanctioned by the Estates General before their execution."[67] The third estate of Troyes urged "that, in the future, commercial treaties with foreign nations will never be concluded without the consultation and approval of manufacturing cities."[68] As France was preparing for the Estates General, its commercial and industrial communities sent more than fifty letters to the king requesting special representation in the Estates General. Their requests were denied, but in March 1789, Jacques Necker, minister of finance, instructed commercial port towns to elect at least one deputy "from the class of wholesale merchants and shipowners."[69] Their representation in the Estates General—soon to become the National Constituent Assembly—was low. To compensate, commercial and industrial towns formed a lobbying group, the Extraordinary Committee of Deputies of Commerce and Manufactures, which the Constituent Assembly formally recognized in October 1789, allowing it to attend assembly sessions and present its views on a regular basis.[70]

By 1789, commerce and industry had a legitimate voice in the political process. What did they do with it? Many demanded the revocation or modification of the Eden Treaty. The issue was relentlessly debated in the Constituent Assembly's Committee of Agriculture and Commerce.[71] In a speech of November 1790, Pierre-Louis Goudard, a national deputy and silk manufacturer from Lyon, distinguished between the "legitimate merchant" and the "cosmopolitan speculator." While the former was a patriot who cared for the nation's interests, the latter was a free-trade extremist who sought the abolition of all tariffs in order to transform the nation into "a giant free port."[72] In his rebuttal, the deputy François-Louis Legrand de Boislandry (an importer of British fabrics and a vocal supporter of the treaty before 1789) insisted on free trade's fraternal effects. Echoing *doux-commerce* arguments, he insisted that "unlimited freedom of commerce binds nations together" and "reduces the jealousies of trade," and he denounced prohibitory tariffs as "a violation of human rights." Ironically, cosmopolitan fraternity gave way to hostile nationalism by the end of the speech. He now argued that if France lowered all tariffs to 5 or 10 percent, that is, lower than the Eden Treaty, it could steal Britain's trade with other countries and "deliver a mortal blow to British commerce and power."[73]

In spring 1791 the Constituent Assembly struck a compromise, passing a law on tariffs that stipulated some prohibitions but, for the most part, set tariffs at 15 percent, three to five points higher than those of the Eden Treaty. These rates were liberal by the standards of the day.[74] Given the chaos at customhouses, which were in the throes of major reforms, and the ongoing presence of free ports, where many British imports were arriving untaxed, it was unlikely that the new tariff regime would check the influx of British goods or generate revenues to help French manufactures compete.[75] Meanwhile, deputies pressed on with economic liberalization, even as they curtailed democracy. Between February and September of 1791, they passed a raft of laws abolishing all institutions regulating the social, economic, and political dimensions of production. The combined effect of the Allarde, Le Chapelier, and Goudard Laws was nothing less than a total liberal-economic revolution. Not only were confraternities, corporations, and chambers of commerce suppressed; so, too, were the government's Bureau of Commerce and Balance of Trade Office, which had overseen regulation, subsidies, and trade statistics. Although deputies promised to provide subsidies and rehouse regulatory agencies within the Ministry of the Interior, they failed to do so, at least in the short run.[76] If their intentions suggest that they were not laissez-faire absolutists, their achievements and failures combined in such a way as to create something approaching a laissez-faire world. This was not a world many wanted, but since economic grievances were now deprived of the institutional means of expression—and even collective petitions were banned—grievances soon spilled over into local politics, which radicalized. How, precisely, the economic liberalization laws of 1791 ended up spawning "sansculottism" or the economic Terror of 1793–94 requires more investigation, but Steven L. Kaplan's hypothesis is compelling: "The [political] section [where sansculottism flourished] functioned to a certain degree as a substitute corporation."[77]

Meanwhile, the Legislative Assembly upheld the Eden Treaty and even sought to extend it. Desperate to secure Britain as an ally in the upcoming war with Austria, the legislature sent Charles-Maurice de Talleyrand-Périgord on a diplomatic mission to London in 1792. Talleyrand proposed making the ten-year treaty permanent. Britain's response was tepid: "The treaty has not yet come to an end. The terms are so beneficial to both nations that we should hope they will renew it when the time comes."[78] The Eden Treaty was certainly beneficial to Britain. Expanded trade with France boosted its commerce, industry, and revenues.[79] That France benefited from the treaty is not evident. Its trade deficit with Britain increased. Calculated by the British, it rose from 166,431 pounds in 1784 to 585,318 pounds in 1791, dropping slightly to 510,531 pounds in 1792.[80] Even if these figures are rough estimates, it is clear that Britain held an increasingly favorable trade balance, that liberalized trade had produced socioeconomic shock and agitation in France, that the French state had failed to prepare for this shock and to assist its industries to cope with it, and that public outrage over the treaty had fueled democratic demands for a say in economic policymaking in 1789.

Ultimately, then, the Eden Treaty was revolutionary, in terms of both motivations and effects. Vergennes's rhetoric, cited above, about "reforming the world," providing "a universal exchange of benefits," and "making all nations one in commerce" certainly anticipated revolutionary utopianism, but the underlying aims of the administration were also revolutionary. Exerting influence over Britain through peaceful, liberalized trade rather than through mercantilist warfare (Vergennes), and creating an international cartel with state backing (Calonne), were novel ways of approaching foreign relations.

Using the treaty to force French industries to modernize, as Rayneval saw it—and the treaty can be seen as perpetuating the physiocrats' assault on corporations—was also revolutionary.

What began as a diplomatic and economic revolution in the mid-1780s helped bring about a political revolution in 1789, when commercial and industrial communities demanded a voice in economic policymaking. They succeeded in getting that voice, but in the clash between economic and political liberalizations, they lost it. Between 1789 and 1791, legislators debated over whether to base economic policy on liberal economic principles—on free trade and deregulation—or on open discussion and negotiation with interested parties. In 1791, they opted for the former. They abolished all corporative and regulatory institutions and banned coalitions of merchants, employers, and workers, even as they upheld the unpopular Eden Treaty and extended its principles to encompass all foreign trade.

Sailing toward the United States, his new homeland, in 1815, Dupont recalled those early years of the Revolution, when he had been a national deputy: "Whenever the issue of commerce or finance came up in the Constituent Assembly, discussion would always begin with violent attacks on the economists [the physiocrats], but deputies usually ended up passing decrees based on their principles."[81] True enough, but the Constituent Assembly's liberal-economic revolution did not last long. In 1793, the National Convention found itself pressured by pike-fisted sansculottes to re-regulate the economy, sending France on a path toward economic modernization more *dirigiste* than that of its neighbor across the Channel.[82] It also found itself at war with Britain, the very crisis that the Eden Treaty was supposed to prevent.

4 1685 and the French Revolution

ANDREW JAINCHILL

In 1685 Louis XIV revoked the Edict of Nantes, ending the religious toleration granted to France's Calvinist minority in 1598 by his grandfather, Henri IV. The presence of France's Calvinists, who comprised approximately 5 percent of the total French population and were known as Huguenots, was seen to constitute a challenge to the French monarchy's traditional adage *Une foi, une loi, un roi* (One faith, one law, one king).[1] As the monarchy increasingly claimed absolute sovereignty in the seventeenth century, the rights guaranteed to the Huguenots by the Edict of Nantes represented a glaring counterexample to the professed unity of the kingdom and the absolute rule of Louis XIV. Louis XIII had ended the Huguenots' rights to maintain fortifications and garrisons, and even laid siege to the Huguenot stronghold of La Rochelle in 1628, but it was not until Louis XIV began intensive persecution of the Huguenots in 1680 and then revoked the Edict of Nantes in 1685 that true confessional uniformity was attempted and nominally achieved. Public Calvinist worship was prohibited (although Calvinist belief was tolerated), children were ordered to be baptized, and pastors were commanded to leave the country. The laity was prohibited from leaving, but 150,000 to 200,000 Huguenots fled France (about a fifth of France's Protestant population), seeking refuge primarily in the Dutch Republic, England, Prussia, and the Swiss cantons, but also in the central German lands, Scandinavia, and Russia. In fact, the Huguenot exiles in England and Holland gave "first circulation" to the term "refugees" as tens of thousands of them took up residence in London, Amsterdam, and Rotterdam.[2] The diaspora created by the revocation of the Edict of Nantes soon stretched across the globe as the Huguenots spread themselves from the Hudson River valley to Suriname to South Africa.[3] The Huguenots who spread out across Europe and the globe augmented existing international networks and established new ones, facilitating future geographical, financial, cultural, and intellectual mobility and communication.[4] This global diaspora injected wealth, talent, and energy into its hosts, predominantly Protestant Europe and its overseas colonies, and conversely deprived France of those same resources.[5] The revocation of the Edict of Nantes fundamentally altered early modern France, Europe, and Europe's colonies.

The revocation of the Edict of Nantes and the creation of the Huguenot diaspora do not occupy the foundational place they once did in accounts of early modern France, displaced perhaps by the great attention paid in recent decades to the austere Augustinian Catholic movement known as Jansenism that was condemned by the papacy and persecuted by the French crown.[6] An older historiographical tradition assigned the revocation of the Edict of Nantes a substantially more central role in the political drama of the day. Jules Michelet observed that "what the Revolution was to the eighteenth century, the revocation of the Edict of Nantes [and] the emigration of Protestants was to the seventeenth."[7] And Paul Hazard judged the revocation of the Edict of Nantes to be at the origins of the "crisis of European consciousness" that for him was the beginning of the Enlightenment itself.[8] This chapter argues that such a perspective merits serious attention and that 1685 needs to be reinscribed into the story of the origins of the French Revolution, especially its long-term intellectual origins.[9] Doing so necessarily trains the historian's gaze beyond France's borders.

The revocation of the Edict of Nantes fits into the narrative of the long-term origins of the French Revolution in numerous ways. On an abstract level, the very existence of the Huguenot diaspora served as a challenge to the sacral absolutism constructed by the French monarchy in the wake of the sixteenth-century Wars of Religion, in a manner similar to and accentuating that of Jansenism as described by Dale Van Kley. According to Van Kley, the fact that "the French monarchy reinvented itself as a religious as well as a political institution" made it "uniquely vulnerable . . . in the longer run" to religious challenges.[10] The Huguenot diaspora constituted just such a challenge. In legal terms, France was unitarily Catholic from 1685 until the Edict of Toleration promulgated in January 1788. The presence of a substantial Huguenot population outside of France that claimed for itself a French identity, coupled with the remaining domestic Huguenot population, was a constant reminder of the fact that France was *not* unitarily Catholic, and thus contributed to the "desacralization" of the French monarchy.[11] This challenge furthermore cut straight to the heart of the Bourbon monarchy's legitimacy, which derived in part from its ability to resolve and transcend the religious conflict that had riven France in the sixteenth century. The revocation of the Edict of Nantes and the creation of the Huguenot diaspora thus played an integral role in the abstract "religious origins" of the French Revolution.

A more immediate manner by which the revocation of the Edict of Nantes contributed to the origins of the French Revolution was the fact that the Huguenot diaspora quickly became a Huguenot international bent on discrediting the French monarchy. Huguenot writers aimed to shape perceptions, especially English and Dutch perceptions, of France. Pierre Bayle, based in the Netherlands, chastised Louis XIV for cruelty, stupidity, and hypocrisy in *Ce que c'est que la France toute catholique, sous le règne de Louis le Grand* (1686), and Pierre Jurieu, also in the Netherlands, accused Louis XIV of tyranny in his *Lettres pastorales* (1686–88) and *Soupirs de la France esclave, qui aspire après la liberté* (1689).[12] In addition, Louis XIV was repeatedly represented as determined to conquer all of Europe and establish a universal monarchy. Collectively, the writings of the Huguenot diaspora contributed mightily to anti-French sentiment throughout Europe, especially in Protestant Europe. Along with the fact of the revocation of the Edict of Nantes itself, Huguenot writers helped to crystallize Protestant Europe's unified opposition to Louis XIV, which was then given further ammunition when French troops devastated the Palatinate during the War of the League of Augsburg (1688–97). The writings of the Huguenot diaspora likewise contributed to the beginnings of France's "second Hundred Year War" (1689–1815) with England after the Glorious Revolution of 1688, which was in no small part a Protestant revolution against James II's Louis XIV–inspired Catholicizing monarchy. The wars that ensued dominated French foreign policy in the eighteenth century and took a devastating toll on France's state finances, feeding the debt crisis that sparked the events of 1789. None of this is to say, of course, that the revocation of the Edict of Nantes played a direct causal role in these developments, only that it contributed in ways that might be easy to overlook, but that a more international vantage point suggests.

The Huguenot diaspora created by the Edict of Nantes furthermore played a transformative role in Europe's intellectual life and helped set the stage for the Enlightenment.[13] Taking advantage of the extraordinary publishing environment in the Dutch Republic—Dutch publishers churned out more books on a greater diversity of subjects and faced less censorship than any others in Europe—Huguenot exiles produced some of the most important works of the late seventeenth and early eighteenth centuries. Most famously, Bayle founded the journal *Nouvelles de la République des Lettres* in 1684 before discontinuing it in 1687 in order to devote his full energies to the *Dictionnaire historique et critique* (1697), which directed withering skepticism and wit at seemingly every institution, belief, and custom in Europe and was later labeled "the Arsenal of the Enlightenment."[14] Jacques Bernard revived the *Nouvelles de la République des Lettres* and directed it successfully from 1699 to 1710 and 1716 to 1718. Jean Frederic Bernard's fictional account of Persian visitors to

Amsterdam in the *Réflexions morales, satiriques et comiques sur les Moeurs de notre Siècle* (1711) had a direct influence on Montesquieu's landmark fictional account of Persian visitors to Paris, the *Persian Letters*.[15] Jean Frederic Bernard and Bernard Picart's *Cérémonies et coutumes religieuses de tous les peuples du monde* (1723–37) has recently been dubbed "the book that changed Europe."[16] And Paul de Rapin de Thoyras's immensely successful *Dissertation sur les Whigs et les Torys* (1717) and *Histoire d'Angleterre* (1723–25), which will be discussed shortly, respectively introduced Continental Europeans to England's seemingly bizarre political system and established the standard account of English history in both French and English (in translation) until David Hume's *History of England* (1754–62).[17] The combination of epistemological skepticism, political irreverence, and religious toleration on display in these works did much to foster the critical spirit that would provide the Enlightenment's sense of itself. The Enlightenment commitment to religious tolerance in particular was powerfully informed by the Huguenot narrative of the revocation of the Edict of Nantes and its depiction of Louis XIV as cruel and myopic—"fanatical" in the lexicon of the Enlightenment—for provoking the emigration of over 150,000 "refugees" who then boosted the economies of France's rivals.[18]

Finally, and more specifically, Huguenot writers based for the most part in the Dutch Republic bombarded France with political writings that aimed to delegitimize Louis XIV's monarchy in the eyes of the French reading public and, at the same time, to mobilize positive principles taken from Dutch and especially English political life and thought. The most prominent, although not unanimous, principle among these writings was religious toleration.[19] In addition, there was a strong, recurrent emphasis on the importance of mixed government in order to prevent despotism or tyranny. Crucially, the terms by which the Huguenot writers argued for the importance of mixed government reprised those of the early modern republican tradition. Early modern republicans looked to the ideal of a mixed and balanced constitution that placed the three classical political forms—monarchy, aristocracy, and democracy, or one, the few, and the many—in a state of balance so that no one form could ever triumph over the others.[20] The Huguenot writers championed this ideal largely through reference to the English constitution, with its balance among king, Lords, and Commons, and which was typically described in post-1688 England in precisely such terms—as a "mixed form of government, combining elements of rule by one, the few, and the many."[21] Such a constitutional arrangement was, of course, deeply antithetical to France's absolute monarchy. The praise of England's mixed and balanced government in the publications of the Huguenot diaspora amounted to a subversive political program that helped to revive the discourse of mixed government in France and thus to establish an alternative conception of sovereignty to that of the absolute monarchy.[22]

The discourse of mixed government took different forms in eighteenth-century France, from Montesquieu's moderate, epoch-making *Spirit of the Laws* (1748) to Mably's radical *Observations sur les Romains* (1751) and *Observations sur l'histoire de la Grèce* (1764) to Jean Louis Delolme's *Constitution de l'Angleterre* (1771), which placed great weight on executive power and was later praised by John Adams as "the best defense of the political balance of three powers that ever was written."[23] Whatever their differences, such works and the discourse of mixed government more broadly posed a critical counterpoint to the absolute monarchy and contributed fundamentally to the intellectual origins of the French Revolution. Once the Revolution was under way, a version of mixed government, more monarchical and more mechanistic than that of the traditional ideal, was advocated by Mounier and the *monarchiens*.[24] During the critical debates in late August and September 1789, the *monarchiens* succeeded in winning a suspensive veto for the king, but their efforts to establish a second legislative chamber were overwhelmingly defeated due to the traditional association of such a chamber with the aristocracy or nobility.[25] As François Furet put it, establishing a senate or the like would have been symbolically tantamount to "repudiating" the accomplishments of the Revolution to that point.[26] The principle of a mixed or balanced constitution was then signally rejected in favor of a more unitary conception of sovereignty when the republic was established in September 1792 and in the radical republicanism that triumphed between 1792 and 1794.[27] It was, however, revived during the drafting of the Constitution of 1795, when the revolutionaries set out to rebuild the republic after the Terror.[28] This trajectory highlights the perhaps paradoxical fact that in France the paramount constitutional ideal of the early modern republican tradition, the venerable tradition of mixed government, contributed to the origins of the French Revolution in the essentially negative sense of posing a critical alternative to absolute monarchy but disappeared at precisely the moment when France first declared itself a republic. The point here is that the Huguenot diaspora played a vital role in the revival of the discourse of mixed government in France and that Huguenot writings thus constituted an important element of the long-term intellectual origins of the French Revolution. Consideration of the writings of the Huguenot diaspora thus begins to cast a decidedly international light on the intellectual origins of the French Revolution due to the physical location of the Huguenot diaspora, their reliance on supranational publishing networks to disseminate their work, and the international character of early modern republicanism.

The story of the Huguenot diaspora's transmission to France of the principle of mixed government as incarnated in the English constitution involved both the communication of republican values more broadly through the translation and presentation of key texts from the English republican tradition, and more specific explanations of the English political system. The effect of the former of these, the Huguenot diaspora's translations and explanations of English republicans, was such that in the 1750s the marquis d'Argenson wrote in his journal of a "philosophical wind" blowing from England that carried "the words liberty and republicanism" and that would lead to a "revolution."[29] D'Argenson rightly identified the source of those notions and words as England, but the wind itself actually blew from Huguenot writers based predominantly in the Netherlands.[30]

The list of seminal works from the English republican tradition that were translated into French by Huguenot exiles is truly impressive. Collectively, it constituted a French-language library of English republicanism: Ludlow's *Memoirs* (1699–1707), Algernon Sidney's *Discourses Concerning Government* (1702), Toland's *An Account of the Courts of Prussia and Hanover* (1706), Molesworth's *An Account of Denmark* (1732), Bolingbroke's *A Dissertation upon Parties* (1734), and Thomas Gordon's commentary on Tacitus (1742) were all translated into French during the first half of the eighteenth century, each appearing with The Hague or Amsterdam as the place of publication. In addition, the Huguenot journals published in the Dutch Republic summarized, explained, and translated the writings of the great English republicans. The *Nouvelles de la République des Lettres* published in 1700 alone a three-part, eighty-two-page, chapter-by-chapter summary of Sidney's *Discourses* and a twenty-page précis of the life and writings of James Harrington upon the publication of John Toland's monumental edition of Harrington's *Oceana* and other works.[31] The journal praised Sidney for his "wisdom concerning all matters relating to government" and introduced Harrington as "a great republican" who "shows that monarchical government is not the most perfect and the most advantageous."[32] The journal then described Harrington's proposed government as a mixture of three powers modeled on the three traditional forms of government, "a Government composed of a Senate that proposes, a People that deliberates, and a Magistrate that executes."[33] If the principle of balance were to be violated, the result would be tyranny, oligarchy, or anarchy. The editor of the *Nouvelles de la République des Lettres* at this moment was Jacques Bernard, a French Protestant minister who had fled France in 1683 and, reports Rachel Hammersley, "appears to have had a particular interest in the works of the English republican tradition."[34] Similar if less strident notes were sounded in the *Histoire des ouvrages des savans* between 1698 and 1702,[35] and then in 1737 and 1740 by the *Bibliothèque britannique*, published in The Hague, when it reported on a reedition of Harrington's *Oceana and other Works* and gave a lengthy introduction to Milton's political writings.[36] Both authors were celebrated as republicans, and the piece on Milton went out of its way to signal Sidney's *Discourses* as the most important work on the right to depose monarchs.[37]

Sidney, who was the most vociferously antimonarchial writer of the English republican tradition, seems to have been the favorite of the Huguenot press. Peter Augustus Samson, a Huguenot living in The Hague, produced a full-length translation of Sidney's *Discourses Concerning Government* in 1702 and stressed in his introduction to the text that Sidney taught the importance of the form of government for maintaining liberty. Sidney, Samson explained, "wanted to establish the rights of peoples, to show them that they are born free, that it depends on them to establish whichever form of government that they believe to be the most advantageous; . . . and that it depends absolutely on them to change the form of their government if they see that it is necessary to do so to maintain and strengthen their precious liberty."[38] The full importance of this statement by Samson—and its emphasis on the form of government—becomes all the more clear in light of Sidney's analysis of forms of government in section 16 of the *Discourses*, titled "The best Governments of the World have been composed of Monarchy, Aristocracy, and Democracy." In this section, Sidney explained that "there never was a good government in the world, that did not consist of the three simple species of monarchy, aristocracy, and democracy." All of history's most successful governments, Sidney argued, had followed this model and "were composed of the three simple species."[39] The Huguenots' efforts to introduce Sidney to French readers were successful enough that Sidney was widely read and discussed in France during the first half of the eighteenth century, more so even than John Locke (later, Sidney would be celebrated in the revolutionary festivals as a martyr for liberty).[40] In fact, Sidney's prominence was such that d'Argenson wrote in his journal of a project to refute the ideas of Sidney, since, as the marquis wrote, "it is the best piece that has been written against the power of a single individual. Reading this book, one becomes a republican."[41]

In addition to providing both a home and printing presses, the Dutch Republic may also have provided a meeting ground for Huguenot writers and English Commonwealthmen or "Real Whigs." John Toland, for example, spent considerable time in the Dutch Republic (and spoke fluent French) and was closely connected to the London-based Huguenot journalist Pierre Desmaizeaux, as was Thomas Gordon, whose discourses on Tacitus and Sallust were so important and were translated into French by the London-based Huguenot Pierre Daudé.[42] In addition, radical or "real" Whigs from England traveled to the Dutch Republic in order to build an international Protestant alliance against Louis XIV's territorial ambitions.[43] It is important to remember in this context the longer-standing ties between English Whigs and the Dutch Republic: Shaftesbury and Locke among others were in exile there before the Glorious Revolution, which itself, of course, saw a Dutch army invade England.

It seems clear, then, that the Huguenot exiles worked to introduce the ideas of the great English republicans to France and that a healthy portion of these texts advocated the ideal of mixed government. It is of course impossible to discern the true influence of such texts, but they were known among France's leading intellectuals, such as d'Argenson. The fact that the Huguenots did so much to introduce English republican ideas to France constitutes a historical irony of sorts. Before the revocation of the Edict of Nantes, the Huguenots had long worked to shed the stigma of republicanism, and of subversion more generally, which had become attached to them due to the Huguenot political theorists of the Wars of Religion and to the presence nearby of the Calvinist republics of Geneva and the Dutch Republic. During the English Civil War and then the Fronde, for example, Huguenot political theorists went out of their way to advocate the most rigorous forms of absolutism.[44] Once in exile, however, they bombarded the French reading public with the tenets of English republicanism, rendering earlier suspicions a self-fulfilling prophecy.

In addition to introducing the ideas of the English republicans to the French reading public, the writers of the Huguenot diaspora also aimed to introduce the English political system and constitution, especially its more republican features. In fact, these Huguenot writers played *the* central role in introducing the English constitution to French readers before the publication of Montesquieu's *Spirit of the Laws*. Their descriptions of the English constitution clearly echoed the early modern republican depiction of the "mixed constitution" and made the latter appear to French readers to be incarnated in a powerful, modern state that incorporated a republican conception of sovereignty within its monarchy. England appeared to be, as Montesquieu would famously quip, "a nation where the republic hides under the form of a monarchy."[45]

The Huguenots' analyses of the English constitution entered a larger French discussion about England at the end of the seventeenth century and during the first half of the eighteenth century. English history and the English political system were the objects of considerable curiosity at the time, with writers such as Pierre-Joseph d'Orléans and the abbé Raynal criticizing the English model, and others, most notably Voltaire and ultimately Montesquieu, celebrating it.[46] Not only was England France's neighbor and rival, but its political system represented the most important extant alternative to France's absolute monarchy. It thus emerged as a privileged site of reflection precisely because of the radical contrast its political system and political life presented to those of France. England was strange and different, yet close enough to represent a real alternative in a way that few other places ever could. Representations of the English constitution were often distorted and even imaginary, but they fit into a developing French discussion about the nature of France's political institutions, especially during the years after the long reign of Louis XIV.[47]

They served, in the words of the historian Edouard Tillet, "in the same capacity as antiquity, [or] the history of the Franks, . . . as a distorting mirror, the echo chamber for the aspirations and questions of an epoch."[48]

Crucially, the terms used by the Huguenot writers to describe the English political system and constitution distinctly echoed those used to describe the classical form of the republic in the early modern period and thus helped to normalize or make real the ideal of the mixed and balanced republican constitution. For example, F.-M. Misson's *Mémoires et observations faites par un voyageur en Angleterre*, published in The Hague in 1698, defined the English constitution as an "aristocratic-democratic-monarchical" government.[49] Tillet, in his exhaustive study of the reception of the English constitution in France, writes that the Huguenot diaspora "gave new vigor to the old idea of the mixed regime. Far from being a historical chimera, . . . this ideal seemed to be realized" on the other side of the Channel.[50]

Just why the Huguenot writers celebrated the mixed and balanced English constitution is impossible to discern exactly, but there seem to have been several reasons. First and most obvious was the Huguenots' experience with absolute monarchy: their repression under Louis XIV led many Huguenot writers, but not all it needs to be emphasized, to distrust absolute sovereignty and thus to advocate constitutional designs that aimed to fracture sovereignty. Second, Calvin had located authority in the entire church just as the conciliarists had located authority in the councils rather than in the papacy.[51] And third, contact with radical Whigs in England and the Netherlands may have helped to push the Huguenots in that direction. Regardless of the reason, the Huguenot writers put forward a republican reading of the English political system. A version of the mixed constitution of classical antiquity was living and breathing across the Channel. Moreover, it seemed to guarantee religious liberty and a certain prosperity. Thus, more than the existing republics of Europe, the English political system helped to establish and to an extent even to normalize republican ideas about constitutions and political life as an alternative to absolute monarchy.

The most important Huguenot writer to explain the English political system to the French reading public was Paul de Rapin de Thoyras, who was, more generally, the most influential writer on the English political system during the first half of the eighteenth century. In a slim volume titled *Dissertation sur les Whigs et les Torys* published in The Hague in 1717, and then in a ten-volume *Histoire d'Angleterre* published from 1723 to 1725, also in The Hague, Rapin explained the curious political system of the English, both its current shape and its historical origins, to seemingly puzzled Continental Europeans.

Rapin was a Huguenot exile who settled in the French-language literary world of The Hague after an extended stay in England. After leaving France in 1686, he first went to London but then relocated to the Dutch Republic after finding his path blocked by the pro-Catholic programs instituted under James II. In the Netherlands, he joined a company of French refugee volunteers who served in William of Orange's army that "invaded" England in 1688. Rapin fought in a number of battles and was shot in the shoulder in 1690 during the Irish campaign. He stayed in England for thirteen years after the Glorious Revolution, serving as governor to the son of the first Earl of Portland and frequently traveling with Portland. He then moved back to the Dutch Republic in 1701 and settled in The Hague, where he founded a literary club along the lines of Benjamin Furly's famous The Lantern (in Rotterdam), and then relocated to the nearby Prussian territory of Wesel in 1707. Rapin devoted the rest of his life to writing about English history and the English political system, the most important results of which were the *Dissertation sur les Whigs et les Torys* and the *Histoire d'Angleterre*.[52]

Rapin's accounts of the English government and English history were extraordinarily influential and almost single-handedly established the basic understanding that would prevail in France until Montesquieu's celebrated description in 1748.[53] His *Dissertation* went through ten French-language editions over the next hundred years and was translated into German, Dutch, Danish, Spanish, and English. The *Histoire* saw six editions printed over the next thirty years and immediate translation into English (followed by multiple English-language editions, including a schoolbook version that itself ran through twenty-four editions in the eighteenth century).[54] The key to Rapin's analysis of the English government was that it was "mixed." He described it as "a unique type; today there is nothing similar in the rest of the World." "It would be in vain," he explained in the opening pages of his *Dissertation*, "to use the usual labels of monarchy, aristocracy, and democracy for this government, none of which apply. It is a *mixed* government . . . composed of a mélange of the three [monarchy, aristocracy, and democracy]."[55]

Rapin's analysis here employed the standard lexicon of the early modern republican constitution. In England, the three classical forms, incarnated in the king, Lords, and Commons, kept each other in check so that no one power could attain a preeminent position. Any attempt to upset this balance amounted to a violation of its "mixed government." Rapin's account of the English Civil War was thus critical of both royalists and republicans: James I and Charles I tried to extend their authority and overturn the system of balance, as did the Independents when they established a unitary republic.[56] Only the Glorious Revolution of 1688 properly restored the ancient balance among the king, House of Lords, and House of Commons. Rapin's history was thus very much a Whig history and has been credited by J.G.A. Pocock and Hugh Trevor-Roper with helping to establish the canonical form of the "Whig interpretation of history."[57] Crucially, the essence of the

English government that Rapin described—and prescribed—was a *political* balance among England's three traditional orders, one that both ensured the continued respect of each order's rights and prevented the undue extension of those rights, and not a more modern juridical or technical separation and then balancing of governmental powers.[58] Rapin's analysis was heavily indebted to Thomas Smith's *De Republica Anglorum* (1583), the sole source on English history that he cited other than documents and to which he referred readers who desired more information on the structure of the English government.[59] Smith's book had provided a partisan reading of the English constitution and has been identified by the historian Patrick Collinson as the key work of "quasi-republican modes of political reflection" in Elizabethan England.[60] Rapin's depiction of the English constitution thus followed the ideal constitutional arrangement of the early modern republican tradition, the "mixed" or "balanced" constitution celebrated by Polybius in his *Histories*. Even if Rapin himself did not use the term "republic" or invoke Polybius, such a reading of the English constitution easily led to inscribing it in the early modern republican tradition. D'Argenson, for example, in his influential *Considérations sur le gouvernement ancien et présent de la France*, penned in the mid-1730s, described the English system of government in virtually the same terms but placed it squarely within the classical tradition. In fact, he criticized the English for hewing too closely to the classical model, which was first established by Lycurgus in Lacedaemon.[61]

Rapin traced the unique character of the English government, specifically the fact that it was "mixed," to the Anglo-Saxon conquest of Britain. When the German peoples overran the ruins of the Roman Empire, they carried their form of government throughout western Europe: the Anglo-Saxons carried it to England, the Francs to Gaul, the Visigoths to Spain, and the Ostrogoths and then the Lombards to Italy. Rapin characterized this "revolution" in government as "one of the most remarkable events in history."[62] The intervening centuries, however, saw the erosion of mixed government and the triumph of absolute monarchy throughout Europe. The English alone "have conserved the form of their government."[63] As Catherine Larrère has nicely put it, in Rapin's narrative England "plays its ecological role as an island: it is the conservatory of extinct species."[64] Rapin furthermore claimed that the Saxons' laws and customs were identical to those of the ancient Germans described by Tacitus in *Germania*.[65] He thus located the deep origins of the English government among the ancient Germans, an argument that Sidney and a number of other radical Whigs had made in England and that Montesquieu would also adopt, and that mirrored François Hotman's account in *Francogallia* of the ancient Germanic origins of Frankish political institutions. In all of these explanations European history contained an alternative tradition of government that predated the absolute monarchies dotting the contemporary political landscape.

Rapin's emphasis on political balance also characterized his portrayal of England's post-1688 settlement. The two sides of the seventeenth-century conflict morphed into England's two great parties, the Whigs and the Tories. The key to England's party system, Rapin argued, was that neither side triumphed and that both parties remained committed to preserving balance among the government's constituent parts. What England needed, wrote Rapin, was to "leave the government on its ancient footing" and for "the People to remain divided. . . . If one of the parties were to acquire superiority over the other, it would be even worse for the public than the discord that follows from equality between them."[66] Thus, Rapin's analysis of both England's history and its contemporary politics emphasized the importance of political balance. The very fact of division as a positive phenomenon pointed in the exact opposite direction of the principles underpinning France's monarchy. Jean Domat had signaled the unity or division of sovereignty as the essential distinction between monarchies and republics in *Les Loix civiles dans leur ordre naturel* (1689).[67] Rapin's analysis of England's constitution and political life presented divided sovereignty as a real, functioning alternative. As a result, the historian Joseph Dedieu even credited Rapin, no doubt hyperbolically, with being "the true creator" of the parlementary "movement" in the eighteenth century.[68] Even if Rapin denied that the English political system was republican, the terms of his analysis pointed in a republican direction and were easily assimilated to the mixed constitution of the early modern republican tradition. Rapin's writings constituted the most influential introduction of the English political system to French readers in the first half of the eighteenth century and two of the most important texts in the broader introduction of the ideal of mixed government carried out by the Huguenot diaspora in the wake of the revocation of the Edict of Nantes.

The writings of the Huguenot diaspora thus helped lay the foundations for the revival of the discourse of mixed government in eighteenth-century France and need to be included in any narrative of the long-term intellectual origins of the French Revolution. At the same time, the subsequent generations of the Huguenot diaspora continued to play an occasional role in French political life. For example, the *Gazette de Leyde*, a long-standing Huguenot journal, functioned as "the opposition press" during the 1750s, reprinting parlementary remonstrances and adopting a pro-parlement and Jansenist line during the refusal-of-sacraments-controversy.[69] Throughout the rest of the eighteenth century and into the Revolution, the *Gazette* remained arguably the most important newspaper of its day, with readers "scattered from Boston to Calcutta, from Glasgow to Constantinople."[70] Elizabeth Eisenstein describes it as "the journal of record that the best informed Frenchmen had to read" and notes that it "consistently upheld the benefits of constitutional 'mixed' governments."[71] In a parallel vein, the Amsterdam publisher Marc Michel Rey, also a descendant of Huguenots, published politically corrosive texts, such as the forbidden works of Voltaire, d'Holbach, and Rousseau, including *Émile* and the *Social Contract*, as well as a variety of anticlerical tracts.[72] Even if the later generations of the Huguenot diaspora did not boast a Bayle or Rapin, they continued to play an important role in the development of French political and intellectual culture over the course of the eighteenth century.

The Huguenot diaspora created by the revocation of the Edict of Nantes was invited to return to France during the French Revolution. The National Assembly decreed equal civil status for Protestants in December 1789 (Louis XVI had decreed a much more limited Edict of Toleration in 1787) and then in December 1790 conferred citizenship on any member of the Huguenot diaspora who sought to return. "All persons who, born in foreign countries, descend in whatever degree from a Frenchman or Frenchwoman expatriated for religious reasons, are declared French natives [*naturels français*] and to possess the rights attached to this quality if they return to France, establish their place of residence, and give the civic oath."[73] In addition, restitution of property was promised. The exact number of Huguenots who took advantage of this legislation and "returned" to France is impossible to calculate, but it seems that their numbers were quite negligible and that the descendants of the original generation of émigrés had adopted the identities of their homelands and did not conceive of themselves as French in the manner of the original diaspora.

Among those who did choose to return were Benjamin Constant and Charles-Guillaume Théremin, both of whom "returned" in 1795 and played a central role in the development of French liberalism.[74] Constant's family had emigrated to Switzerland during the sixteenth-century Wars of Religion, not because of the revocation of the Edict of Nantes, but the legislation applied to the descendants of anyone who "expatriated for religious reasons." Théremin's family had fled to Prussia following the revocation of the Edict of Nantes. Constant became an active politician and writer upon his arrival in France and is now remembered as a founding thinker of French liberalism. Théremin took up a position in the French Ministry of Foreign Affairs and wrote a series of political pamphlets in which he outlined a vision of the international order with an expansionist France at its center, articulated a liberal political philosophy for the still new French republic, and advanced an important argument for extending political rights to women. Théremin openly announced his status as the descendant "of a Protestant who left France for religious reasons" in his tract *De la Situation intérieure de la République* (1797) and, two years before, upon his arrival in France, explained in a letter to Emmanuel-Joseph Sieyès: "I descend from refugees from the time of the revocation of the Edict of Nantes."[75] The full story of 1685 and the French Revolution thus includes the origins of French liberalism and the noteworthy fact that it emerged in no small part at the margins of French political culture in the works of the descendants of Huguenots.[76]

In conclusion, I would like to suggest that reinserting 1685 into the narrative of the origins of the French Revolution and even into the origins of French liberalism compels historians to look beyond France's borders. The revocation of the Edict of Nantes was originally a specifically French event, but one rooted deeply in Europe-wide questions. The creation of a Huguenot diaspora that spanned the globe had important implications for the intellectual, religious, and economic lives of Britain, Prussia, and especially the Dutch Republic. The Huguenot diaspora then turned their pens against the French monarchy, directing withering criticism against Louis XIV and inundating the French reading public with antimonarchial and prorepublican writings. The result was the introduction to the French reading public of a number of key principles from the early modern republican tradition, especially its English variant. Foremost among these was the ideal of mixed government, which had occupied such a central place in the republican tradition and which presented such a radical contrast to France's absolute monarchy. The transmission of this ideal helped lay the foundations for the broader revival of the discourse of mixed government in eighteenth-century France and contributed in a fundamental manner to the intellectual origins of the French Revolution by posing a critical alternative to absolute monarchy. It was then subsumed under progressively more unitary conceptions of sovereignty during the early years of the French Revolution before playing a constitutive role in the post-Terror Constitution of 1795. The story of the Huguenot diaspora's transmission of the ideal of mixed government needs to be counted among the intellectual origins of the French Revolution.

PART II

"Internal" Dynamics

5 Colonizing France

REVOLUTIONARY REGENERATION
AND THE FIRST FRENCH EMPIRE

WILLIAM MAX NELSON

In 1791, the great chronicler of revolutionary displacement and loss, François de Chateaubriand, fled the tumultuous circumstances of France in search of safety in the United States. He hoped to find the vitality of a new nation and unspoiled wilderness. While he found some of this, he also found that his expectations were repeatedly frustrated. In several of his written works, he returned to one of the events from this trip that seemed to capture his misguided preconceptions and his disappointment with the New World. As a self-professed "disciple of Rousseau," Chateaubriand was dismayed that on his first encounter with Amerindians, he found them dancing a French country-dance led by "a little Frenchman" in powdered wig.[1] Three years before Chateaubriand met these frenchified Native Americans, the English traveler Arthur Young had an almost inverse experience when he traveled through the French town of Combourg, where the brother of Chateaubriand lived and where François himself spent some of his childhood. Young found the nearby countryside to have a "savage aspect." It was inhabited by "people almost as wild as their country" and "husbandry [was] not much further advanced . . . than among the Hurons."[2] Chateaubriand's anecdote of frenchified Amerindians and the mirror image of Indian-like peasants in Chateaubriand's France point toward the way that by the era of the Revolution, France and the New World were deeply and surprisingly intertwined through the movement of people, the ties of colonial commerce, the proliferation of written works about distant lands and peoples, and the formation of intellectual and cultural dispositions built from the collision of worlds that were both far apart and strangely close.

The use of Native Americans as a reference point in discussing French peasants was not merely a practice of foreign travelers like Young. Comparisons had long been made between French peasants and the "savage" native peoples of the New World, from the writing of the early Jesuit missionaries in New France to Voltaire's observation that there were still savages in Europe.[3] During the French Revolution, urban travelers in the countryside and local elites often referred to peasants as "savages" and occasionally compared them to Amerindians. One French nobleman complained of local peasants dancing "like Hurons and Iroquois," while a provincial informant wrote to Paris about the local "savages" and "men of nature" whose language he compared to that of the Iroquois.[4] The perception of Indian-like peasants is a striking example of the way that even metropolitan people, places, and events deep in rural France and seemingly unrelated to the colonies of the first French Empire could be affected by the history of colonialism.

This chapter focuses on several of the ways the long history of colonialism played a role in France during the Revolution. The last few decades have seen the development of an excellent scholarship focusing on French colonial history and the Atlantic world, but the less direct influence of the first French Empire—what we could call its obscured metropolitan afterlife— is at an earlier stage of study. Recently, scholars of the eighteenth century have fruitfully highlighted the meaningful silences in metropolitan literature about the colonies and have demonstrated the ways that material artifacts like furniture and fabrics reveal surprising connections between the colonies and the metropole, while also bringing attention to experimental "internal colonies" in France and arguing that even the development of sciences as rarified as astronomy were intimately related to the colonial project.[5]

I hope that looking at the indirect or seemingly silent ways that Old Regime colonialism continued to play a role in the development of ideas and practices during the French Revolution suggests how deeply and broadly the colonial project had affected France. Furthermore, it may allow us to see important aspects of the Revolution differently. For example, the long history of colonialism informed one of the greatest problems of revolutionary governance: how to transform people and make them capable of creating the radically new future envisioned by revolutionary leaders? Although it has been underappreciated, the very concept of "regeneration" was entangled with the history of the colonies, as were the many projects envisioned and enacted to bring about regeneration. These projects were some of the primary means by which the revolutionaries faced the dilemma that sprang from the political necessity of national unity and the reality of social and cultural diversity. At the outbreak of the Revolution, France was a country of profound differences of language, law, custom, and belief. As one scholar has put it, the bond that was necessary to unite the French people and provide the foundation for the nation was "a political proposition before it [was] a sociological fact."[6] Revolutionary leaders needed to find ways to fashion the "new men" of the Revolution and to transform the disparate peoples and practices of the hexagon into a more homogenous and unified nation. This problem of regeneration became all the more pressing after the first years of the Revolution failed to bring about miraculous regeneration and the Terror made people sensitive to forms of regeneration that appeared coercive.[7]

In addressing this central tension of the Revolution, many political and scientific elites drew on ideas, dispositions, and practices that developed in the colonies or where constituted through a significant engagement with colonial issues. These colonial resources were sometimes invoked in a fashion that made their relation to the colonies explicit, but more often than not, this colonial trace remained a silent force and a hidden reservoir of intellectual and practical resources. Sometimes it was even hidden to the historical actors that drew on these resources, since people often acquired the ideas and practices through indirect means. They may not have even realized that some of their intellectual arsenal was a result of the long history of interaction between France and its colonies. The abbé Grégoire, for example, became the most famous advocate for the rights of the slaves and free people of color during the Revolution, but he had no real engagement with, or apparent interest in, colonial issues before becoming a revolutionary leader.[8] Nonetheless, well before 1789, he drew on naturalists' theories of physical regeneration and the ethnographic practices of travel literature, both of which developed through France's colonial engagement with the extra-European world, particularly its colonies in North America and the Caribbean.

As I will discuss below, the abbé Grégoire was one of the central theorists of regeneration and one of its strongest political advocates. In fact, his case, along with the examples of Nicolas-Louis François de Neufchâteau and the Society of the Observers of Man, demonstrates how the new anthropological perspective that emerged in part from the Enlightenment engagement with colonial people and places was refashioned through projects of revolutionary regeneration. This new anthropological perspective was exemplified and popularized through a new subgenre of internal ethnographic literature and was first institutionalized with the grand statistical project of the Ministry of Interior in the late 1790s and 1800s, the founding of the Society for the Observers of Man in 1800, and the formation of the Celtic Academy in 1805. To put it another way, the internal anthropology that took shape during the Revolution and focused on knowing and transforming the French peasantry was linked to the earlier history of external colonization and external ethnography in ways that have not yet been articulated.[9]

In *Voyage dans le Jura*, a piece of internal travel literature published in year IX (1800), Joseph-Marie Lequinio, a former deputy to the Legislative Assembly and fervent "representative on-mission" during the Terror, chose to start his long narrative with a detour. En route from Paris to the mountainous Jura region of eastern France, Lequinio took the reader to the estate of the famed natural historian Georges-Louis Leclerc, comte de Buffon. Lequinio lingered in the great man's workroom, hoping to draw inspiration and maybe some authority from an association, however distant and contrived, with the deceased master whose very name stood for natural history well into the nineteenth century.[10] This symbolic invocation is a good representation of how the literary form of voyages through the provinces that took shape in the last decades of the Old Regime transformed during the Revolution and became a new literary form by the beginning of the nineteenth century. The voyages in the provinces became voyages in the *départements*. In addition to using the newly formed administrative units to define their purview, the authors of this subgenre also responded to the political imperatives of the era by exhibiting a new interest in culture of the local inhabitants and the triangular relationship between this culture, the physical characteristics of the inhabitants, and their environment. The gathering of knowledge of local particularities had two primary purposes: to discover what was already common and shared so as to foster political and social unity; and to find the true extent and nature of local differences so as to lessen them. The "universality" of France could be discovered in the particularities, but so too could the targets of regenerative projects intended to homogenize the people and make them into a unified nation.

This was a relatively new endeavor because while there were Old Regime traditions of gathering knowledge of the kingdom for the king, it was only in the last years of the regime that authors showed an interest in detailed information focusing on local inhabitants. Works of internal travel literature began to appear in these years as "philosophical-travelers" began moving beyond the vague and often-repeated clichés of regional character that had dominated literary accounts of the provinces for centuries.[11] This process of transformation was not complete until the political imperatives of the Revolution created a corresponding epistemological imperative. The two editions of *Voyage d'Auvergne* published by Pierre-Jean-Baptiste Legrand d'Aussy in 1788 and 1794 captured the transformation of this literature during the Revolution. After being criticized for caring more about rocks than people, Legrand d'Aussy expanded his second edition with a significant amount of information on the local inhabitants, discussing their *mœurs* and customs as well as the physical characteristics of the "races" in the region.[12]

The changes brought about by the political imperatives of the Revolution and the desire to grasp the whole of France in its particularities and commonalities can also be seen in the heightened interest in statistics among bureaucrats and savants in this era. Like internal travel literature, this revitalized field grew in popularity and became increasingly institutionalized. The numerous projects to gather statistics on the departments and their inhabitants also reflect an anthropological shift. For example, in the 1790s, when a minor forestry official won a major prize for the creation of a set of guidelines and questions that travelers could use in gathering statistics about the departments, he included the customs and *mœurs* of local inhabitants as well as physical (or "racial") characteristics such as the color of their hair and skin.[13] This is the same type of detailed anthropological information found in the works of Enlightenment naturalists, as well as in the questionnaires and instructions written for foreign travelers embarking on scientific expeditions in this era.[14] This similarity between the internal and external anthropology is but one of the indications of the new orientation toward human variation and the question of "the other" within France. It also points toward how the development of the internal and that of the external anthropological orientation were connected, as they would remain through their further institutionalization in the nineteenth century.

The new anthropological approach that these travel writers and revolutionaries employed was drawn from the cluster of Enlightenment human sciences that contemporaries often referred to as "the natural history of man" or "the science of man." This new approach to observing and understanding humans developed primarily within the broad field of natural history but also drew on philosophy, medicine, foreign travel literature, theories of language, and political economy. It was characterized by a new attention to the global variation of human types, or "races" as they were beginning to be called; firsthand empirical observations made by "philosophical travelers," naturalists, and colonial correspondents; the systematic collection and presentation of evidence in widely circulated printed works; the attempt to understand the relationship between the "physical" and the "moral" dimensions of human beings, that is, the functioning and interaction of physiological, anatomical, cognitive, linguistic, moral, and emotional dimensions of existence; and, finally, the way that these characteristics of humans were affected by their physical and social environments. While most of these ideas and practices existed to some degree in the human sciences before the Enlightenment, they received a new intensity of attention and philosophical importance in the middle of the eighteenth century.[15] They were also combined in a new way in order to understand the causes of differences between peoples and to learn how the characteristics of humans changed over time. Many naturalists attempted to harness this knowledge of causes for the good of humanity and to gain some degree of mastery over the processes of change. The practitioners of this Enlightenment science of man aimed to find ways to "improve" and "perfect" people, both individually and as a species.

The Enlightenment science of man in France was particularly bold and influential because many of its leading practitioners broke free from the perspective of "physico-theology," which attempted to demonstrate divine creation and predetermined natural order through empirical evidence. French savants, such as the distinguished scientists, friends, and collaborators Pierre-Louis Maupertuis and Georges-Louis Buffon, were among the most important Enlightenment thinkers who formed naturalistic explanations that avoided recourse to supernatural forces and divine agency to explain the characteristics of the natural world. They approached nature as a complex system determined by immanent forces and open to significant historical transformation. Among the new possibilities that emerged from this revolution in natural history, sometimes referred to as the "Buffonian revolution," was the ability of humans to transform living organisms through active intervention in reproduction and maturation.[16] Throughout his body of work, Buffon emphasized the ability of humans to improve nature and control the development of species, which eventually came to include the human species itself. More than ten years before Condorcet went into hiding during the Terror and wrote his celebrated essay that probed the limits of progress and the human ability to bring it about, Buffon asked of man: "And what could he not do to himself, that is to say his own species, if the will was always directed by intelligence? Who knows to what point man could perfect either his moral or physical nature?"[17]

The Enlightenment science of man was not, of course, the only reservoir of resources that revolutionaries drew on in the development of regenerative ideas and practices. The Catholic Counter-Reformation, early modern philosophies of education, ideas relating individual bodies and the body politic, and classical republicanism were all resources.[18] Nonetheless, the radical reconceptualization of nature in the French Enlightenment, particularly by Buffon and his associates, was a major factor in determining Enlightenment ideas of regeneration that Grégoire and other revolutionaries employed. The Enlightenment transformation of the related ideas of nature, human perfectibility, and regeneration cannot be disconnected from the long history of European colonization.[19] To take the case of Buffon, not only did he ground his central concepts of "degeneration" and regeneration (or "improvement," as he usually expressed it) on comparisons of animals from the Old and New World, but he also relied heavily on the reports of foreign travelers and colonial correspondents for much of his detailed evidence of animals, as well as humans. There are telling examples in the work of Buffon, such as the authors and correspondents that he used as sources of material for a supplementary article on varieties of the human species: a naturalist in Grenada, a naturalist in the French colony of the Île de Bourbon in the Indian Ocean, European travelers in Africa, a doctor in the French colony of Saint-Domingue, a doctor in the former colony of Quebec, and a doctor in the French colony of Guiana.[20] Furthermore, much of Buffon's work at the time of this article was accomplished with the help of his assistant Sonnini de Manoncourt, a former resident of Guiana.[21]

The study of the variation of the human species was not simply the result of European travelers and residents of the colonies gathering information about the native peoples of the world; the specific character of colonial commerce and the slave trade influenced its historical development. For example, when Buffon discussed the difference between the various peoples of Africa, he drew on a history of Saint-Domingue and its account of differences among slaves taken from Africa rather than on just naturalistic or historical descriptions of Africa.[22] Furthermore, some of the most important natural historical work was driven by the economic incentive of finding new plants that could be commodified as pharmaceuticals or acclimatized so that they could be grown in Europe. Crossbreeding and acclimatizing foreign varieties of animals was also important in the development of natural history. In addition to relying on colonial sources for his writing, Buffon was the director of the King's Garden, which functioned as one of the major nodes within the global network of naturalists and travelers. Although Buffon was an unusually important figure in Enlightenment natural history, the global scale of his work and his colonial connections were not atypical for naturalists of the era.[23]

An analysis of abbé Grégoire and his approach to regeneration suggests the ways that we can find echoes of colonial history on different levels of the development of ideas and practices in the Revolution, from the more epiphenomenal to the more foundational. In Grégoire's work as a revolutionary, the colonial world was present as a series of small reference points, a topic for explicit analysis, and a silent factor in the formation of some of his fundamental concepts and dispositions. Grégoire is a fascinating example because he was a prominent leader in many phases of the Revolution and one of the leading theorists of regeneration, for which he drew on an eclectic combination of intellectual and religious beliefs.[24] The philosophical abbé from the eastern region of France was directly involved in many of the most important and representative projects of regeneration; he undertook a project to gather information on the many languages and dialects spoken in France with the goal of "annihilating the patois"; he presented ideas for the education of children and was a member of the Committee on Public Instruction; he advocated for the political rights and cultural assimilation of Jews and people of color; he was a "representative on-mission" to the countryside during the Terror; and he was involved in numerous attempts to improve French agriculture. Through the vicissitudes of the Revolution, Grégoire remained one of the most articulate and strenuous advocates for the creation of the "new man" and the large-scale improvement of the people. While he claimed that revolutionary "France is truly a new world," the government still needed to be extremely active in order to achieve a complete regeneration.[25] He wanted nothing less than to "reconstruct human nature," and he tirelessly worked to bridge "the enormous distance between what we are and what we could be."[26] Like most of the revolutionary leaders calling for this type of dramatic transformation, Grégoire drew on numerous models of improvement and discourses of regeneration that came from the religious, classical, and Enlightenment traditions. Throughout his work, as in this synthetic discourse of regeneration more generally, we find evidence of a strong natural historical and anthropological perspective, even before the Revolution.

Three of Grégoire's activities best demonstrate his anthropological orientation before the Revolution. These are his involvement with the Société des Philantropes of Strasbourg and the affiliated society in the city of Nancy, the trips he took through the regions of eastern France and Switzerland in the 1780s, and his writing on the "physical, moral, and political regeneration" of the Jews, which earned him a prestigious essay prize from the Metz Academy in 1788 and was his first high-profile contribution to the Republic of Letters. As a member of the educated elite of Alsace and Lorraine, Grégoire was a cofounder of a philanthropic society in Nancy that was associated with the quasi-masonic Société des Philantropes of Strasbourg.[27] These philanthropic societies were provincial sites of learning and charity that cultivated fraternity among a small group of members and were one of the primary institutional forces of the Enlightenment in the region. As the members of the Nancy society announced in their programmatic founding document, they aimed to be "practical-philosophes" working for the "moral, political, and physical perfection" of humanity, with a special focus on enlightening local farmers and the "simple inhabitant of the countryside."[28] Along with the cultivation of political economy and agriculture, one of their central goals was to encourage members to take ethnographic journeys to study the "laws, *mœurs*, principles, and the religious and political practices" of various peoples, reporting on "the number of inhabitants, the nature of the climate, [their] needs, products [*productions*], commerce, finances, monuments of art, and the state of their letters and sciences."[29] In the 1780s and the 1790s, Grégoire fulfilled the ethnographic goal of the philanthropists with journeys through the Vosges, Alsace, and Switzerland, writing several published and unpublished reports on his travels in the Vosges. One of his accounts of a trip in the late 1790s is full of ethnographic observations and references to naturalists and internal travel literature from the last years of the Old Regime.[30]

In his written work considering the regeneration of populations, Grégoire revealed that the Enlightenment natural history of Buffon and his associates was another important source of his outlook. In Buffon's early works, the regenerative powers of systematic crossbreeding were the preeminent example of the human ability to restore nature and transform degenerated organisms. Buffon developed these ideas in his influential discussions of the natural history of humans and applied them to questions of racial *métissage* (mixing) that would be used and developed by a number of savants, such as the physician Charles-Augustin Vandermonde, who wrote an important book about improving people through a variety of means, including selective breeding.[31] This approach developed into a substantial literature in the late eighteenth century that often directly focused on issues of race and colonial *métissage*.[32] In fact, a number of well-known revolutionaries, including Condorcet, Sieyès, Cabanis, and Volney, as well as lesser-known figures like Julien-Joseph Virey, François-Emmanuel Fodéré, and Louis-Joseph-Marie Robert, suggested that *métissage* or some more selective form of human breeding should be a part of the larger project of regeneration.[33] Grégoire was a part of this discourse before and during the Revolution, and he often used the naturalistic and racialized sense of regeneration, as can be seen clearly in his writing about the physical improvement of people through *métissage*. He first used this concept in his 1788 essay on the regeneration of the Jews, in which he directly named Buffon and Vandermonde as authoritative sources.[34] He went on to develop this point about *métissage* in his famous writings about people of African descent, eventually calling for the intermarriage of blacks and whites, Greeks and Turks, Catholics and Protestants, and Europeans and South Asians.[35] These ideas fit within Grégoire's vision of the creation of a universal Catholic Church, but they never lost their natural historical and colonial relevance. Even though some of Grégoire's political and religious ideas had changed by the time of the Restoration, when he called for the intermarriage of blacks and whites in the 1820s, he again echoed Buffon and built on the theoretical foundation that had been laid in the Enlightenment.[36]

Grégoire was involved in several projects to improve agriculture as a means of morally and economically regenerating the nation. "The two most useful and neglected sciences," he claimed, "are the cultivation of man and that of the earth."[37] The agricultural projects offer further evidence of the role of Enlightenment natural history in his thought and the ways that it allowed him to see *métissage* as a powerful source of regeneration. He spoke of how practicing crossbreeding, studying natural history, and viewing dissections held people's attention and how these practices provided "illumination to philosophy."[38] To make this illumination more widely accessible throughout France, Grégoire proposed that the government establish rural agricultural centers in each department. In collaboration with one of Buffon's most important subordinates from the King's Garden, Grégoire envisioned centers where peasants would learn new farming techniques and the skills to acclimatize foreign plants and animals in France.[39] Through these centers, Grégoire wanted the government to "multiply the attempts to cross the races [of animals] and obtain the mixed species of the highest value," and he encouraged French generals fighting abroad to bring home foreign species for crossbreeding.[40] In addition to facilitating the biological *métissage* of domestic animals, the centers would facilitate an epistemological and technological *métissage* in service of the economic and political regeneration of the nation. They would be nodes in a new national network enabling an unprecedented sharing and mixing of tools, techniques, and theories of agricultural production. He believed that bringing the disparate parts of France together through communication and the sharing of knowledge was a vital step in national regeneration, since many parts of the kingdom languished because "before the Revolution, the various parts of France were, so to speak, strangers to each other."[41] This is the same expansive sense of the regenerative benefits of *métissage* that can be found in Grégoire's more famous project to annihilate the patois and replace it with a common language that would facilitate the mixing of the disparate cultures and peoples of France.[42] For Grégoire, the body politic, like the animal body and the human body, greatly benefited from *métissage*.

To exemplify some other types of quiet, but recognizable, echoes of the first French Empire in the French Revolution, I turn to the revolutionary career of Nicolas-Louis François de Neufchâteau. Even though he rarely made explicit references to the colonies after 1789, François de Neufchâteau's belief in the state's need for detailed and reliable knowledge of the natural variation of its territory and the cultural variation of its people can be traced to his formative experience as a magistrate in Saint-Domingue at the end of the Old Regime. As he made clear during the Revolution, this kind of knowledge was crucial to the state's ability to effect true regeneration and to consolidate and stabilize the republic. Although greater uniformity and national unity were the goal, François de Neufchâteau recognized that laws, agricultural production, economic reforms, and tactics of cultural regeneration and education had to be adjusted to fit local circumstances. The massive statistical project that he undertook as the minister of the interior in the Directory was meant to represent these circumstances in unprecedented detail and thoroughness.

During the first years of the Revolution, François de Neufchâteau played a role in organizing the department of the Vosges. Later, he was a deputy to the Legislative Assembly and was elected to the National Convention, although he never sat. During the Directory, he became a *commissaire*, the minister of the interior (twice), and a Director. Before this revolutionary career, he had been a precocious poet and a teacher until he turned to the practice of law. After five years as a magistrate in Lorraine, François de Neufchâteau sought and received a position as a magistrate in Saint-Domingue. His time in the colony proved to be formative, and in fact, he was politically radicalized during his four years in Saint-Domingue. It was there that he developed ideas on popular sovereignty, the links between public credit and political representation, and the disassociation of rights and privileges that would play an important role in his political career, as well as in the Revolution more generally.[43]

His experiences in the colony were also formative in the development of his legal philosophy and his ideas of the relationship between law and politics. After initial frustrations, he abandoned the traditional role of the magistrate and adopted a voluntaristic approach to positive law that focused on the ability of the law to be quickly and appropriately created for—or adapted to—specific circumstances. In Saint-Domingue, he became more of an active creator of the law than a passive representative of the monarch's authority and its expression through the law. As the intendant of Saint-Domingue wrote in a letter to François de Neufchâteau, this approach "would seem to have arrogated some of the power reserved to the sovereign."[44]

In addition to becoming a political radical through his experience in the colonies, François de Neufchâteau developed several administrative dispositions that would play a role in the project for which he is best known: the attempt to create a comprehensive statistical survey of France during the Directory. This massive project to create a broad and detailed representation of the nation enlisted officials from all over France to gather information about an extremely wide variety of commercial, political, religious, agricultural, natural, and cultural topics. Although statistical projects in the service of centralized power had been slowly growing in importance since the late seventeenth century, François de Neufchâteau's grand project was the first to attempt to integrate both qualitative and quantitative information from all regions of France. Many subjects of the survey, such as the cultural beliefs and customs of the peasantry, had never before been included in a large, centralized statistical project. This grand statistical project of the minister of the interior reflects the interest in statistics that he developed while a magistrate in the colonies. Additionally, it bears the stamp of the much longer history of statistics in the colonies.

Although it is often overlooked in the scholarship on the development of the state and its tools of knowing and managing the population, since the seventeenth century the colonies played a crucial role in the development of comprehensive surveys of populations and commerce. The first complete nominative census in French history was taken in the colonies, and scholars have identified a total of 286 censuses taken in the French colonies from the beginning of the eighteenth century to 1790.[45] The colonies were laboratories for the development of these biopolitical tools because the populations were small enough to make comprehensive surveys appear practical, because masters were required to provide inventories of their slaves for the purpose of taxation, because the health and size of the free and enslaved populations were always precarious and in need of attention, because of the importance of commerce and productivity in the colonies, and because people saw statistical knowledge as instrumental in creating and maintaining order in slave societies where slaves often outnumbered free people by significant numbers.

It is not coincidental then that it was in the colony of Saint-Domingue that François de Neufchâteau developed his concern with statistics as an administrative tool of knowledge and improvement. This new interest was evidenced in his books on Saint-Domingue, which included numerous discussions of the population, as well as tables that enumerate the population and detail the varieties of agriculture in in the colony.[46] In these writings, he also demonstrated a new attentiveness to the particularity of regional variations based on differences of climate and location. François de Neufchâteau discussed natural differences between the colony and the metropole that would necessitate differences of government, law, agriculture, and commerce, and he also divided Saint-Domingue into its three regions and analyzed internal differences with greater detail.[47]

Building on this new interest in statistics and local variation, the grand statistical project of the Directory brought together descriptive and quantitative traditions in the service of a comprehensive survey of France. This effort represented a new attempt to relate the variety of particular differences to the newly conceived whole of France.[48] The new administrative importance of the relation between the departments and the nation—the parts and the whole—resulted in a new epistemological importance that was reflected in the statistical project. As François de Neufchâteau explained in his instructions to the officials gathering the information, "the grandest knowledge of localities" was necessary in order to "embrace the universality of France."[49]

In 1800, as a major state-sponsored expedition prepared to set out for Australia, the government called on the newly formed Society of the Observers of Man to advise the expedition's scientists on the study of the cultural and racial characteristics of the native inhabitants that they would encounter.[50] The author of the resulting "Consideration on the Various Methods to Follow in the Observation of Savage Peoples" attempted "to present a complete framework that might bring together all of the points of view from which these [savage] nations might be envisioned by the philosopher."[51] Joseph-Marie Degérando was the author of this document, noted in the history of anthropology for its adherence to comprehensiveness and many of the methodological principles that came to define the modern discipline. Degérando was also an official in the Ministry of the Interior who took part in the massive statistical survey of France.[52] He was not, therefore, merely an important historical figure in the formalization of the anthropological study of exotic others in far-off lands. He was also an associate of Grégoire and François de Neufchâteau who was at the forefront of the creation of the anthropology of the internal other and the institutionalization of statistics as a major tool of the state. In fact, the connections between the global and the local, internal anthropology and its external variation were a fundamental focus of the Observers of Man. It was something of which they were aware and about which they were explicit. As the perpetual secretary of the society announced in one of its founding documents, the members intended to study people that originated in different continents and countries, but also people from different cities and villages within the same country.[53] They would try to find objective racial differences between people of African and European descent, but they would also create an "anthropological topography of France" and reveal an "anthropology of the different regions."[54]

Through the anthropological orientation developed in the Enlightenment and refashioned during the Revolution, the Observers of Man oriented themselves toward the new imperial ventures of the nineteenth century as well as the process of "internal colonization" that aimed to complete the construction of the nation by making "peasants into Frenchmen."[55] The traditional separation between the historiographies of France and its colonies has obscured the fact that the development of ideas and practices in one place was never truly separate from that in the other, even while the places themselves were. The two have always been connected in a circular fashion with neither the metropole nor the colony exclusively influencing or being influenced by the other. Whether in the form of commerce, politics, science, food, or fashion, the colonial found its way into the metropolitan as the metropolitan found its way into the colonial. This is true even on the highest plains of abstraction and in some of the most refined philosophical systems of the era. Even Hegel's master-slave dialectic, one of the most powerful concepts of nineteenth-century European philosophy, appears to have emerged in part from an encounter with the Haitian Revolution.[56]

By focusing on these developments—the suggestive traces of the first French Empire in the French Revolution and the early Napoleonic era—I do not want to downplay the importance of the many direct engagements with colonial questions during the French Revolution. Clearly, questions like the abolition and reintroduction of slavery continue to be of the highest historical importance. But a fuller sense of the manner in which colonial history played a role in shaping the ideas and practices of the revolutionary actors may help us better understand these explicitly colonial concerns and the role they played in the Revolution. We may also be able to see in a new light, some aspects of the Revolution that at first appear to be unconnected to colonial history but nonetheless—like the perception of Indian-like peasants in the French countryside—speak to a longer and deeper connection in which the metropole and the colonies were not as easily separated as they have traditionally appeared.

6 Foreigners, Cosmopolitanism, and French Revolutionary Universalism

SUZANNE DESAN

24 August 1792. Two weeks earlier the monarchy had been overthrown. Within the last week, General Lafayette had defected, the Prussians had invaded, and the fortress town of Longwy had just fallen, though Paris did not yet know. Verdun would tumble a week later. In the midst of this ferment, the playwright Marie-Joseph Chénier led a delegation of Parisian citizens to the bar of the Assembly, petition in hand. He urged the deputies to offer full French citizenship to a list of "courageous philosophers who have sapped the foundations of tyranny." The Legislative Assembly, facing not only the war but also a domestic political struggle with the Paris Commune and a full reform agenda, took time for a hot debate of Chénier's proposal. Two days later, eighteen foreigners—ranging from British abolitionist Thomas Clarkson to writer of the United States Constitution James Madison—were pronounced French citizens, with full political rights.[1]

Certainly, this act was meant to play on the cosmopolitan stage of the Enlightened public sphere of Europe. But this granting of citizenship was not purely performative or honorary. Three of the adopted citizens—Tom Paine, the Prussian Anacharsis Cloots, and the Englishman Joseph Priestley—were soon elected as deputies to the new Convention, though only the first two would serve. The decree's supporters made the politics clear: if the republic was to be universal, it must be a global creation from the outset; the National Convention would be, in Chénier's words, "a congress of the whole world." This idea immediately provoked the resistance and anxiety of some deputies. "You are delivering the Convention to foreigners!" exclaimed the deputy Claude Basire at one point mid-debate. And invasion by outsiders was not the only threat. Lasource warned that the Assembly should not give away this glorious title of French citizenship so lightly. To build a republic was a fragile and controversial act. "If you set about giving this title to those who have not asked for it, wouldn't you risk suffering the humiliation of a refusal?"[2]

When exploring this striking move by *la patrie en danger*, historians have either seen it as a diplomatic "gesture of defiance," or most often, inquired what this incident meant for the treatment of foreigners and the creation of citizenship. They have variously interpreted the 26 August decree as a high point of cosmopolitan openness before its demise or as a step toward politicizing citizenship and clarifying the exclusionary meanings of universalism.[3] I reverse the citizenship question and ask instead: what could the act of adopting these foreigners possibly do for the nascent republic? Ask not what your country can do for foreigners; ask what foreigners can do for your country.

On one level, the events of 24–26 August 1792—tied to a particular political moment—show how issues of foreigners and foreign policy became entangled with domestic politics: in the tense weeks after the overthrow of the king, the Legislative Assembly sought to stake out its legitimacy and future Girondins worked indirectly to defend their foreign policy. On another, broader level, this event performs crucial ideological work for the new republic. I will argue that this debate illustrates how the emerging republic laid claim to universalism by incorporating foreigners. Historians have largely situated the origins of republican universalism in the Enlightenment discourse of natural rights. For the French revolutionaries, "universalism" meant that the legitimacy of the nation—the very sovereignty of the nation itself—rested on the defense of universal human rights and on guaranteeing equality before the law. While some scholars have stressed the exclusionary contradictions of this ideology, others have emphasized that it also enabled various groups of people to demand rights.[4] Republican universalism had both exclusionary and liberationist potential, and the issue of inclusion/exclusion is clearly pivotal.

However, to focus primarily on the issue of how Enlightenment ideas about rights promoted inclusion or exclusion obscures another aspect of republican universalism: its hybrid construction[5] through interaction with foreign peoples and powers. In this chapter, I will analyze the 24–26 August event to suggest how multiple international forces—people, ideas, geopolitics—fundamentally informed the French national act of claiming a universal basis for their republic. In order to ground the republic in a claim to worldwide validity, the revolutionaries had to figure out how to incorporate various aspects of foreignness: I argue that they drew legitimacy and vital energy from the presence of foreigners—from their ideas, their representation, and their participation in a shared crusade to alter history.

To build universalism, the revolutionaries appropriated and politicized Enlightenment cosmopolitanism. Cosmopolitanism provided a frame for imagining relationships among foreign individuals, and also foreign powers. I examine how this cosmopolitan frame influenced notions of global fraternity and regeneration. I also show how geopolitics was entangled in building republican universalism, and suggest the limits and contradictions of this ideology on both the domestic and the international stage. For the revolutionaries, to root the republic in universal rights was an international act: they claimed to defy the whole system of aggressive, monarchical geopolitics and take up the cosmopolitan pursuit of peace. Parallel to the rights of individuals were the rights of whole peoples to liberty and reciprocal respect. But at the same time, from 1789 on, the universalizing impulse carried a contradictory message—the sense that the French should spread their Revolution, whether by example, missionary zeal, or eventually, by force.[6] As the revolutionaries embraced leading foreigners as citizens in August 1792, they simultaneously expressed their cosmopolitan renunciation of conquest and their commitment to an international crusade—a nutshell of the dilemmas emerging in republican universalism. In the months after this debate, once France repelled the Prussian invasion and began to advance into neighboring territories, the National Convention repeatedly disputed whether universalist ideology guaranteed each people the right to determine their own sovereign status or whether France should take the lead in regenerating, liberating, and colonizing areas such as the Savoy, Belgium, and the Rhineland.

This chapter, then, explores a brief but revealing incident—the debate over adopting foreigners—to ask how the revolutionaries laid claim to universalism in part by incorporating foreign peoples and projects and by politicizing cosmopolitanism. The event also sheds light on tensions within universalism. I will weave together analysis of the debate and press responses with examination of the foreigners chosen.

Foreigners, Global Fraternity, and Regeneration

When Chénier led a delegation of Parisians to petition for adopting fourteen strangers, he intended to combine performance and politics. This well-known playwright was already tuned in to the symbolic power of foreigners. In April 1792 he had helped orchestrate the festival of Châteauvieux, which featured liberated Swiss soldiers, American and British radicals, and images of Algernon Sydney, Ben Franklin, and William Tell, with a javelin at his feet for slaying the Austrian governor and emancipating Switzerland.[7]

Four months later, when Chénier and his Parisians brought their list of proposed citizens to the Assembly, the political situation was heated. Enemy troops had crossed the French border. Meanwhile, the 10 August uprising that overthrew King Louis XVI had ushered in a moment of tense power-sharing between the Legislative Assembly and the Paris Commune, newly triumphant after spurring on the attack on the monarchy. The Assembly, and its leading political group, soon known as the Girondins, had been reluctant to suspend the king. Pressured by popular activism and the Commune, the Assembly had agreed to imprison the king and call elections for a new legislature to lead France, a National Convention to be elected by universal manhood suffrage.[8] In short, at this moment when France worked toward defining its emerging republic, it faced both foreign invasion and divisive domestic politics.

In this loaded context, the debate over foreign citizens held significance and sparked controversy because it cut to the heart of key matters just when France set out to invent its republic. First, legitimacy. How could the embrace of universal values, drawn largely from the Enlightenment, legitimize and unify the fragile act of building the republic? Second, sovereignty. If the sovereignty of the republic rested conceptually on the defense of rights, did that mean that non-French defenders of rights could participate in building the sovereign nation? Did their commitment to universal goals trump their outsider status? Third, international relations and the Revolution beyond the hexagon. How could the revolutionaries' new vision of sovereignty garner transnational legitimacy and also challenge traditional geopolitics of "tyrannical" states? And what did the claim to universalism mean for exporting revolution to other peoples or colonies?

Chénier's delegation, with its list of Enlightened foreigners, offered one response to these large questions. After a lively discussion, the deputies agreed that the Committee of Public Instruction should draw up a list of meritorious "philosophes who had had the courage to defend liberty and equality in foreign countries." On 26 August, the Legislative Assembly voted to grant citizenship to eighteen individuals. Presented as "citizens of the world," these men did not represent the whole globe. Rather, they embodied the European and American Enlightenment, its assertion of cosmopolitanism, and the commitment to certain revolutionary political stances. Their names, exactly as listed in the 26 August decree, are as follows: "the doctor Joseph Priestley, Thomas Payne, Jérémie Bentham, William Wilberforce, Thomas Clarkson, Jacques Mackintosh, David Williams, N. Gorani, Anacharsis Cloots, Corneille Pauw, Joachim-Henry Campe, N. Pestalozzi, Georges Washington, Jean Hamilton, N. Madison, H. Klopstock, and Thadée Kosciusko." The deputy Philippe-Jacques Ruhl successfully added the German playwright Friedrich Schiller.[9] Seven of the new citizens hailed from Great Britain, four from German states, three from the new United States, and one each from Italy, the Netherlands, Switzerland, and Poland.

In imagining and claiming these European and American writers, generals, and politicians as representatives of humanity as a whole, the French revolutionaries espoused and built on a logic drawn from Enlightenment cosmopolitanism, a concept with multiple meanings. First, it refers to a set of ideals about human emotions and morals: as a philosophical stance, cosmopolitanism held that core human qualities and moral characteristics transcended national, religious, or linguistic differences. Hope for progress lay in the fact that all human beings shared moral commitments to the world at large and emotional bonds to one another. Second, in geopolitics, cosmopolitanism signified the ideal of perpetual world peace. Third, cosmopolitanism could also suggest a set of practices, of transnational interconnectedness, correspondence, dialogue, and rubbing shoulders with people of other nations, often imagined as an elite experience. Fourth, cosmopolitanism could be a rhetorical strategy, a positioning of oneself as impartial, and therefore uniquely capable of offering insight from above the fray. Finally, a fifth meaning: even as they discussed universal human qualities, proponents of cosmopolitanism were intrigued by the comparative study of different cultures. They explored and assessed—often in judgmental ways—the diverse customs, histories, religions, and values of peoples from various geographies, climates, or regions of the world. To put this last point succinctly, some peoples seemed to have progressed more than others, and it was important to figure out why.[10]

The revolutionaries did not enact cosmopolitanism as an ideal. Instead, they used one set of ideals and practices, cosmopolitanism, to inform another ideal: universalism—a legitimizing ideal under construction in practice. Rather than simplistically positioning cosmopolitanism as an ideal that was opposite to nationalism, I argue that cosmopolitan assumptions and practices informed the republican universalism that at times underpinned nationalism. As they recruited certain foreigners to help them define republican universalism, the revolutionaries drew on and politicized these cosmopolitan claims.

Cosmopolitan language and assumptions provided a frame for expressing the fraternity of the revolutionary crusade and giving it emotional power that could spring across borders. Chénier, Antoine-Adrien Lamourette, and Pierre Vergniaud linked France's mission to the fate of "the human race," "all the peoples of the world," the "free world," and the "liberty of the world." Both the initial debate and the final decree invoked "universal fraternity"—the ultimate global, emotional bond. At one point in the deliberations, Claude Fauchet leapt up to embrace François Chabot as he stepped down from the tribune.[11] Adopting foreigners could tie this ardor and fraternity of revolutionaries in the Assembly and in France to the cosmic wave of revolutionary zeal abroad. Even as these outsiders became French, they retained their foreignness and made manifest the universalism of transnational revolution.

In fact, some of the chosen foreigners clearly personified this transnational passion for revolution and had cultivated it in their writings. For example, in his 1789 work, *Briefe aus Paris* (Letters from Paris), the adoptee Joachim

Heinrich Campe, swept away by the energy and harmony of the Revolution, longed to spread this joy back home: "My heart heats up and expands as I contemplate . . . all the consequences that it will bring for Europe, for the world! . . . I'd like to cry for joy as I anticipate springtime and the general happiness of peoples." In choosing Campe, the revolutionaries blended revolutionary fervor with geopolitical motives. Beyond his heartfelt defense of spreading revolution, Campe's hometown origins helped him make the list: now back in Germany, he had been publishing a reformist newspaper in the duchy of Braunschweig or Brunswick, the very principality whose duke was invading France.[12]

If the adopted foreigners embodied the emotional power of global fraternity, according to their supporters, they were also bringing about the moral transformation of the world at large. Marguerite-Élie Guadet listed the moral and political accomplishments of several of the nominees: "Wilberforce pleaded the slaves' cause with an energy that shamed greed. . . . Priestley has taught men the secret of their power." To adopt such figures would put humanitarian goals of political and social reform at the heart of republican universalism. In an analysis of late Old Regime cosmopolitan writers, the historian Sophia Rosenfeld has argued that by taking a stance as "citizens of the world" or "friends of humanity," anonymous authors could make powerful international critiques of despotism or unjust warfare precisely because they situated themselves as impartial, as outside national politics, as vessels who allowed the forces of "reason, compassion, and imagination" to speak on behalf of humanity at large. While Rosenfeld is interested in individual authorial strategies, her point applies also to the self-conscious, cosmopolitan positioning of the revolutionaries who collectively claimed to conduct transparent politics for the liberty of the whole globe, politics without partiality, and as I will discuss below, the spread of revolution without conquest. As Marie-Jean Hérault de Séchelles promised, free France would not look, as the self-interested Louis XIV had, for adoring savants in foreign courts to be paid off with gold robbed from "sweat and blood of the people." No, "free France [would be] satisfied to associate with her glory these great men from distant countries who had dared to speak the language of liberty and equality."[13]

In building their claim to republican universalism, the French revolutionaries drew on the iconic, moral pull of leading humanitarians who above all had defended human rights in action. In its report on the debate, the *Journal des débats et des décrets* made clear that the selected foreigners had "proclaimed the rights of man," and thereby "prepared the reign of universal liberty." The Assembly chose men who embodied the quest for rights and the Enlightened reform of education and justice: abolitionists like Wilberforce and Clarkson, educators like Pestalozzi and Campe, theorists of natural rights and democratic politics like Paine and Mackintosh, a justice-system reformer like Bentham—whose prison design, the Panopticon, was under review by the legislative committee. Their "philosophical ties of blood"—to use Lamourette's phrase—brought "glory" and grandeur to France and philosophers alike.[14]

In some cases, these rugged crafters of universal liberty, equality, and rights generated even more moral and affective pull because they had been victimized, like France herself, by kings, the evil defenders of the status quo. Because France was struggling to repel invasion by some of these kings and carve out new republican politics, this move held all the more power. Expelled from Habsburg lands, his property seized, the Milanese novelist and economist Giuseppe Gorani had been "honored and made famous by the hatred and persecution of the house of Austria, this great enemy of the happiness of mankind." The "court of Saint James" had targeted Paine. And as for Priestley—whose home had been ransacked by Church and King rioters in the Birmingham riots of 14 July 1791—his "misfortunes had covered him with glory as much as did his virtues and his genius."[15]

As the revolutionaries associated themselves with this coterie of great philosophers, for all their global claims, they laid out an imagined geographic hierarchy that placed France at the pinnacle, standing on the base of Europe, which in turn represented the world as a whole. When he depicted Priestley as "cosmopolitan, and consequently, French," Chabot pithily encapsulated the bond between France and the global, Euro-elite. Two months later, in October, when the Convention invited intellectuals to offer their suggestions for France's constitution, the future Montagnard Bertrand de Barère enunciated the architecture of this joint creation of republican universalism most clearly: "The Constitution of a great Republic cannot be the work of a few minds; it should be the work of the human mind. . . . Anyone . . . in France, in Europe, in the whole world, who is capable of drawing up and writing a plan for a republican Constitution, is necessarily a member of the Committee of the Constitution." He envisioned a constitution generated by the cosmopolitan dialogue of the educated and Enlightened public sphere. The Constitutional Committee should draw on "all the luminaries, interrogate the genius of liberty everywhere, . . . reap the benefits of the freedom of the press." It should "establish political and moral correspondence with philosophes and publishers, bring together all the minds to better band together all the wills, and give the solemn initiative to public opinion."[16]

Public opinion, print culture, correspondence networks—a textbook model of the Enlightened, cosmopolitan public sphere, one to be guided by an elite corps of writers, by "great men" who combined the power of the pen with their innate genius. "Why wouldn't [France] consult these foreigners who have taught her how to be free?" asked the *Courrier des 83 départements*. "Why wouldn't all the geniuses of Europe sit in the National Convention?" As the *Annales patriotiques et littéraires* stated, the Assembly offered citizenship "to the men in Europe who had most gained fame through their love of liberty. . . . France declares that they are her children because they are the children of liberty."[17]

Encompassed within this avowedly open model of creating republican universalism lay limits and tensions generated in part by its construction out of the old Republic of Letters. How could the cosmopolitan model of sovereignty set up by elite, "grands hommes" encompass a new, broader definition of popular sovereignty and grassroots public opinion? The popular insurrection of 10 August brought this question to the forefront. Mid-debate, Basire, advocate of universal manhood suffrage, attacked the elitist assumptions of the decree when he exclaimed against the adoptees: "It's the aristocracy of half talents!"[18] And what was the role of each nation's sovereignty and self-governance in this republicanism led by France, to be seconded by Europe, and spread from there to a global universal republic, no doubt a colonial one? Revolt in Saint-Domingue and the imminent success of French armies in Europe would soon pose this question acutely and repeatedly.

For the supporters of the decree, cosmopolitanism, as appropriated by the revolutionaries, could provide a bridge across those tensions and contradictions with its ideals of human diversity, progress, and regeneration. Most of the adopted citizens of France were writers who used their words not only to reveal, unmask, and critique, but also to regenerate and civilize. Within their cosmopolitan appreciation of human variety, within "their writings that promise the triumph of liberty in all the climates of our globe," some had assessed the readiness of different peoples for liberty. The adoptee Cornelius de Pauw, who had written on the Americas, China, and ancient Egypt, was celebrated for theorizing a climatological hierarchy: in contrast to Europe's temperate readiness for civilization, the wet, cool climate of the Americas had a degenerative effect, both moral and physical.[19]

Although   de Pauw was not fully optimistic about the possibilities for universal progress across climates and geographies, most French revolutionaries, and their newly adopted citizens, argued that such differences among people—both within France and far beyond—would be repaired by institutional political reforms coupled with revolutionary regeneration. Nominee James Mackintosh waxed poetic about the "energy of freedom" and praised the French for beginning "her regenerating labours with a solemn declaration of . . . sacred, inalienable, and imprescriptible rights." Setting himself up as the "orator of the human race" and the "prophet of universal regeneration," adoptee Cloots argued tirelessly that the Revolution would bring about the regeneration of humanity by destroying Catholicism's hold on the popular imagination and creating a vast republic. In contrast to his uncle de Pauw, Cloots believed that the human thirst for liberty overcame cultural and climatological varieties among peoples. To see the universal "instinct for liberty," one only had to look at the "experience of Boston and Charlestown, the patriotism of Indians in Pondicherry, the Africans of the Ile de Bourbon, the Americans of Saint-Domingue, the independence of blacks in the blue mountains of Jamaica and the thick forests of Guyana, the voice of nature that preached liberty to the Iroquois and the Samoyeds."[20]

For all that he championed liberty as a shared human quest, Cloots also epitomized the view that regeneration and republican politics should be built outward from France and Europe to span the globe. By tapping into the fervent beliefs of new citizens like Cloots and Mackintosh, the revolutionaries staked out not only their cosmopolitan belief in global fraternity and their moral commitment to human rights and Enlightened reforms, but also their investment in the loaded and unequal politics of regeneration from above.

This vision of republican universalism faced some pointed opposition within the Assembly. Notably, opponents voiced anxiety that this ideal rested on a perilous confidence in human emotions of fraternity and moral commitment to the collective good. Taking a realpolitik position in this time of war, Jacques-Alexis Thuriot bluntly exposed the fault line underlying the universalist claim to fraternal transcendence and impartiality. Emotions on behalf of humanity did not necessarily trump national feeling. While it was true that great men belonged to all of humanity, if an Englishman, a Prussian, and a German were adopted as French citizens, and if France were at war with their countries, no one could expect them to reliably support measures to repel the enemy. He proposed that the nominees be granted citizenship but not the right to become representatives. Also mistrustful of the intentions and loyalty of strangers, Lasource objected to offering citizenship to those who had not asked for it, to those who had in effect not voiced their political will.[21]

Attacking the cosmopolitan assumptions from a different angle, Basire impugned the sincerity of elite authors called on to regenerate France and the globe. Written words alone did not prove the purity and truthfulness of emotions, he warned. External style did not necessarily reveal the true workings of the heart. According to Basire, authors of public writings could show talent and even offer "dazzling ideas," but they could also mislead the people and, once in the Convention, "betray the public good. . . . Do not expose your fellow citizens to seductions like these." This future Montagnard called into question the false expressions of fraternity by "famous foreigners"—an "aristocracy of half talents"—and implicitly aligned himself with the ordinary citizens who had overthrown the crown on 10 August.[22]

His objections spotlight the extent to which domestic political positioning mixed with the ideological attempt to hammer out revolutionary ideals. Chénier, and most likely his fellow Parisian delegates, had backed the Commune. In contrast, many, though not all, of the deputies who picked up his proposal and carried it forward belonged to the Girondin faction. For these deputies, to adopt foreigners marked the opportunity to move attention away from Parisian leadership and seize a transnational mantle for the Revolution, even as they outlined its universalist claims. With the exception of Lasource, the leading opponents of the 24 August petition were future Montagnards, aligned with Paris and suspicious of the Girondins.[23] The alignments, however, were complex and fluid. Chabot, future Montagnard and backer of the Commune, favored the decree and connected the foreign defenders of liberty with the "brave French citizens [who] had poured forth in a majestic front on 10 August." Why hesitate to make international heroes into citizens? "Did we wait for the sansculottes to ask for liberty to give it to them? No, principles pleaded in their favor for four years, they have conquered this right, and you have declared that it belonged to them."[24] By drawing a parallel between foreign philosophes and sansculottes in the quest for rights, Chabot reinforced the leadership role of Paris in creating the incipient republic, allied 10 August with the transnational pursuit of liberty, and reiterated the commitment to universal manhood suffrage that the Assembly had been pressured into allowing.

In the 24 August 1792 debate, the selective assimilation of foreigners became a site for articulating domestic political alignments and for working out the ideological underpinnings of the new republic. As they wrestled over incorporating foreign people and ideas as part of creating the republic, the revolutionaries tapped into the emotional and moral power of cosmopolitanism and also politicized its cultural assumptions to build a regenerative vision of universalism. At the same time, this domestic forging of republican universalism became bound up with geopolitics.

Cosmopolitan Geopolitics

Strikingly, when the Assembly offered full citizenship to these eighteen outsiders, the supporters' speeches, press accounts, and the decree itself also directly espoused the cosmopolitan renunciation of conquest by force. The 26 August 1792 decree announced that "friends of liberty and universal fraternity" should be "cherished by a nation which has proclaimed its renunciation of all conquest and its desire to fraternize with all peoples." After all, noted the decree boldly, the National Convention would soon set "the destiny of France, and perhaps that of the human race."[25]

The historian Marc Belissa has shown how French revolutionaries were influenced by Enlightenment attempts to envision a cosmopolitan system of international or inter-European peace: over the early 1790s, the revolutionaries escalated their militancy, and wrestled with their earlier goal of forming a "universal republic," an Old Regime phrase often used— in opposition to "universal monarchy"—to refer to a loose confederation of states agreeing to follow international laws in order to avoid war. If individuals had rights, whole peoples also had sovereign rights that should be reciprocally respected. In the spring of 1790, the Assembly had decreed that France renounced wars of conquest and would never use its forces against the liberty of any people.[26]

Two years later, when the supporters of the 26 August decree invoked this cosmopolitan language of renouncing conquest, they made clear that inventing the republic was a geopolitical act. In effect, they defined the creation of a new nation as an *international challenge*, as a geopolitical move whose significance far transcended the borders of the hexagon. They boldly claimed that the French republic would inaugurate a new kind of state: it would not be led by tyrants and would not engage in the endless rounds of destructive warfare and territorial aggrandizement.

In reporting on the adoption of foreigners, the journalist Antoine-Joseph Gorsas provided the most in-depth commentary on this tie between cosmopolitan geopolitics, adopted foreigners, and the regenerative republic. He first excoriated the monarchical "scoundrels who had divided Europe between them, . . . cultivated national hatreds and put the globe into a state of perpetual warfare." He then praised the nominees, these "ardent cosmopolitans" and "enlightened philosophers" who had dared to challenge the tyrants. France had been the first to answer their call and should now "hasten the *resurrection of the world* . . . and present all peoples with the olive branch of fraternity" (emphasis mine). With feigned disbelief, Gorsas brushed aside Thuriot's objection that warfare could shatter the cosmopolitan emotion of loyalty to universal liberty (and France). The journalist dismissed this pragmatic argument with vaunted praise for the brave, disinterested, and enlightened citizens-to-be who had forsworn "all national prejudice."[27]

As Gorsas made clear, the new republic would regenerate not just individual citizens but also the whole system of geopolitics. Along these same lines, in his introductory speech, Chénier depicted the French constructing their cosmopolitan republic, against "diplomatic ineptitude [and] the tortuous negotiations between courts who have agreed on mutually deceiving one another." Those old squabbles would never produce "universal fraternity" or enable "all nations to rest in the shade of equality." Bentham had written a plan for perpetual peace, and several of the other adopted foreigners, including Mackintosh, Paine, and Friedrich Klopstock, had celebrated the French renunciation of conquest in 1790. At a prorevolutionary festival in Hamburg on 14 July 1790, an ode by Klopstock had proclaimed: "War, the most horrible of monsters, has been enchained by her [the Assembly.]"[28]

In effect, as part and parcel of republican universalism, with the 26 August 1792 adoption of foreigners, the revolutionaries appropriated the cosmopolitan image of the universal republic—as a peaceful alliance of nations against the universal monarchy. To root the creation of the republic in the universalist claim of forging international peace had great moral potency. With the Prussian army bearing down on the emerging republic, this renunciation of conquest positioned France on the defensive in the war that it had declared four months earlier. In this mode, not only did the 26 August decree voice "the desire to fraternize with all peoples," but it also claimed as allies men who had been victimized, like France, by powerful monarchs, malevolent defenders of tyranny at home and incessant warfare abroad. With this stance, France's defensive war took on the resonance of a crusade in the name of all humanity. As the *Chronique de Paris* commented, the Assembly invited these eighteen outsiders to "defend the cause of the human race against tyrants and their slaves."[29]

For the Girondins, who faced the political rivalry of Paris and who could be accused of leading France into the current disastrous war, the language of renouncing conquest had particular appeal. By claiming to act on a much larger global stage, they implicitly downplayed the activism of Paris, defined their war as a defensive war, and simultaneously raised the Revolution above territoriality into the realm of the universal. As Vergniaud stated in the Assembly, "It is not only for this little part of the globe that we call France that we have conquered liberty; it is not only on the Place Vendôme [i.e., in Paris against Louis] that we should concentrate the attack against despotism. . . . What means could be more sure, more effective, for assuring French liberty than associating with our dangers the philosophes from foreign nations, who have defended it?" In the *Patriote français*, Jacques-Pierre Brissot likewise called for a philosophic alliance shielding liberty against despotism: "May this wise and philanthropic decree win over for France this crowd of philosophers who have built respect for the Revolution in their countries; this is the only kind of conquest that we cannot renounce."[30]

From cosmopolitanism, the revolutionaries built the powerful notions of regeneration from above and a global fraternity of nations; however, they further recast cosmopolitanism by hitching these aspirations to an inevitable tide of international revolution moving through time and space. For the revolutionaries, the chosen foreigners laid out a geography of transformation. "Payne, Priestley, and Mackintof [*sic*] in England; Pitalozzi [*sic*] in Switzerland; Gorani on the banks of the Tiber, and Malakowski on the banks of the Vistula have successfully pleaded the cause of humanity against tyranny, and laid the foundations of the universal Republic."[31] While the claim to universalism lifted the cause above territory, the very spatiality of this imagery—the banks of the Tiber, the banks of the Vistula—gave this movement a romantic allure and a sense of spatial destiny. It could not but unfold.

The crafters of the 26 August decree endorsed international revolution selectively, in dialogue with current geopolitics. No Dutch patriots or Belgians, whether Vonckist or Statist, found their way onto the rolls. Instead Chénier more cautiously invoked those whose "luminous writings had served either American liberty or French liberty," and the list would include a marked number of British individuals battling for republican principles. While Tom Paine's transatlantic activism made him an obvious choice, David Williams, minister and political theorist, had written a universalist, deist liturgy and had just published a work diagramming the progress of revolutionary, political reform in Britain, America, and the new France. Both Paine and Williams demonstrated revolution on the march. Spanning revolutions in action, the Polish general Thaddeus Kosciusko had fought in the American Revolution and had led the recent Polish attempt to defend their new constitution against Russian invaders.[32]

The American Revolution, safely across the sea, also offered James Madison, George Washington, and oddly enough, Alexander Hamilton. When he praised Madison for "in the *Federalist* developing in depth . . . the system of confederations,"[33] Chénier effectively drew a parallel between the American federal system and the cosmopolitan quest for a universal republic. Madison and other drafters of the Constitution had feared that the individual American states would emulate the geopolitics of European nation-states, jealously guard their own interests, and splinter into warfare: Madison's "compound republic," a federative system, offered the promise, as yet untested, of peaceful union among the American states, a possible model for Europe. The Assembly's choice of these Americans simultaneously linked France to the transatlantic wave of revolution and reiterated the cosmopolitan claim that the republic should promote respect between self-governing states.[34]

As the French enlisted foreigners, they voiced the conflicting international impulses of their universalist project, supporting both the transnational spread of regenerative revolution and the peaceful defense of each people's autonomy. While there is no room here to explore the varied responses of the adopted foreigners, two replies suggest how much these tensions within universalism opened the door to malleable interpretations on the ground. Republican universalism could be evoked for and against conquest and colonization, for and against various peoples' autonomy and liberty. Swept up in the zeal for revolution, the adoptee Cloots pushed for a "universal republic," defined not as a confederation of republican peoples, but as a republican empire distributing rights from above. "Let us push war with vigor, it will be decisive. . . . The universal republic will replace the Catholic Church." In contrast, Bentham treated the French Convention to his opinion on their overseas empire: "Your predecessors made me a French Citizen: hear me speak like one . . . EMANCIPATE YOUR COLONIES. . . . Do you seriously mean to govern the world, and do you call that *liberty*? What is become of the rights of men? Are you the only men who have rights?"[35]

The adoption of foreigners by the French revolutionaries was in some ways a curious event: a divided nation under threat of invasion asserted that its politics of liberty and self-invention had global significance, voiced its intent to transform geopolitics in the name of peace, and enlisted leading European and American philosophes and activists in its cause. Curious as it may have been, this adoption of foreigners, just when France struggled over how to create a republic, reveals several key facets of France's emerging claim to universalism. Far from being a unified discursive claim, republican universalism developed as a vital terrain of debate, as a field for struggling over the direction and validity of the republic. Different groups would work to stretch and shape its elastic meanings in various ways to fit their particular goals in domestic politics and geopolitics. The August debate offered future Girondins in particular the opportunity to affirm the power of the weakened Legislative Assembly and to defend their war in universalist, cosmopolitan terms.

This August 1792 event also suggests more broadly how the revolutionaries built republican universalism by assimilating and altering some aspects of Enlightenment cosmopolitanism. The deputies tapped into its unifying emotional power, its moral authority, its practices of sociability, its roots in print culture and elite correspondence, its internationalist vision of peace among nations, and its claim to transcend the particular even while believing in a hierarchy of civilization among the diverse peoples of the world. Nationalism did not just bump cosmopolitanism out of the way. Rather, to fuel a political crusade, the revolutionaries both drew on and transformed cosmopolitanism. Certain cosmopolitan assumptions helped to render revolutionary universalism less than fully universal, riddled with tensions and contradictions, open for debate. The cosmopolitan celebration of great men's genius stood in uneasy relationship with the republic's proclaimed roots in popular sovereignty. Likewise, the concept of regenerating the diverse peoples of the earth—from France to Europe and then beyond—made room for a colonizing republic and seemed to validate a cultural and political hierarchy with France at its pinnacle.

The act of granting citizenship to foreigners also helps us understand the French Revolution as an international creation. As they strove to shape and claim universalism, the revolutionaries also debated how to incorporate foreignness, foreign people, and transnational concepts into the very foundations of the republic. Republican universalism had many sources, including, of course, the powerful Enlightenment ideologies of natural rights and popular sovereignty. But because these ideologies held power only as global assertions, the revolutionaries had to root their legitimacy in claims that transcended France and articulated its relationship to foreign peoples and ideas. War accentuated this ideological need and made it concrete. Within weeks after the 26 August decree, French armies reversed the war's direction and invaded Savoy, and then the Austrian Netherlands and the Rhineland. The issue of defining universal rights became all the more entangled with conflict over sovereignty and territory. The French themselves and their allies and opponents abroad engaged in repeated debate and conflict over whether universalism legitimized conquest in the name of liberty or guaranteed each people's right to sovereignty.[36] This international conflict over sovereignty, the foundational claim to defend universal human rights, and the transnational, Enlightenment origins of revolutionary ideas—these three forces accentuated the centrality of foreigners and foreign issues to the Revolution. Republicanism—born at war and based in universalism—could not be simply a national product.

7 Feminism and abolitionism

TRANSATLANTIC TRAJECTORIES

DENISE Z. DAVIDSON

"Men are born and remain free and equal in rights. Social distinctions may be based only on common utility." So proclaimed the first article of the Declaration of the Rights of Man and Citizen, completed in August 1789 by the new National Assembly. The Declaration's claim that all men are equal and that they have "natural and imprescriptible rights" built on eighteenth-century transatlantic ideals and set in motion two centuries of global conversation about the nature of rights, the political expression of those rights, and the constitution of a democratic society.[1] Much of that conversation concerned questions that had not been answered in 1789. Did the "men" of the Declaration include women, people of color, and slaves? And what exactly constituted "common utility"?

In the early 1790s, these unanswered questions combined with revolutionary violence in France and slave revolts in the French Caribbean colony of Saint-Domingue to open a space for the radical expression of both feminism and abolitionism. These movements drew on and in turn inspired other transatlantic and European expressions of feminism and abolitionism, which are too often considered separately and in exclusively national contexts. While the trajectory toward granting rights to women and people of color included many reversals, the transnational rights talk that grounded these actions and debates could not be suppressed. That these questions were not settled in any meaningful way until the mid-twentieth century indicates how important they were, both at the time and for many decades afterward.

Modern feminism emerged in the cauldron of this era of political experimentation, which encouraged men and women alike to question their assumptions about the entire political and social order of the Atlantic world. Feminism was, and remains today, an effort to attain rights for women equal to those accorded to men, and therefore a battle against women's subordination within society. Voices fighting against women's oppression go back hundreds of years, but the revolutionary era initiated a shift as the language and logic of natural, universal rights entered feminist arguments.[2] Many feminists began to view their project as not solely about women's position vis-à-vis men, but rather as part of a broader humanistic challenge, a sense of collective responsibility to fight against all forms of inequality.[3] In particular, they linked their critique of the subordinate place of women to the status of slaves. "Slavery," with reference to black slavery in the colonies, came to serve as an analogy for all kinds of oppression. Early feminist thought, even at the grassroots level, was thus informed by thinking about the abuses of colonial slavery. This humanist feminism continued to reverberate in more muted form during the Napoleonic period (1799–1814) and the Bourbon Restoration (1814–1830), as slavery emerged as a key concern among early liberals who stood for individual rights and constitutional government.[4]

While existing scholarship has examined revolutionary-era feminism and abolitionism in great detail, only a few studies have considered the connections between them. A large body of work exists on connections between women's abolitionist work and the rise of later nineteenth-century feminism, particularly in the United States.[5] The few studies that have examined women's interest in slavery in this earlier period suggest that attentiveness to this issue grew out of women's sense of oppression and their resulting identification with slaves.[6] Questions about the gender consequences of the French Revolution have inspired more intense debates. For many years, the dominant view held that the Revolution fostered a hardening of gender roles as the new politicized public sphere it helped to create was conceptualized as essentially male, while women were marginalized in the apolitical private sphere.[7] More recent scholarship emphasizes how the Revolution empowered women and encouraged debates about women's rights. Revolutionary legislation requiring equal inheritance among siblings and legalizing divorce enhanced women's position within the family at the same time that new approaches to citizenship and nationality shaped debates all over Europe. In addition, women continued to influence public life in the wake of the Revolution, despite the conservative consensus that emerged under Napoleon.[8] A handful of radical texts published between 1789 and 1793 addressed women's political and legal subjugation and have been the subject of much historical discussion, but the actions taken by thousands of ordinary French women demonstrate that many simply took political action without questioning their right to do so.[9] In making it possible to take such actions, and to argue that women deserved the full rights of citizenship, the French Revolution inaugurated modern feminism.[10]

The Revolution also had an impact on the movement to abolish black slavery. Founded in 1788, the French abolitionist organization the Society of the Friends of Blacks followed the model established by the London Society for the Abolition of the Slave Trade, which British abolitionists had founded the previous year. Both the Paris and the London groups focused on the slave trade, in the belief that once it ceased, slavery would necessarily come to an end.[11] They did not base their arguments on racial equality but instead focused on the abuses of slavery and the notion of universal human rights. French abolitionism stands out for its limited impact on public opinion, particularly in comparison with English and American abolitionism.[12] Still, the topic of slavery had emerged as a matter of public debate in France before the Revolution. Following 1789, the issue received greater attention, particularly as news of the 1791 slave revolts in Saint-Domingue began to arrive.

Revolutionary rights talk inspired both women and free people of color to stake their claims to political participation. The cultural work of the Revolution—embodied clearly in the night of August 4, when the National Assembly abolished the privileges associated with nobility—produced a transnational logic of equality. An October 1789 text addressed to the National Assembly drew attention to women's continued oppression: "You have broken the scepter of despotism; you have pronounced the beautiful axiom [that] . . . the French are a free people. Yet still you allow thirteen million slaves shamefully to wear the irons of thirteen million despots!"[13] As the most extreme form of the denial of rights, slavery here served as an analogy for the legal subordination of wives to their husbands. In using the term, feminists hoped to drum up sympathy for their own cause. At the end of the petition was a list of proposed decrees, the first of which referred to the August 4 decrees: "All the privileges of the male sex are entirely and irrevocably abolished throughout France." A delegation of free men of color submitted a similar demand to the National Assembly in October 1789, arguing that they deserved full equal rights as well. The National Assembly did temporarily grant citizenship rights to free men of color in 1791, in the hope that they would help put down slave riots that had broken out in Saint-Domingue, but any attempt to dismantle slavery remained off the table.[14] As unfree human beings, slaves were by definition ineligible for the rights of citizenship.[15] The various revolutionary constitutions likewise defined women, along with children and domestic servants, as dependent beings, whose political voices would be incorporated into the rights and privileges granted to men, whether their fathers, husbands, or masters. Such logic would underlie suffrage laws in France until 1848, when the revolutionary government enfranchised all men, regardless of wealth or property holdings, and decreed full emancipation of slaves in the French colonies.[16]

Feminism and abolitionism shared more than just linguistic similarities. Virtually all of the thinkers and writers we associate with revolutionary-era feminism—including Mary Wollstonecraft and Olympe de Gouges—were also passionate abolitionists. Among the founders of the Society of the Friends of Blacks was the marquis de Condorcet, the one philosophe who devoted significant attention to the plight of women. Jacques Brissot, the person most responsible for creating the Society after observing American and British abolitionists firsthand, also voiced support for women's causes, particularly the legalization of divorce.[17] The fight for greater equality between the sexes emerged from the same intellectual terrain as opposition to slavery and the slave trade, namely, the concept of natural rights based on the human ability to reason. In addition, feminist consciousness largely revolved around the recognition that women's legal situation represented a kind of slavery. Prevailing attitudes toward women's and slave emancipation were similar too: both were viewed as something that would come gradually. Even the members of the Society of the Friends of Blacks opposed immediate emancipation, proposing instead various schemes in which gradual emancipation could take place. While drafting the preamble to the constitution in July 1789, the abbé Sieyès explained that active citizens were those who could contribute to upholding public institutions. He excluded children, foreigners, and women "du moins dans l'état actuel" (at least in the current state of affairs), leaving open the possibility for an eventual reversal.[18] Many believed that women's limited education precluded their access to the full rights of citizenship, and dozens of pedagogical projects launched during the Revolution attempted to address this deficiency.[19] Efforts to push for faster change, however, such as the slave uprisings in Saint-Domingue, and women taking matters into their own hands through their participation in the revolutionary *journées* and in political clubs, shocked even those who supported equality and freedom in theory.

The defenders of women's rights during the revolutionary period may have been few in number, but they argued their case vociferously. In 1790, for example, Condorcet proposed that women receive full political rights. His reasoning linked women's rights with the rights of all human beings: "Now the rights of men result only from this, that men are beings with sensibility, capable of acquiring moral ideas, and of reasoning on these ideas. So women, having these same qualities, have necessarily equal rights. Either no individual of the human race has genuine rights, or else all have the same; and he who votes against the rights of another, whatever the religion, colour, or sex of that other, has henceforth abjured his own." Condorcet insisted on the *universality* of rights: in arguing for women's rights, he connected them to the rights of other oppressed groups.[20] Olympe de Gouges's Declaration of the Rights of Woman and Citizen (1791) made similar claims. De Gouges's Declaration offered a revision of the official Declaration, with seventeen articles calling for equal participation and equal rights for men and women based on their shared humanity. The text concluded with a "social contract between man and woman" united for the duration of their inclination, demonstrating again the centrality of marriage in the minds of these writers who sought to end women's oppression. De Gouges also wrote *L'esclavage des noirs*, an antislavery play that, after many years of negotiation and revision, was finally performed in December 1789. The play so angered the owners of colonial plantations and their supporters that they organized a counterattack, heckling loudly throughout the performance.[21] De Gouges's interest in writing the play and the effort she expended to have it staged demonstrate the centrality of slavery in the minds of the few writers espousing feminist views. In addition, Condorcet and de Gouges had numerous opportunities to discuss the parallel plight of women and blacks, as they attended many of the same intellectual gatherings before and after 1789.[22]

From the outset, feminism emerged as a transnational project inspired directly by events and debates taking place during the Revolution.[23] The English writer Mary Wollstonecraft, author of the most influential feminist text of the period, *A Vindication of the Rights of Woman* (1792), had been following the events of the Revolution from its beginnings. She moved to Paris in December 1792 to observe developments firsthand and remained in France even through the year of the Terror, departing only in April 1795. Her earlier work, a rebuttal to Edmund Burke's diatribes against the Revolution, was published as *A Vindication of the Rights of Man* (1790). Wollstonecraft decided to write a sequel addressing women's rights after Talleyrand argued in 1791 that "the common happiness . . . requires that [women] not aspire to exercise rights and political functions."[24] Wollstonecraft argued that women's apparent weakness was caused by society and the education they received, and in doing so she laid the philosophical foundation for feminism. And like many other feminists of the era, Wollstonecraft made constant reference to slavery as an analogy for the tyranny that women experienced in their daily lives.[25] One of the most outspoken feminists in France during the Revolution, Etta Palm d'Aelders, a Dutch woman who settled in France in 1773, also used the slavery analogy: "Deprived of a civil existence; subjected to the arbitrary will of those closest around them . . . from the cradle to the grave, women vegetate in a kind of slavery."[26] The explosion in political debate and rights-based language inspired others outside of France as well. Writing in East Prussia, Theodore Gottleib von Hippel developed an argument similar to Condorcet's in his 1792 tract *On Improving the Status of Women*: "Do I go too far in asserting that the oppression of women is the cause of all the rest of the oppression in the world?"[27] Von Hippel's assertion underscores the link between feminism and humanism in European thought, a link that necessarily evoked the colonial world and the problem of slavery.

Like de Gouges, Condorcet, and von Hippel, other early proponents of women's rights in France saw a logical connection between the oppression of women in Europe and that of slaves in the colonies. In a text presented to the National Convention in the spring of 1793, the deputy Pierre Guyomar made this link explicit: "White or black skin will no longer characterize exclusion from sovereignty in the human species than a male or feminine sex. . . . I submit that half the individuals of a society do not have the right to deprive the other half from the imprescriptible right of expressing their wish [*vœu*]. Let us free ourselves henceforth from the prejudice of sex, just as we have freed ourselves from prejudice about the color of blacks."[28] In retrospect, it is obvious that Guyomar was being overly optimistic in pronouncing the end of racial prejudice in 1793. What is important here, however, is his argument that both women and people of color deserved to be included in the rights of man. In his view, the term "man" in the Declaration of the Rights of Man meant all human beings, regardless of skin color or sex, but only a small minority of deputies supported Guyomar's views.[29]

Legislation passed during the Terror temporarily silenced debate on both the woman question and the problem of slavery. On 9 Brumaire, Year 2 (30 October 1793), the National Convention passed a law forbidding women from forming or joining political clubs. The language of the decree focused on women's duty to care for their households and families. Speaking on behalf of the Committee of General Security, the deputy Jean-Baptiste André Amar argued that women should be prohibited from meeting in clubs "because they will be obliged to sacrifice to them more important cares to which nature calls them. The private functions to which women are destined by nature itself follow from the general order of society."[30] According to his logic, it was "unnatural" for women to concern themselves with politics. Of course this was also a self-serving argument, as the male deputies preferred to keep the women in their lives available to cook, clean, and raise their children so that they could focus on more "important" matters. Amar further claimed that women did not have the mental or emotional capacity to participate in political assemblies.

Legislation treating the problem of slavery came up at nearly the same time. In late 1793 the Montagnards remained divided over the issue. Some argued for immediate emancipation; others, including Robespierre, opposed the idea.[31] In the end, the French granted something the slaves in Saint-Domingue had already taken themselves, their freedom. The law abolishing slavery in the colonies passed without discussion on 4 February 1794 when a three-man delegation from the island—a free black, a white, and a mulatto—announced that emancipation had already taken place.[32] The limits of the possible may explain the Convention's contrasting treatment of women and slaves. Its members *could* ban women's clubs. They *could not* force slaves who had successfully fought for their freedom to return to slavery, although that is exactly what Napoleon would attempt to do a decade later. Women had also proven themselves capable of shaping the political terrain. Many even pushed the Committee of Public Safety to move in more radical and violent directions.[33] Silencing women contributed to the committee's larger goal of ending all political opposition.

The more moderate government formed after the Terror, the Directory (1795–99), permitted freer discussion, but political clubs no longer served as the spaces for these debates. Instead a vibrant print culture took shape, along with intellectual institutions and less formal discussions in salons.[34] These private gatherings gave women access to the world of ideas, but other developments limited women's ability to shape political discussions. In response to a large group of women who marched into the legislature in May 1795 demanding a return to the Constitution of 1793, the Directory deputies voted to forbid women from attending legislative debates. The same law prohibited groups of more than five women from gathering in public places.[35] While it diminished women's freedom to act and speak in public, the law did not defeat feminism. Writers in France and elsewhere continued to speak out in support of women's rational and moral capabilities and the necessity to improve women's education. In addition, the mother-educator role grew in significance during these years, giving women a public role as they helped to raise virtuous citizens.[36] Feminist texts and discussions became less strident than they had been during the early 1790s, but more women than ever claimed the right to shape public opinion as they crafted careers as writers.[37]

Rights talk burst forth again during the Directory, helping to inspire modern liberalism, and reshaping both abolitionism and feminism. Republicans of the period, fighting against growing counterrevolutionary movements that would have reversed French policies in the colonies, emphasized the granting of rights to people of color as a symbol of the regime.[38] Liberalism's earliest proponents, among them Benjamin Constant and Germaine de Staël, continued to argue against slavery and the slave trade and kept alive efforts to improve women's status. Constant especially admired Condorcet, who died in 1794, and built his political theories on the same foundations.[39] Unlike Condorcet, however, Constant grew skeptical about using legislative innovations to remake society, turning instead to the private sphere as the source of liberty. Expressing views that could be labeled libertarian, he argued that the freedom to enjoy private pleasures best guaranteed individual liberty. At the same time, both Constant and de Staël critiqued Rousseau's arguments that women should not concern themselves with public matters.[40]

Other writers continued to push for women's rights and abilities as well, including Constance Pipelet (later Princesse de Salm), author of a 1797 poem entitled "Epître aux femmes" in which she demanded legitimate rights for women so they could stop using "ruses" and "trickery" to exercise power.[41] In 1798 she gave a speech praising the artistry and technical innovations of *la citoyenne* (the female citizen) Roux-Montagnat, who ran a business in Paris making artificial flowers. Roux-Montagnat received a medal from the Lycée des Arts recognizing her accomplishments, and Pipelet used the ceremony as an opportunity to discuss women's talents and the need to encourage their productive abilities.[42] Then, in a response to a book about women published in 1800, Pipelet bemoaned the fact that after ten years of proclaiming "liberty and equality," half of humanity continued to be denied rights. While she did not go so far as to demand that women receive the right to vote, she made clear that women's capacity to reason made them eligible for basic human rights, a fact that the male legislators in France had chosen to ignore.[43] Clearly feminism did not die after 1793, but references to slavery seem less abundant in texts by and about women from this later period than had been the case earlier. After emancipation, the issue may have lost its pertinence, and the slavery analogy probably seemed less effective in the wake of destructive revolts in Saint-Domingue, particularly in the more conservative atmosphere of the Directory.

Once Napoleon Bonaparte came to power in 1799, he worked to reinforce the power of fathers and husbands and even to reinstate slavery in the French colonies, actions that had global consequences visible to this day. Troops sent to the Caribbean in 1802 succeeded in reenslaving former slaves in both Guiana and Guadeloupe, although not without a fight. In Saint-Domingue, however, the French forces were defeated, resulting in the creation of the independent state of Haiti in 1804.[44] The French Civil Code, which was also completed in 1804 and is often called the Napoleonic Code, represented a step back in terms of women's rights, too. It made divorce more difficult and explicitly stated (Article 213) that "the husband owes protection to his wife, the wife obedience to her husband."[45] Although the Napoleonic Empire (1804–15) represented a low point for French feminism, female *salonnières*, writers, and artists nonetheless continued to shape public opinion.[46] For example, Marie Benoist painted an image of a beautiful woman of color: her *Portrait d'une négresse* (1800) became an emblem of both women's and slave emancipation. While most female artists painted portraits, a genre defined as suitably "feminine," some began to move into other genres, notably history painting, which was deemed a masculine preserve because of the political messages it typically carried.[47]

Like feminism, abolitionism waned under Napoleon, although an undercurrent of popular antislavery thinking remained visible. One scholar describes French abolitionist activity as "reduced to a trickle"; another argues that slavery and especially the slave trade were largely ignored by the French public until later in the nineteenth century.[48] Antislavery sentiment continued to surface nonetheless. Soldiers sent to Saint-Domingue in 1802 deserted in exceptionally large numbers, in part because they sympathized with the former slaves. In addition, Napoleon chose to imprison the captured Toussaint Louverture in the Fort de Joux in eastern France because he feared that any location near the Atlantic coast would facilitate efforts to bring Toussaint to freedom.[49] Further proof that abolitionism remained alive during the Napoleonic Empire is the publication of *De la littérature des nègres* (1808) by the abbé Grégoire, one of the most influential voices in support of abolition during the Revolution. In emphasizing the talents and capabilities of people of color, Grégoire kept alive the fight for emancipation. And in dedicating his book to "the courageous men who pleaded the case for the unfortunate blacks and people of mixed race," Grégoire reinforced the notion that revolutionary activism could be maintained. Although he was far from a feminist, Grégoire included one woman on his list of courageous "men": Olympe de Gouges.[50]

Colonial interests carried more weight during the Empire and the Restoration than the arguments espoused in antislavery literature. Nonetheless, abolitionism emerged as an important theme among a handful of thinkers associated with early liberalism, and many of these liberals supported, even when they did not actively fight for, women's rights. In looking back on the revolution in Saint-Domingue, the abolition of slavery, and the ensuing unsuccessful effort by Napoleon to reinstate slavery there, liberals rediscovered a tool to voice their opposition to all kinds of oppression. Discussion of such issues became easier during the Restoration as liberals began coalescing into a political opposition. In 1814, as Napoleon's (first) fall seemed eminent, Constant published a critique of imperial conquest, *De l'esprit de conquête*, and the 1820s brought a spate of publications that drew attention to the questions of slavery and the slave trade.[51] A philanthropic organization founded in 1821, the Société de la Morale Chrétienne, created a slave trade committee in 1822 to further the goal of abolitionism. It included the most prominent leaders of the liberal opposition: Constant, François Guizot, and Germaine de Staël's son-in-law Victor de Broglie.[52] In the context of negotiations over French recognition of Haitian independence, both Constant and de Broglie gave impassioned speeches to the Chamber of Deputies on the need to end French involvement in the slave trade, a goal they viewed as more realistically attainable than full abolition.[53]

Though less strident than in the early 1790s, both abolitionism and feminism remained visible thanks to the efforts of Restoration-era liberals. One publication in particular served as a venue for young liberals seeking to voice their opposition to Restoration policies: *Le Globe*.[54] Charles de Rémusat, one of the members of the "generation of 1820" and a frequent contributor to *Le Globe*, wrote a play entitled *The Saint-Domingue Plantation; or The Insurrection* that includes sympathetic characters involved in the slave revolts of 1791.[55] Unpublished until the 1970s, the play circulated widely among liberals in the 1820s. The issue of slavery weighed on the minds of these intellectuals, who defined their movement as fighting for the cause of "liberty." Abolitionism lay at the heart of their stance as opposition figures. Rémusat's parallel interest in keeping the woman question alive is visible in his decision to publish posthumously a text written by his mother, Claire de Rémusat, in which she argued for the importance of educating women.[56] Though less radical than some of the texts cited earlier, these early nineteenth-century liberal writings continued in the same path.

Debates about colonial slavery, gender roles, and women's rights shaped political developments in revolutionary and postrevolutionary France and elsewhere as those ideas spread. Rights talk necessarily brought to mind the denial of rights, and the most thorough form of such denial, the problem of slavery. As demonstrated by the ever-present metaphor of colonial slavery, global concerns entered into revolutionary-era feminist thinking, even at the grassroots level. Those concerns remained vibrant as early liberals sought to define their movement against Napoleonic and Restoration policies, particularly around the issue of slavery and to a lesser degree around questions about women's rights and roles in society. Current and future research will no doubt reveal other ways that global concerns reverberated within France. Studies of how slavery and colonialism were brought up in various contexts during and after the Revolution, in the popular press and in political clubs, could reveal the ways in which ordinary French men and women viewed their actions within France as part of a larger set of transitions. To what extent did the men and women fighting for and against the revolutionary project view what they were doing as having global consequences—consequences that could spread beyond Europe and even beyond the Atlantic world? How did discussions of the colonial question and slavery change as the tide of revolutionary politics shifted? Much work remains to be done on these issues, but it is clear that European feminism emerged out of a context in which the *universality* of rights seemed essential. The fight for women's rights was, and remains, part of a broader fight against oppression of all sorts.

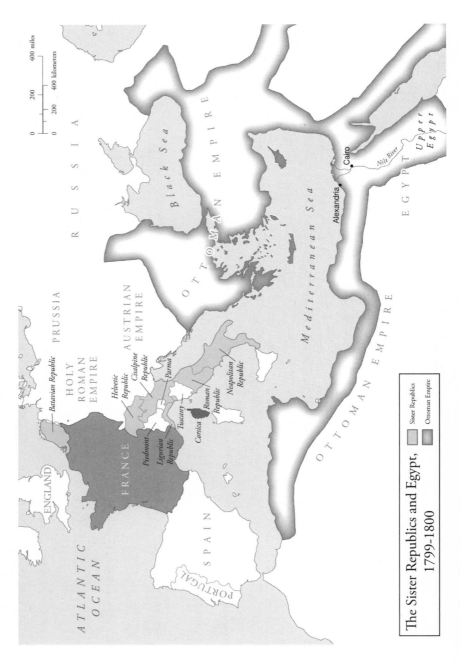

The Sister Republics and Egypt,
1799-1800

- Sister Republics
- Ottoman Empire

Map 2. Sister Republics and Egypt, 1799–1800

PART III

Consequences

8 Egypt in the French Revolution

IAN COLLER

The story of the French occupation of Egypt from 1798 to 1801, and its failure, has been retold many times over two centuries. It has often served as a touchstone for modernity's encounter with its ostensible opposite: a Muslim society that has often been painted as isolated, theocratic, deeply conservative, and resistant to change.[1] But the arrival of French troops on the shores of Egypt just nine years after the storming of the Bastille should tell us quite the opposite—and something that should be quite self-evident— that Egypt was in every way a part of the world in which these revolutionary transformations were taking place. Once we take the global view of the French Revolution as our starting point, we can begin to see the complex ways in which the societies of France and Egypt were linked, the evolving logic of postrevolutionary politics that gave rise to the failed occupation, and the impact that the attempt to unroll the republic in Egypt ultimately had on both France and Egypt.

The year 1798 was once considered a kind of watershed in the history of Muslim societies in the Middle East and North Africa, and while many historians have rightly criticized this Eurocentric presumption, this should not lead us to neglect the significance of the events unleashed in that year, either for Egypt or for France. The principles under which the French occupied Egypt were as radical and transformative for Egyptians as they had been for French, Italian, or Irish men and women. But the invasion and occupation also provoked bitter conflict and resistance, which itself had complex ramifications in the longer term.[2] The French set out to "unroll" the republic in Egypt, while bringing the very birthplace of civilization into the French orbit, and it was for this reason that Bonaparte recruited so many scientists, engineers, technicians, and draftsmen for what some historians have aptly described as the "Egyptian Laboratory."[3] The technocratic nature of this project was one element in the failure of the republican model in Egypt: while Bonaparte and his administrators learned quickly, they were unable to keep pace with the consequences of their early mistakes, particularly in regard to religion and its place in Egyptian society. On the larger canvas, the Directory had miscalculated the Ottoman response and its resonance in Syria and Egypt— whether innocently or disingenuously, it is hard to tell. Bonaparte met insurmountable opposition to the French advance in Palestine, and violent insurrection in Cairo.

In a purely mechanical sense, the consequence of this concatenating disaster was Bonaparte's departure from Egypt to seize power in France. But the relationship between Egypt and the "ending" of the Revolution was not a wholly aleatory one. Egypt was Bonaparte's first experience of direct rule and shaped his vision of personal power. In particular he consistently cited his religious policy in Egypt as the precedent for the Concordat. As Louis Bergeron noted, he surrounded himself with the "Old Boys from Egypt" in his imperial administration in Europe. More than a third of French prefects had cut their teeth in Egypt.[4] Transforming that defeat into a victory was a preoccupation of the Napoleonic regime. The giant canvases of Gros and Girodet addressed key accusations leveled at the occupation, including poisoning soldiers infected with plague and massacring the insurgent population of Cairo. The emperor kept close by him a Mamluk servant, Roustam, and a praetorian guard (composed in part of Egyptian and Syrian soldiers) dressed in expensive Oriental fabrics. Josephine's palace at Malmaison was redecorated in the Egyptianizing style he favored during the Consulate.

But such fripperies should not disguise the ongoing strategic significance of a possible return to Egypt, which closed only with the consolidation of Muhammad Ali after 1810. For this reason, the most strategically sensitive parts of the *Description de l'Égypte,* the great scientific publication on Egypt, did not appear until the Restoration. Egypt would drag France back into international power struggles in 1840, 1880, and 1956, and each time the result would be failure and a major shift in France's foreign policy. In this sense, the door that opened in 1798 never quite seemed to close.

The story of Egypt in the French Revolution has always been treated as a case apart. If it has been connected to anything beyond rampant exoticism, it has been to France's later aggressive colonial expansion in North Africa, and certainly not to contemporaneous events in France and Europe. Such colonial connections certainly exist, although they are complex and deserve more nuanced analysis. But the occupation of Egypt was also, and crucially, an event of the French Revolution. It must be understood within the evolving politics of the post-Thermidorean regimes. Egypt can illuminate in important ways some of the key processes at work in this second phase of the Revolution, a phase in which the Revolution was no longer simply "French"—if it had ever really been so. Moreover, that quicksand-like involvement in Egypt would help bring this second phase of the Revolution to a close. By any reckoning, Egypt was the high watermark of the global territorial expansion of the Revolution. The transformations we can observe within the occupation itself conform to the shift within the French regime, away from a set of republican ideals of liberty and equality to the kind of imperial *machtpolitik* that would predominate under the regime of Napoleon Bonaparte, the former governor of Egypt.

Eighteenth-century Egypt was a society rocked by fierce struggles between different parties competing for power. If there is little evidence that these internecine conflicts bore the hallmarks of what have conventionally been claimed as "democratic revolutions" in the Atlantic context—representative bodies, an expanding print culture demanding liberty from censorship, the push for the enfranchisement of a middle class—we should not be too quick to dismiss them simply as peasant rebellions or opportunistic power struggles.[5] Instead they may be considered in terms of what Christopher Bayly has provisionally described as "conjunctural revolutions"—a set of major social changes, expressed in quite different ways, but responding to the same broad set of global conditions across this period.[6] The references for revolution in the Muslim world were different: the forms of consultation and legitimacy prescribed by Islam, new theological challenges coming out of the Arabian Peninsula, and a vast Islamic ecumene stretching across Africa and Asia as well as parts of Europe.

Another great difference between Ottoman and western European societies was the toleration—prescribed by Islamic law—of large religious minorities, whose boundaries ran across conventional class lines. Thus, many of those pushing for entry to the privileged upper ranks of Ottoman society were Christians and Jews.[7] In Egypt these minorities were principally Copts and Syrian Catholics, but they also included "Franks" or local Europeans. These groups are key in understanding the chain of connections linking France and Egypt. Like the professional classes in France and Europe, they constituted a primary constituency for the revolutionary ideas of the French in Egypt: indeed, their awareness of such ideas preceded the arrival of the French in Cairo, and they quickly demanded from the French regime equality of rights and the removal of traditional restrictions. But local Franks took an even more critical role: like other local revolutionaries in Belgium, Italy, and the Netherlands, and like the "Black Jacobins" of the Caribbean too, they played a leading role in both invoking and contesting the aegis of France at a crucial moment in the development of the Revolution, helping to drag the "French" Revolution out onto the world stage, making it a world-historical event. Moreover, there are indications that revolutionary sympathies were considerably more widespread in Egypt (and even beyond) than we have imagined. One result was the formation of a network of independence-minded "patriots" across the religious spectrum in Egypt: the expatriation of a part of that group would have consequences for both Egypt and France, and for their relationship over the following century. It is along these three lines of development—the evolving politics of the sister republics, the role of local revolutionaries, and the development of a prorepublican party in Egypt—that this chapter will trace an initial response to the complex question of Egypt and its role in the French Revolution.

The Sister Republics and the Politics of La Grande Nation

Marc Belissa has compared the period from 1795 to 1802 with the redefinition of the "new world order" after the fall of the Berlin Wall.[8] What emerged during this second period of the French Revolution was a profound shock to an ancien régime "world order" based on the relationships between sovereign rulers, and represented a major turning point in world history that would ultimately result in the decisive shift toward an "international" world order of states. But, as Bernard Gainot has written, French revolutionary foreign policy between 1796 and 1799 was not "discreet, specialized, and secondary to the internal issues of the period," but rather a highly public matter of concern.[9] Indeed, it may be considered the defining question facing the republic. Just as the situation of continental war and the terrifying threat of invading armies helped shape the internal emergency conditions of 1793 and 1794, the euphoria of victories in 1795 and 1796 turned the attention of revolutionary leaders, journalists, and the public outward to France's boundaries. We may distinguish three tiers of this thought: the self-interest of the French state; a limited expansionism to protect smaller republics or fledgling republican movements; and a more radically universalist republicanism that looked beyond the limits of Europe, to Asia and Africa in particular. These questions no longer applied solely to French men and women, but to millions of others whose destinies were now deeply entangled with that of France.

Shortly before the fall of the Jacobin government in 1794, revolutionary France had at last begun to win military successes not only against the counterrevolutionary insurrection in the west of France, but also at its borders with the Netherlands and Italy. Consequently, it found itself in a position to determine the political direction of peoples not considered "French" in any conventional sense. New questions now arose regarding the boundaries of republican France and the French place in a "new world order." Should the republic simply stabilize its place in a Europe of monarchies, or use its growing military force to republicanize the Continent? Some conservatives pushed for a return to older French boundaries, while others insisted French sovereignty should extend all the way to the Rhine and the Alps, which they called the "natural frontiers" of France. Yet, as Andrew Jainchill has observed, "the history of republics and early modern political philosophy both taught that republican liberty and territorial expansion were fundamentally incompatible."[10] This doctrine of republican constraint was compromised by the existence of vulnerable republics on France's borders, claiming the ideological aegis of France. The decision to support the "sister republics" created a new ground that helped expand and modify the political understanding of the republic. It is by following this development that we can better understand both the origins of the "expedition" to Egypt and its impact on the political trajectory of the First Republic.

The city of Liège in Belgium had declared itself a republic as early as 1789, long before France became a republic in 1792, and the fledgling Republic of Basel had voted for absorption into France in 1793. The following year Amsterdam was reborn as the Batavian Republic after the defeat of Dutch and British forces. This situation helped the party that insisted France's security would be best assured by a ring of republics sharing the same political commitments and naturally friendly to France. But other members of the Directory—some hoping for a restoration of the monarchy—were fiercely opposed to any expansion of France's frontiers or interference in neighboring states.[11] Others, particularly those fighting on the eastern boundary of France, felt that the republic should be a unitary and universal principle, regardless of territorial boundaries. With the spectacular success of the French army in Italy under the command of General Bonaparte during 1796 the pendulum swung strongly in the expansionist direction.

Over the three years that followed more than a dozen different republics were created in the Italian Peninsula, including Roman, Parthenopean, and Etruscan republics and a host of others, large and small. Many Italian patriots were deeply disappointed in their hopes for a single national entity, while others quarreled over local rivalries. The French seemed only too happy to tolerate or even encourage this infighting, so long as the new republics provided France and its army with sorely needed funds. Despite the unification of patriots in the northern Italian cities, elections produced a mixed bag of patriots and ancien régime notables. The Directory concluded that the Italians "are not yet ready for liberty, or rather that they have been rotted by slavery and the vices it brings in its train."[12] The Directors allowed their representatives, particularly General Bonaparte, a much greater role in nominating administrations and drawing up constitutions on the model of the French constitution of 1795. The ideological vagueness of these "republics" was demonstrated in the Treaty of Campo Formio of 1797, which handed over to Austrian rule the most ancient republic of all: Venice. Bonaparte was, in Michel Vovelle's words, "the propagator of new republics, but in the framework of a project which diverged more and more from the aspirations of the patriots it had awakened."[13] If this policy seemed inchoate, there is no indication it was simply the cover for a policy of "divide and rule." Indeed, the creation of the Helvetic Republic in April 1798 seemed to reflect a significant recalibration toward a unitary republicanism: despite having preserved strict neutrality in the revolutionary wars, the Swiss cantons were abolished, and the confederacy was declared a single republic "one and indivisible."

What is clear throughout this process is that the reshaping of the political landscape outside France was not taking place simply through the will of one man. Bonaparte's decisions certainly made reference to his own ideology and ambition, but they were fundamentally shaped by other factors: the context of the internal politics and financial requirements of the regime in Paris, the military situation of the army on the ground, and the desires, ambitions, and conflicts of "patriots" and their adversaries in the newly occupied territories. Many patriots sought to use the French occupation to further the existing cause of reform: in response, large sectors of the population joined bloody revolts, often expressed through the defense of religion and the traditional order of the pope, the Virgin Mary, and the saints, as the Egyptian revolts were energized by Islam and the call to defend the Ottoman caliphate.[14]

It is perhaps in part as a result of the challenge presented by these European republics that in late 1797 the second Directory began to turn French external policy away from the idea of Républiques Soeurs and toward a new expression—la Grande Nation. The origins of this term are disputed: certainly it appeared in an indefinite form (*une grande nation*) throughout the revolutionary period, in the writings and speeches of Volney, Robespierre, Constant, and others. The conception of revolutionary France as a vanguard or a liberator of other nations was common both to revolutionary ideologues and to foreign "patriots" seeking French intervention. But with the shift to the definite article this expression acquired a far more specific political content: *grande* came to mean more than simply "powerful" or "glorious"; it also took on an expansionist geographical connotation.

In 1796, General Bonaparte was established in Milan, previously a key Austrian city, looking east toward Venice and its possessions in the Ionian Sea. In the Treaty of Campo Formio, Bonaparte handed over the Republic of Venice but annexed for France the seven Venetian-ruled islands west of Albania and Greece. Crucially, these islands were not declared separate republics, but rather territorially integral *départements* of revolutionary France.[15] Bonaparte insisted that these new territories "are worth more to us than all of Italy together. The Turkish Empire is collapsing day by day, and possessing these islands will allow us to support it as much as that is possible, or to take our proper share."[16] In his letter to the Directory, he claimed that when General Gentili stepped onto the beach in Corfu, the grateful "pope" of the local religion handed him a copy of Homer's *Odyssey*. Bonaparte continued: "The islands of Zante, Cephalonia, and Lefkas share the same desire and express the same wish, the same feelings for liberty: liberty trees are in all the villages; municipalities govern all the communes, and these peoples hope that with the protection of the *great nation* they will restore the science, the arts, and the commerce they have lost under the tyranny of oligarchs."[17] Henry Laurens has argued that the new expression was in fact suggested to Bonaparte by the Ottoman notables seeking French assistance in their attempts to achieve autonomy from the Porte: he cites the notes of General Desaix, which made reference to "the Pasha of Bosnia who calls the general *the strong man of the great nation.*" Whether this is indeed the origin of the term is less important than its emergence or resurgence at this crucial moment when the boundaries of the French republic reached the edge of the Muslim world. In his notes, Desaix continued: "The general has a great and shrewd policy, which is to give all of these people a grand idea of the French nation. He has received orders from the Directory to spread this idea across the whole of Africa, and Greece, through pamphlets and proclamations."[18]

The idea of la Grande Nation served to reconcile the idea of liberating other peoples from tyranny with the preservation of the interests of the French republic. It was a grandiose rhetorical formulation that resolved none of the underlying tensions but offered an ideological context in which Bonaparte's authority could move from military into civilian administration, as a natural consequence of the defense of the republic. Two important elements emerged from this synthesis. First, an indigenous revolution or republican movement was no longer necessary in order to "liberate" a country—indeed, such "patriots" could now be a significant source of irritation. Adherence, or even submission, to the "Great Nation," combined with the fantasy of the reawakening of ancient civilizations, could now substitute for evidence of ideological alignment with revolutionary principles. Second, the vocation of this new policy was global, and no longer confined to the land borders of France. The conception of the "Great Nation," in its elegant fusion of political virtue with territorial enlargement, offered a space for imagining the extension of the republic not only into Europe, but also into Asia, Africa, and beyond. It was the ideological hinge that connected the politics of the sister republics to the claims of France's wider geopolitical interests—interests stretching back to the Seven Years' War and France's losses to Britain in Asia. Bonaparte made full use of this formula in his letters to the Directory, and it helped a group of key members of the political and military establishment obtain final agreement for the proposal to invade Egypt.

The French Revolution in Egypt

Because Egypt was itself in the throes of internecine struggles, its response to and participation in the early stages of the French Revolution was limited. But as France confronted postrevolutionary stabilization and the challenge of repositioning the republic in a new global order, Egypt became crucial, and was drawn more fully into the Revolution. Although it did not border France like Italy, the Netherlands, Spain, or the German states, Egypt, straddling the isthmus connecting Africa and Asia, represented an important axis of France's competitive global interests. By the second half of the eighteenth century, although France had been largely pushed out of India and North America, French interests in the Levant trade had become dominant. Egypt was the link between these Mediterranean interests and global empire in Asia, particularly for the British in India.[19] The last independent rulers in India sought French aid in resisting British advances, and control of Egypt could offer a means to support Tipu Sultan, who was fighting a war of resistance against the encroachments of the East India Company.[20] General Bonaparte maintained a correspondence with Tipu, in the hope of connecting with the insurgent forces in India. Egypt offered further connections with the sharif of Mecca and rulers in Yemen and Oman through the Sudan to Ethiopia and across the northern coast of Africa to Tripoli, Tunis, and Algiers. All of these powers maintained consistent neutrality after the Revolution and had shown themselves open to entertaining political alliances with France.

Moreover, although Egypt was neither part of French territory nor on its borders, for historical reasons it was not completely external to French sovereignty. Merchants from Marseille were well established in Egypt even before Provence became a permanent part of France in the fifteenth century. Egypt at that time was ruled by a dynasty known as Mamluk (owned) because they were bought as slaves and trained as warriors. The Provençal merchants concluded a treaty with the Mamluk sultan that ensured them protection and trading privileges. When the Ottomans conquered Egypt in 1517 they maintained the Mamluk ruling institution and continued these arrangements, extending them to European merchants in other parts of the empire through agreements known as "Capitulations." Extraterritorial sovereignty over French subjects in Egypt was a valuable prerogative of the ancien régime

French monarchy. Because of these long-standing arrangements, French merchants mixed with a multiplicity of other categories—including other Europeans or "Franks," local Christians, Jews, and Muslims—as an element of the Ottoman urban fabric, and never as an isolated and distinct foreign colony.[21] Indeed, Raoul Clément suggests that until the reign of Louis XIV the French in Egypt had lived "a life almost independent of [French] royal power," in their own quarter or "country" of Cairo, and in Alexandria in a walled "okelle" (*wakil* in Arabic).[22]

These older liberties played a role in the strong republican tendencies of the French in Egypt. In the course of the eighteenth century, Paris inexorably tightened its grip on the populations of the Échelles, rescinding the traditional authority of the Chamber of Commerce in Marseille and instituting heavy regulation by central committees and royal ordinance.[23] The ostensible motivation for imposing increased state control over the Echelles was the threat of an *avania* or collective retribution against the "nation" by Muslim authorities. But, as Merlijn Olnon has argued, these *avanias* have been misunderstood as arbitrary exercises of despotic government: in fact they were "negotiations between merchants and local Ottoman officials about how the law could be interpreted, stretched or bypassed to the benefit of both sides."[24] The wiliest of these intermediaries in Egypt was the merchant Charles Magallon, who managed to build close personal relationships with key political figures in Cairo during the 1780s, aided by his wife, who made a fortune selling French fashions to the women of Cairene high society.

French misunderstandings of Egypt were promoted by the sheer complexity of the political situation there, in large part due to the revival of the Mamluk system in the eighteenth century, as a kind of aristocratic resistance to Ottoman government. But no single *bey*, as the Mamluk lords were known, was able to unite that resistance, and protracted struggles raged on throughout the second half of the century. In France, the Mamluk regime could equally be represented as a tyranny or as a rebellious republic resisting Ottoman imperial domination. In the rapidly changing winds of revolutionary rhetoric, these two contradictory understandings could sometimes coexist.[25]

In 1785 the Ottoman admiral Hasan Pacha was dispatched from Istanbul to reassert imperial suzerainty and drove the warring beys, Murad and Ibrahim, out of Cairo into Upper Egypt, replacing them with a single *sheikh al-Balad*, Ismael Bey. Ismael was favorable to the French: in March 1789 he summoned Magallon to a private meeting to request French military assistance against his rivals, and to construct a fleet for the defense of Egypt. Magallon wrote to the minister on Ismael's behalf, but the events of July 1789 intervened, and Magallon was forced to apologize to Ismael for a delay "founded in the disorders that afflict our government."[26] It is clear, then, that just weeks after the fall of the Bastille, the authorities in Egypt were aware of the situation in France, and that the balance of power in Egypt was affected by its outcome.

But the revolutionary upheaval did not long remain just a distant clamor from metropolitan France. By 1790, the French consul in Alexandria was complaining about a "plague of insubordination and licentiousness" spreading through the French extraterritorial communities.[27] Visiting sailors brought with them a fierce attachment to the Revolution, insisting that all French subjects don the revolutionary cockade. In 1790 the sailors revolted en masse against their captains. Jacobins in the Échelle began to call for the abolition of the whole consular regime in the Levant, as a reflection of royal tyranny and privilege. The situation became further embittered as members of the consular staff began to "emigrate," taking refuge with the British or Austrian consuls. In Cairo, the radical faction purchased weapons and formed a "national guard" that met every day. These Jacobins even sought permission from the authorities to build a temple of Reason.[28] But Ismael Bey, the protector of the French, died suddenly during an epidemic in Cairo in 1791, and his rivals Ibrahim and Murad returned in force from Upper Egypt. They blamed the French for provoking the intervention that had driven them from power.

Other powers could now exert a greater influence in Egypt. One French visitor in 1795 wrote: "Since the beginning of the French Revolution, and particularly since the overthrow of the monarchy, the enemies of the French people have worked in Egypt with the same ferocity as in all parts of Europe."[29] The hostile parties suggested that the French no longer had any government at home, and thus had no protection under the former agreement with the sultan. The French merchants, exposed and uncertain, protested their unconscionable neglect by "a Republic that is the lawgiver to Europe, and whose name strikes terror among tyrants," declaiming: "Oh take from us the title of French citizen, or give us our rights!"[30] The envoy Guillaume-Antoine Olivier agreed: "Could we remain in Egypt in such a humiliating position?" he asked. "Should the French Republic, so accustomed to victories, submit to such humiliation?"[31]

In February 1793, after the execution of Louis XVI, Britain had joined the coalition against the republic, throwing France into a war that was increasingly global rather than continental. The counterrevolution was gaining strength in western France, Federalists were rising in the South, and the British fleet occupied Toulon, the chief French Mediterranean port. Egypt was an important, though not yet central, question for the global geopolitical calculations of the revolutionaries. They were still ill informed about the situation there: Charles Magallon had fled to Paris after Ismael's death in 1791 and besieged the ministry with demands for compensation of his losses. The decision to send him as consul general to Cairo in 1793 rid them of a nuisance but only aggravated the tensions between the French and the new rulers in Egypt. Magallon was unceasing in his denunciations of the despotism exercised by the beys and his demands for forceful intervention. The authorities in France replied that force was not a possibility "at the moment," and therefore Magallon should seek a "kind of conversion" in the attitudes of the beys toward the republic. But Magallon's ideas would eventually find their champion in the form of Talleyrand: François Charles-Roux suggests that the minister effectively cribbed his project for Egypt from a report provided by Magallon.[32]

In February 1798, the influential republican Charles-Guillaume Theremin wrote a report for the minister of foreign affairs in which he argued that Ottoman power was on the point of collapse, confronting the republic with a difficult question. The Ionian islands, now part of France, demonstrated that France could expand into the Mediterranean without undermining the republic. But Egypt was another matter. "As for Egypt, since the republic cannot have subjects, and since conquest will not make the Egyptians into French citizens, we will have to establish armed trading posts in Alexandria, Rosetta, and Cairo."[33] Thus, the intervention of Magallon on behalf of the French merchants in Egypt helped to broach the apparent contradiction between revolutionary ideals and aggressive conquest, offering the bridgehead of "armed trading posts" that would rapidly expand into a full-blown territorial conquest of Upper as well as Lower Egypt. Less than a year later, reporting in the same register on "the presumed progress of the army of Egypt" another author imagined Bonaparte at the head of an army composed of 30,000 Frenchmen and 60,000 Greek and Arab auxiliaries. Such a picture raised the same concerns about "subjects" and "citizens," but the report's author now made it clear that a fundamental difference of rights and privileges could exist between different groups, even in the armies of the republic. The general would be sure to make the sacrifices fall on the auxiliary troops: "This is how the European powers conduct themselves in India in regard to the Sipahis in their pay."[34] This striking statement suggests that even before Bonaparte's return to France, the French involvement in Egypt was already contributing to the shift away from a conception of republican equality.

The Republican Implantation in Egypt

The frontispiece of a book entitled *Bonaparte au Caire*, published anonymously in Paris in 1798–99, shows the general pointing to the projected canal of Suez (which French engineers concluded to be impracticable) in front of the fascia of the republic. The crescent of Islam is depicted on the most prominent of the many flags clustered behind this potent republican symbol (fig. 4).

Figure 4. Image of Bonaparte with a map showing Egypt. Frontispiece of *Bonaparte au Caire* (1798–1799). Reproduced by kind permission of the Bibliothèque Nationale de France, Estampes.

Figure 5. Earlier image of Bonaparte with a map of Italy and Europe. F. Bonneville, *Bonaparte: Dédié aux armées françaises* (1798). Reproduced by kind permission of the Bibliothèque Nationale de France, Estampes.

Bonaparte stands straddling the Mediterranean on the map he is unrolling over the symbols of Islam and the republic, as though seeking to wrap them together through technical prowess, while an obelisk stands behind him, adorned with a blank plaque, ready to monumentalize this new stage of "civilization." The curious thing about this image is that it is a near-exact copy of another image published a year earlier (fig. 5), which showed the same elements in the conquest of Italy: the Muslim crescent now stands where "Arcole" was previously written, and "Suez" in place of "Rastad" (the location of negotiations for the Treaty of Campo Formio). This image suggests at once the parallelism between the "unrolling" of the republican projects in Italy and Egypt, and the difference in their conceptions of the future of the Revolution—one pointing toward a durable place for the republic in Europe, the other gesturing to a global expansionism.

The loss of the French fleet at Aboukir shortly after the arrival of the French in Egypt, which Talleyrand identified as the turning point in cementing the coalition against France, perhaps made the recreation of the republic on Egyptian soil all the more urgent.[35] But its provisions had been prepared before departure, like a vast prefabricated republican kit ready to be assembled once victory was assured. Bonaparte had enlisted 167 engineers, technicians, artists, and experts in natural history. These were joined by the French in Egypt, already fiercely republican, and their associates, particularly local Christians, who acted as interpreters and intermediaries. Magallon's son joined Bonaparte aboard ship before it reached Alexandria, and helped guide the first steps of the expedition.

In the first months of their occupation of Egypt, the French launched an extraordinarily ambitious program of social and political transformation, creating a central consultative body called the Diwan, composed of Muslims, Copts, and Syrian Catholics, to rule the country, with a local equivalent in each province. They began reshaping the urban fabric of Cairo and other cities, demolishing buildings, clearing boulevards, erecting bread ovens, restaurants, and theaters, dredging canals, and constructing windmills. The large body of scholars, along with at least one local participant, was immediately formed into an academy—the Institut d'Égypte—which met regularly. Its reports were printed by a press that also produced Egypt's first newspapers, *Le Courier de l'Égypte* and *La Décade Égyptienne*. As in France, the year was divided up into ten-day weeks, marked not by religious holidays, but by revolutionary festivals. These days were celebrated in Egypt, with all the republican trappings— tricolor flags, sashes and cockades, liberty trees, and fireworks.

On the first day of Vendémiaire, Year 7 (22 September 1798), a festival to celebrate the seventh anniversary of the republic was ordered in Ezbekkiya Square, in a great field "decorated with as many columns as there are departments in the French republic, in the centre of which a pyramid will be erected with seven sides on which the names of those brave soldiers killed in liberating Egypt from the tyranny of the Mamluks will be inscribed."[36] The authorities "both French and Turkish" were ordered to process toward the palace of the general in chief, Bonaparte, who would appear on a platform with an obelisk, to the acclaim of the troops singing hymns and patriotic songs "to the prosperity of the French republic and the friendly republics [républiques amies]."[37] The festival was celebrated not only in Cairo but in all the towns and villages where French contingents were stationed. In the town of Atfiéli, the *Courier de l'Égypte* reported, French officers, members of the Divan, and the aga of the Janissaries gathered with a crowd of inhabitants: "The general read to the Arabs a speech written in their language, containing an account of the principal events of our Revolution and bearing witness to the wish and hope to see these peoples enjoy the same happiness as the French, and return to their former greatness."[38] This was as ambitious an installation as had been attempted in any of the other territories annexed or invaded by the French to that time.

In 1799, Bonaparte departed Egypt in haste on hearing of the shifting political situation in Paris, leaving his army stranded and his "breeches full of shit" according to his successor, General Kléber.[39] The republican project quickly disintegrated into its two opposing streams: one deeply republican and insisting on an immediate withdrawal from Egypt, and the other forming a colonial lobby seeking ways to preserve a permanent French presence in Egypt. But as observers noted at the time, these contradictions had existed within the republican project since the very beginnings of French expansion: Bonaparte had held them at bay with his stream of conquests, but they were bound to come unstuck, as they did now in Egypt.

General Kléber was a committed republican: unlike Bonaparte his chief motivation was to remove the French from Egypt as quickly as possible. As he famously declared to the Directory in 1796: "I do not wish to be, nor will I ever be, the passive instrument of any system of conquest that could defer for an instant the happiness of our citizens."[40] Kléber's opposition to colonialism emanated primarily from his commitment to a republic defined within French borders, despite his origins in Alsace and youthful service in the Austrian army. His primary motive for joining the military expedition to Egypt had been the desire to deliver Britain a blow through its communication with India, and when this goal became unachievable he opposed the attempt to transform Egyptian society by force. Yet he too was caught in the inevitable contradictions of the occupation: Egypt was now already "republicanized" in part, and parties calling for independence, as well as those supporting the Islamic legitimacy of the Ottoman government, were in conflict. Kléber had little choice but to support the republican elements, while working toward a return to France, the true home of the republic.

But with the news of 18 Brumaire from France, Kléber saw that the republic now no longer existed in France any more than in Egypt. He scribbled in the margin of his journal that a republican was constituted more by "moeurs" (moral qualities) than by "connaissances" (knowledge): a kind of opening toward the possibility of an alliance beyond the boundaries of France, or even of Europe. Indeed, betrayed by both France and Britain, he turned to one of the chief Mamluk leaders, Murad, recognizing him as "prince-governor of Upper Egypt" in exchange for support against the Ottoman army—a treaty that was later destroyed and kept a secret, except for a single remaining proof.[41] Kléber's assassination by a young Syrian Muslim, and Murad's death from plague, ended this brief attempt to forge a different kind of republic on Egyptian soil. The policy of his successor, General Menou—who had converted to Islam in order to marry the daughter of a local notable—was colonial in style, dictated in part by the new policies emanating from France under the Consulate of Bonaparte, and by the predominance of Talleyrand in external policy. But the republican impetus in Egypt continued in clandestine ways, as it did in Italy, Greece, and elsewhere in Europe.

The Last Sister Republic? The Republican Legacy in Egypt and France

By 1801, the French were packing up what remained of their flags, their libraries, and a not inconsiderable number of looted artifacts to take ship for Marseille aboard British frigates, as the Ottoman governor moved back into his Cairo palace. Along with the troops returning in the British frigates were many hundreds of Egyptians and Syrians of all backgrounds—both Muslim and Christian—who had chosen to leave Egypt for Marseille. Alongside them were "Franks," French subjects settled in Alexandria and Cairo. Some of Egyptians and Syrians were fleeing Egypt because they had joined the French as soldiers, interpreters, or officials. But others had developed a common political project for the independence of Egypt and hoped to appear at the peace conference in Paris to present their case.[42]

What the documents left by this group, calling itself the "Egyptian Legation to the European Governments," suggest is that ideological alignment with the ideals of republican self-determination was not confined to the French subjects in Egypt, nor even to the Christian minorities in Egypt, but was a larger network with connections across all levels of Egyptian society. It is more difficult to gauge from the documents how Egyptians presented this alignment among themselves, but it is clear that it was not a simple calque from either French or British models, since the members of the Legation sought diplomatic contacts with both major powers and expressed their project differently according to the values of each state. To the French they wrote of "civilization" and "science"; to the British, of "commerce" and "stability": if they avoided direct reference to the republic, it nevertheless permeates their conceptions.

The letters of the "Egyptian Legation" do not present the project of a French colony in Egypt, but rather the creation of an independent republic that would help stabilize the global situation of conflict between the superpowers. In arguing their case, they referred, not to European politicians or political theorists, but to the Mamluk ruler of Egypt, Kléber's ally Murad Bey: "Egypt was actually so well known by the infidels of the West," they quoted Murad as saying, "that, because everyone wants to possess it, it would be the object of their eternal discord."[43]

The language of these documents demonstrates not only how the ideas and ambitions of the French Revolution had taken root in Egypt, but also how these people brought back their own conceptions to France. They spoke of a "revolution" but one emerging specifically from Egyptian conditions:

> The system of government . . . will not be in this case a revolution made by the spirit of enlightenment or by the fermentation of opposing principles, but a change occasioned by absolute necessity in a community of peaceful and ignorant men. . . . Let the new government be just, severe and *national* . . . as that of sheikh Amam in the Sa'id . . . and it is certain that it would be respected, obeyed and loved.[44]

The Legation insisted that it remained in close contact with all the "sects" of Egypt "without partiality," while taking necessary precautions against "the permanently suspicious despotism which would not hesitate to sacrifice even the last of the *independent brothers* if it could identify them."[45] It would seem then that a significant party seeking national liberation existed in Egypt by 1801: the members of the Legation were prepared to take the risk of expatriation on the basis of that network.[46] In the event, the death of their leader, General Ya'qub, during the crossing to Marseille, and the new conditions of France under the Consulate and Empire, would leave this movement at best clandestine, if not entirely extinguished.

This coda can tell us something crucial about the shift in the trajectory of the French Revolution that the failure of the global strategy in Egypt helped bring about. These Egyptians were among the last "independent brothers" fleeing to republican France. What they found instead was the beginnings of a police state, at the heart of an absolutist empire: there would be no peace conference, and they would not be permitted even to travel to the French capital for almost a decade, as the new regime sought to mend its ruptured alliance with the Ottomans.

Egypt demonstrated the ultimate failure of the project to combine republican freedom and equality with territorial expansion, to which the collapse of the Italian and Swiss republics had already gestured. In suggesting that the Revolution could not be exported, it helped convince those at home that the "manifest destiny" of the Revolution had come to an end, and to accept that personal rule by Bonaparte against which the Egyptians had so violently rebelled. The irony of this lay in the fact that, in a way that few historians have acknowledged, the Revolution *was* in fact exported, embraced, and taken up by Egyptians of different creeds and classes, and brought back to France with their emigration in 1801. It was Napoleon's France, however, that now proved a stony ground for the ideas of freedom, equality, and independence that the Egyptians had embraced.

9 *abolition and Reenslavement in the Caribbean*

THE REVOLUTION IN FRENCH GUIANA

MIRANDA SPIELER

In April 1794, the popular society of Loudun (Vienne) congratulated the Convention for abolishing colonial slavery: "The soil of liberty must not be inhabited by slaves! . . . Liberty or death!"[1] This and similar petitions from that spring expressed exuberance for slave liberation in phrases that owed much to the political moment. The abolition of slavery occurred at a time of global war and overlapped with the Terror. The same terms that revolutionaries used to cheer slave liberation also figured in contemporary celebrations of violence. "Liberty or death" was France's wartime slogan. The "soil of liberty," which the Jacobins of Loudon invoked to convey their support for abolition, was the noble aim that sanctified killing and banishing regime enemies; it was an ideal that became concrete in cleansing acts of destruction. The popular society of La Rochelle paid tribute to legislators for abolishing slavery, annihilating political enemies, and ruling dictatorially. All three acts extended from the same principle: "In decreeing revolutionary government, the liberty of men of color, and the exportation of suspects, you continue to be just . . . in purifying the soil of the republic."[2]

Uses of the phrase the "soil of liberty" to describe the empire at the time of emancipation implied that France and the colonies comprised a single terrain under a common legal regime. French colonial historians have also depicted revolutionary France after the abolition of slavery as a single polity that stretched across the sea and included the colonies. More than a century ago, the political economist Arthur Girault described the French legal order after 1794 as "assimilation violente, à outrance" (violent, extreme assimilation); he meant that colonial soil became indistinct from the metropole in a legal sense.[3] More recently, Bernard Gainot has depicted the relationship between metropolitan and colonial soil as "complete fusion . . . unity of the republic, the guarantor of general freedom."[4] Laurent Dubois similarly observes: "France and its colonies had become one, legally consistent, a nation-state."[5]

The remaking of France circa 1794 into a transoceanic democracy would suggest that global war in the age of revolution had extremely positive effects in French slave colonies. Of the war's role in establishing racial concord and imperial citizenship, Dubois notes that "the idea of whites, blacks and *gens de couleur* joined together in a struggle for liberty was the foundation of France's colonial policy."[6] In this view, war democratized the Revolution overseas as on metropolitan soil and created conditions that made slave emancipation possible. This picture of the war's imperial consequences is somewhat misleading, however. Ultimately the war affected French colonial subjects in a twofold manner. While helping slaves to acquire their liberty, the war also thwarted emancipated people's enjoyment of newfound rights to the point of unsteadying their future status as freedmen. The war led imperial citizenship to become a formal goal of the French state while obstructing imperial civic practice.

Long periods of global war in early modern societies are known to have weakened the bonds between center and periphery in multiple imperial contexts while promoting divergences in outlook and institutional design.[7] War during the French Revolution produced effects following that general pattern. War stunted the growth of revolutionary institutions in French colonies during the 1790s while magnifying the authoritarian character of French imperial rule. War strengthened the colonies' legal and institutional distinctiveness in relation to each other and to France. It did so by causing the power of colonial administrators to expand and grow independent from metropolitan authority, so that each colony became subject to decrees that reflected the predilections of local dictators and circumstances on the ground. There could not have been a less propitious moment for "complete fusion" between the French empire and the metropole to occur than during the French Revolution.

To explore the effect of war on the French empire during the 1790s, I shall focus on French Guiana, which was then a wild, untouristed, and economically irrelevant piece of northern South America that so differed from other slave societies in the region, French or otherwise, that it might be tempting to question the colony's broader relevance to the French imperial experience and even to global history. On the eve of the Revolution, the free inhabitants of French Guiana—763 white men, 330 white women, 253 white children, and 483 free people of color of all ages and sexes—had virtually no commercial dealings with the metropole.[8] Scarcely any of the colony's 10,430 slaves worked on sugar plantations, and indeed the plantation reached French Guiana only in the final years of the Old Regime as a heavily subsidized imperial experiment that met with spirited local resistance.[9] French Guiana's economic backwardness increased its isolation from the mother country and from other French colonies while encouraging legal anomalies to proliferate there. As a concession to the poverty of Guianese masters, royal statutes pertaining to slave treatment applied there only selectively.[10] The crown also did not bother imposing mercantile restrictions on a place where commerce did not exist.[11] The colony's reputation as a remote and unsettled wilderness led revolutionary legislators to designate Guiana as an exilic depot for enemies of state—mainly priests—who lost their citizenship as punishment for their treason, real or imagined.

During the Revolution, French Guiana managed to exist simultaneously in a state of perfect union with France and in total estrangement from it; to the extent that any colony attained what Gainot calls "complete fusion" with the metropole, it was this one. French Guiana was one of only three colonies— with Saint-Domingue and Guadeloupe—where slave emancipation took effect during the 1790s, despite the broader intentions of the 1794 abolition decree. Slaves in Saint-Domingue attained their freedom from a 1793 local act born of military necessity.[12] By contrast, in French Guiana and Guadeloupe, slaves owed their freedom to the 1794 abolition decree. The 1794 document also incorporated them into the revolutionary nation; it declared that "all men without distinction of color who are domiciled in the colonies are French citizens and will enjoy all the rights of the Constitution."[13] In fact, only two colonies—French Guiana and Saint-Domingue—were ever governed according to metropolitan public law in the sense that administrators in these places enacted the 1795 constitution, which declared the overseas empire to be one with France in a legal sense: "The colonies are integral parts of the Republic and subject to the same constitutional law."[14] As for the other colonies, Martinique, Saint Lucia, and Tobago all fell to the British, and slavery persisted there. Lobbying efforts by East Indian deputies to the Convention helped slavery to persist on the Île de Bourbon (present-day Réunion) and the Île de France (present-day Mauritius).

The case of French Guiana during the 1790s reveals the paradoxical effects of the war in the colonial empire among slaves and freed slaves with particular sharpness of line. As an indirect consequence of the war, the colony merged with the imperial center and became an extension of the French republic; yet the war also led the colony to veer sharply away from metropolitan society. In French Guiana as elsewhere, yet perhaps more extremely, war conferred rights and also stripped them away. The ironic fate of black citizens in this colony resulted from the concatenation of four legal problems that either originated with the war or thrived on it: (1) the legal regime that the French government applied to the whole Atlantic empire beginning in 1792; (2) the legal regime of metropolitan France following the suspension of the 1793 constitution; (3) the international law of the seas in wartime; (4) the legal consequences of France's foreign policy during the late 1790s at the time of French military expansion on the European continent. These four elements interacted with conditions on the ground in Guiana to remake everyday life and transform local events into expressions of global history.

France's Atlantic colonies came under a wartime regime that gave administrators robust discretionary authority. By the decree of 28 March 1792 the Legislative Assembly invested special envoys to the colonies called "civil commissars" with the power to override and remove existing officials and to govern by extraconstitutional dicta. In March 1793, the Convention declared the Atlantic colonies to exist in a "state of war," which expanded the commissars' repressive powers.[15] As for the 1795 constitution declaring the colonies "integral parts of the Republic," the full text of this document envisaged quite a different system of rule than this phrase might suggest.[16] The real novelty of the 1795 constitution, with respect to the colonies, was to transform emergency rule by dictatorial officials into a permanent technique of government. What had been a temporary wartime system became a legal norm through that document.

The revolutionary model of imperial rule, which legislators devised between 1792 and 1795 in the name of wartime necessity, sabotaged black citizenship everywhere it emerged during the 1790s—French Guiana, Guadeloupe, and Saint-Domingue. This outcome cannot be mistaken for a random, and hence unintended, consequence of the war arising from *la force des choses*. The war supplied a convenient rhetoric of crisis and a range of legal tools to deputies who sought the withdrawal of former slaves from the new political order on the unspoken grounds that these people were inapt for citizenship and perhaps for freedom; by enabling the suspension of French legal norms overseas, the war made it possible for revolutionaries to perform a sweeping, racially inflected act of exclusion without needing to repudiate their creed of liberty, equality, and fraternity.

Wartime measures in metropolitan territory played a considerable role in shaping the exceptional character of imperial rule in the era of slave liberation. Although the 1794 emancipation decree granted freed slaves the constitutional rights of citizens, there was no constitution in effect on metropolitan soil at the time. Earlier, on 10 October 1793, the problem of civil war and international war had inspired the Convention to suspend the newly drafted French constitution while bestowing new emergency powers on the Committee of Public Safety.[17] The emancipation decree, despite its promise that "all men without distinction of color who are domiciled in the colonies . . . will enjoy all the rights guaranteed by the Constitution," needs to be read through the prism of France's extraconstitutional wartime regime, which was known as "revolutionary government." At the time of emancipation, metropolitan France no less than colonial France was a domain of suspended legal norms.

Despite a few isolated calls for the abolition of privateering, revolutionaries understood the law of nations in wartime to authorize and even to require the pillage of commercial vessels by licensed raiders.[18] Liberated slaves in French colonies not only took part in these seafaring expeditions but also risked being seized at sea and reenslaved by British seamen. In French Guiana, the ubiquity of privateering altered the relationship of local people to nearby colonies and passing ships. The southern Atlantic ceased to be a domain of commercial networks that excluded this forlorn outpost; the war transformed French Guiana into a base for French corsairs and gave this otherwise obscure place a new regional prominence.

The republic's foreign policy toward European states proved unexpectedly central to black experience in northern South America. During the latter 1790s, the relationship between French Guiana and neighboring slave regimes resulted, at least in part, from the marked difference between French policy toward European and non-European peoples. In *La grande nation*, Jacques Godechot evokes France in the late 1790s as a republic on the march whose armies and collaborators spread its constitutional principles throughout Europe.[19] The republican project that France proved uninterested in exporting to foreign lands, and that patriot collaborators also failed to embrace, was slave emancipation and the application of the constitution to colonial territory. That reluctance became a stark feature of the republic's policy toward the Low Countries after French soldiers toppled the stadtholder and helped to found the Batavian Republic in 1795.[20] Inaction by French officials and resistance by Dutch patriots assured the survival of slavery on Dutch colonial soil. French Guiana, which borders Suriname, lay adjacent to the notoriously brutal slave colony of a sister republic for nearly the entire postemancipation period. That curiosity should not be mistaken, however, for an anomaly of the hinterland. Residents of Saint-Domingue lived in a similar predicament after the republic chose not to emancipate the slaves of Santo Domingo when the Spanish colony passed to France in the Treaty of Basel (1795).[21] French Guiana and Saint-Domingue, two of the three colonies where slaves were emancipated during the French Revolution, both lay adjacent to land where slavery persisted through the complicity of French officials.

After the local enactment of the emancipation decree on 14 June 1794, French Guiana became an isolated pocket of black liberty bounded by slave colonies to the east (Brazil) and west (Suriname) and by the Atlantic, which then served as a highway for slave ships and privateers. The danger posed by the world of slavery that edged the colony became evident when local authorities first considered whether Guiana should count as "the soil of liberty" in a formal sense by providing asylum for slaves from neighboring colonies. After the abolition of slavery, a great number of slaves from Brazil sought refuge in French territory, raising panic among Portuguese administrators.[22] In October 1794, the governor of Brazil's Para province dispatched troops and boats to patrol the Oyapock River on Guiana's eastern frontier and issued a bellicose demand to Henri Benoist, Guiana's dying governor, that he render slave fugitives. With manifest reluctance, a council of war composed of planters and administrators decreed on 25 October 1794 "relative to the desertion of slaves now said to be in French territory, [that] there can be no action with respect to them, because of the promulgation of the law concerning the abolition of slavery in the colonies, solemnly published in Guiana."[23] To mark its opposition to slave emancipation, the war council refused to enforce its declaration by sending troops to stave off Portuguese encroachment. Emboldened by French inaction, the governor of Para expanded his presence in the borderlands; in February 1795, Portugal occupied both banks of the Oyapock River, Guiana's eastern frontier, and patrolled the waterway.[24] During the borderlands crisis, a sense of endangerment swept through the colony, triggering uprisings by emancipated people against a rumored Portuguese attack.[25]

French colonies after 1794 became destinations of choice for seafaring slaves in the Americas. As with Guiana's overland migrants in 1794, the discovery of maritime fugitives obliged administrators to decide whether the republic would render slaves to owners and foreign governments. Guadeloupe under Victor Hugues, the republican commissar sent in 1794 to reconquer the colony and emancipate its slaves, did not offer a haven to enslaved refugees. In 1795 a correspondent in Pointe-à-Pitre informed New York's *Gazette française et américaine* that "Hugues has ordered the departure of some negroes who had made their escape from the neuter islands, and who were claimed. On their refusing to obey, he ordered their arrestation, and delivered them up."[26]

Officials in Guiana did not render slaves during the 1790s. There, however, it was the asylum principle and not its avoidance that exposed the ambivalent attitude of colonial officials and even of metropolitan legislators to emancipation. In 1798, when a slave woman fled to Cayenne from an American ship, the captain asked Juriaan de Frederici, governor of Suriname, to intercede with Nicolas-Georges Jeannet-Oudin, Guiana's chief administrator. This rendition dispute would not have occurred in the first place had France sought to diffuse the republican constitutional model, in its entirety, on the European continent. The persistence of Dutch colonial slavery with French assent, and the amity between revolutionary France and the Batavian Republic, acted as conditions of possibility for this affair.

The hostile relationship between the French and American republics during the Quasi-War (1798–1800) also contributed to this dispute. The American captain would have sought Dutch help in recovering his slave had the United States then enjoyed normal relations with revolutionary France.[27] Since the affair coincided with the Quasi-War, Jeannet-Oudin also had no reason to be indulgent toward an American seaman. Yet the political rupture between France and America also increased Jeannet-Oudin's economic dependence on Suriname, making his reply to the Dutch governor Frederici far from certain. Because of the Quasi-War, American ships ceased to stop at Cayenne in 1798. Paramaribo, Suriname's capital, became the point of sale for export crops from French Guiana and for booty seized by French privateers. After Britain conquered Suriname in August 1799, both Jeannet-Oudin and his successor, Etienne-Laurent-Pierre Burnel, drafted schemes for retaking the new "comptoir of the French colony" (Burnel's phrase). Neither plan mentioned liberating slaves there.[28]

Jeannet-Oudin refused to render the slave woman, citing "one of our constitutional laws."[29] He quoted from the law of 1 January 1798 in his response, by which "every black individual, born in Africa or in neighboring colonies, transferred to French islands, will be free the moment he sets foot in the territory of the Republic." This restatement of the asylum principle appeared in broadly conceived legislation that otherwise traced a framework for practicing citizenship in the empire. The law of 1 January 1798 answered the plea of representatives from Saint-Domingue, who in September 1797 had sought the application of the French law to their colony as a matter of the greatest urgency. No one in the delegation had sought a renewed commitment to slave asylum, which was too obvious to bear repeating. When situated in the context of French imperial practice since 1794, the unsolicited article about the granting of freedom to foreign fugitives offers a glimpse of the war's pernicious effect on slave emancipation. Through the maritime practices that it legitimated, the war transformed the asylum principle into an exploitative device that subverted the status of imperial citizens.[30]

Jeannet-Oudin did not resist the demands of the governor of Suriname because of a scrupulous regard for French constitutional law. He took the high ground on slave rendition because the granting of asylum to slaves had become the cornerstone of his foreign policy and the key to Guiana's economic future. On 3 October 1796 Jeannet-Oudin wrote Admiral Laurent Truguet, minister of the navy, about a new privateering campaign whose "principal object will be to intercept and to direct to Cayenne the floating dungeons that carry sixteen thousand Negroes from Africa to Brazil each year." Privateers had no incentive to deliver slaves to the soil of liberty. They could not sell their booty in colonies where bodies no longer had a price. In contrast, French privateers sold 2,105 Africans from intercepted ships into slavery in Brazil between the abolition of slavery in 1794 and its revival in 1802 by Napoleon (see fig. 7). Wielding the threat of court-martial, Jeannet-Oudin forced three crooked captains to execute his scheme after he discovered them plundering and burning Portuguese supply ships.[31] Burnel, who replaced Jeannet-Oudin in November 1798, proclaimed his own campaign against slave ships: "The pavilion of the republic, in removing these unfortunates from slavery, would perform a philanthropic action."[32]

Neither Burnel nor Jeannet-Oudin was an innovator. The plunder of slave ships by privateers became a commonplace of maritime war in the second half of the eighteenth century, when the Atlantic slave trade reached its apogee. Most English and French privateers originated in ports tied to the slave trade; their backers traded in slaves, and their vessels might even be slave ships. French privateers had cruised for British slave ships during the Seven Years' War and sold the captives for a discount to Guiana's penurious burghers. Burnel and Jeannet-Oudin simply provided a new rationale—humanitarian benevolence—for an old looting practice.

Beginning in 1795, French sailors and administrators began promoting the maritime seizure of enemy slave ships as a philanthropic enterprise. In a 1795 memorandum for the navy, Captain Joseph-Jacques Eyriès advised an aggressive campaign against British slave ships and trading posts in Africa: "It is necessary to fall on the ships engaged in the trade and seize them; to destroy their establishments, to remove the cannons, and to carry the unhappy slaves to the land of liberty."[33] In this account, privateering and naval warfare in conjunction with the asylum principle offer a panacea to the misery of the African. The commercial war advised by Eyriès was under way when he wrote this text. In autumn of 1794, French warships and privateers attacked British ships on the African coast and along rivers that served as collection points for slaves, which brought the British slave trade to a temporary standstill. From 1793 to 1794, the number of slaves embarked on British vessels fell an astonishing 59 percent from 46,236 to 27,454. The republic's assault on Britain's Africa trade prevented at least thirty-nine British vessels from embarking slaves (see fig. 6), which provoked a political crisis on the African coast.[34] Lacking buyers, slaves in the region of Sierra Leone fled their keepers by the thousands and began "devastating the neighboring countries."[35]

After 1794, the French war against the slave trade ceased to be preemptive. Instead of obstructing the departure of slaves from Africa, French privateers cruised for British ships full of slaves on the Middle Passage. The practice of seizing Africans at sea raised the question of what legal status these people would have on French soil. Daniel Lescallier, director of colonies in 1797, believed that "new negroes . . . cannot, without endangering the plantations . . . be given liberty."[36] French captives aboard *The Swallow*, a British slave ship, who commandeered the vessel to Cayenne in 1798, later sought compensation per head of Negro from the

Figure 6   Interceptions of Slave Ships in the Revolutionary Era

	1793	1794	1795	1796	1797	1798	1799	1800	1801	Totals for 1793–1801	1802	1803	1804	Totals by category
British [BR] ships intercepted by French before embarkation of slaves /no slaves embarked [NSE]	2	39	5	6	7	6	13	2	0	80	0	1	3	84
Ships of other nationalities [OTH] intercepted by French before embarkation of slaves / NSE	0	0	0	0	0	0	0	0	0	0	0	0	0	0
BR by French before embarkation / slaves disembarked in Americas [DIA]	0	2	1	0	0	0	0	0	0	3	0	0	0	3
OTH by French before embarkation of slaves / DIA	0	2	0	0	1	0	0	0	0	3	0	0	0	3
BR by French after embarkation of slaves / DIA	3	3	10	9	4	2	2	2	0	35	3	12	11	61
OTH by French after embarkation of slaves / DIA	0	4	0	0	1	0	3	0	1	9	0	1	0	10

BR by French after disembarkation of slaves	3	2	1	4	4	4	0	5	1	24	0	1	1	26
Total French interceptions	8	52	17	19	17	12	18	9	2	154	3	15	15	187
BR by ships of unknown nationality after disembarkation of slaves	0	0	1	0	2	2	0	1	2	8	0	0	0	16
BR by unknown ships before embarkation / NSE	0	1	0	0	2	1	3	0	1	8	0	3	1	20
OTH by unknown ships before embarkation / NSE	0	0	0	0	0	0	1	0	0	1	0	0	0	2
BR by unknown ships after embarkation / DIA	1	3	2	2	3	1	0	0	0	12	0	2	2	28
OTH by unknown ships after embarkation / DIA	0	0	0	0	0	0	1	2	0	3	0	0	0	6
Total interceptions by ships of unknown nationality	1	4	3	2	7	4	5	3	3	32	0	5	3	40
Total French and unknown ship interceptions	9	56	20	21	24	16	23	12	5	186	3	20	18	227

Source: Voyages Database, 2009, *The Trans-Atlantic Slave Trade Database*, http://www.slavevoyages.org (accessed 23 April 2012).

Note: This chart tracks slave ship interceptions by French and unknown parties after Britain entered the war in 1794 and reflects French efforts to destroy the British slave trade in 1794 after a series of military defeats in the Caribbean that resulted in the loss of Guadeloupe, Martinique, and portions of Saint-Domingue. Although most of the period covered here coincides with the short-lived era of revolutionary emancipation, data have been included for several years after the return of slavery to French colonies to provide a point of comparison. The ships called "other" in this chart were Portuguese in all but two cases.

Navy, alleging that gratuities "had been allotted numerous times in such cases to French corsairs."[37] As for Jeannet-Oudin, his attitude toward African newcomers can be inferred from a report he sent to Bonaparte in October 1800: "That the liberty of the blacks is desired by nature I shall not bother to prove or to deny; but it is permitted to consider men in general as instruments of work, as causes of production, and the negroes can be classed as such."[38]

The applied history of the asylum principle in French Guiana, alongside these observations about African status by prominent administrators, supply a context for interpreting the law of 1 January 1798, which Jeannet-Oudin quoted when refusing to render the American captain's slave. At the time of the drafting of that law, French privateers had directed at least 9,251 slaves to the Americas since 1794, of whom 4,230 are known to have reached French colonies (see fig. 6 and fig. 7). Thousands more were expected to follow. The law of 1 January 1798 did not merely restate the republican commitment to slave asylum; it also defined newly arrived Africans as foreigners. According to the 1798 text, refugees who set foot on the soil of liberty would become eligible for French citizenship "subject to the conditions prescribed by Article 10 of the Constitutional Act."[39] Under the provisions of the 1795 constitution, to which this law referred, "the male foreigner becomes a French citizen when, after reaching the age of 21 and having declared his intention to remain in France, he resides there for seven consecutive years, so long as he pays direct taxes, owns landed property or an agricultural or commercial establishment, or marries a French woman." The new law could not reduce such people to slavery. Yet the ghost of slavery was still in the text. An earlier French text of 1791 had called slaves "individuals of a foreign nation," who thereby became ineligible for the rights of man.[40] The law of 1798 resolved the question of African status in conformity with the views of officials who saw free soil as a device for creating a new colonial underclass.

The Africans who reached Guiana during the Revolution dramatically altered rural life. In 1796, the year he began interception efforts, Jeannet-Oudin estimated the number of agricultural workers at 4,000 out of approximately 9,500 freed people.[41] Both Jeannet-Oudin and his successor, Burnel, distributed Africans from seized slave ships to state plantations and to private employers. It is possible that these newcomers comprised one-third of Guiana's rural work force at the turn of the nineteenth century. In all, from 1796 to 1800, seven captured ships delivered 2,163 Africans to Cayenne.[42] During roughly the same period (1795–1800), seven ships carried 2,128 Africans to Guadeloupe—a colony with nine times Guiana's population (see fig. 7).[43]

The arrival of intercepted slave ships in Guiana coincided with increasingly restrictive work legislation and policing measures. Anecdotal evidence suggests that the colony's new relationship with Suriname, together with

Figure 7   Slaves Delivered aboard Intercepted Ships, 1793–1804

	1793	1794	1795	1796	1797	1798	1799	1800	1801	Totals for 1793–1801	1802	1803	1804	Totals by destination for 1793–1804
To Martinique	328	0	0	199	0	0	0	0	0	527	0	0	279	806
To Guadeloupe	0	0	922	328	355	328	195	0	0	2128	529	529	1395	4581
To French Guiana	0	0	0	523	656	328	0	656	0	2163	0	0	0	2163
To Saint-Domingue	283	328	575	344	0	0	0	0	0	1530	0	0	0	1530
To USA	0	0	0	0	0	0	0	0	0	0	0	0	279	279
To Cuba	0	0	0	0	0	0	0	0	0	0	0	126	0	126
To British Caribbean	0	0	158	0	0	0	0	0	0	158	0	0	122	280
To Rio de la Plata	0	0	0	0	0	0	555	0	0	555	0	18	192	765
To Bahia	0	1424	0	0	328	0	0	0	353	2105	0	0	0	2105
Total to French colonies	611	328	1497	1394	1011	656	195	656	0	6348	529	529	1674	9080

(continued)

Figure 7 *(continued)*

	1793	1794	1795	1796	1797	1798	1799	1800	1801	Totals for 1793–1801	1802	1803	1804	Totals by destination for 1793–1804
Total to known destinations	611	1752	1655	1394	1339	656	750	656	353	9166	529	673	2267	12635
Total conducted by French interceptors to unknown destinations	339	687	1323	1274	93	0	309	0	0	4025	279	0	432	4736
Totals	950	2439	2978	2668	1432	656	1059	656	353	13191	808	673	2699	17371

Source: Voyages Database, 2009, *The Trans-Atlantic Slave Trade Database*, http://www.slavevoyages.org (accessed 23 April 2012).

Note: This chart reflects the fate of slaves aboard vessels intercepted by France during the revolutionary era. As the chart shows, a number of people were sold into slavery in locations such as Bahia and Rio de la Plata by French privateers after the Convention abolished slavery in French colonies by decree of 4 February 1794, and a large number of people were taken to unknown destinations by French privateers, who may have been more involved in slave trafficking than the chart indicates. Unfortunately, there is no equivalent database for France's Indian Ocean colonies of Île de France (Mauritius) and Réunion.

the rising number of foreign laborers, lay behind draconian measures that applied to both emancipated slaves and African newcomers. A glowing account of Burnel's administration by Charles Malenfant, who commanded the Battalion of Guiana, recalled that "Surinam became the storehouse and the treasury of Cayenne. From this commercial liaison, agriculture in Guiana became ever more flourishing." According to Malenfant, two groups drove the revival of agriculture: African newcomers and young men who moved to Cayenne after emancipation "in the hope of going to sea with the corsairs" and had since been run out of town.[44] In Malenfant's summary of Burnel's achievement, Guiana's rising prosperity depended on the colony's access (1) to cash, supplies, and markets through a neighboring slave society and (2) to Africans seized at sea aboard slave ships. The soil of liberty had become a place organized around the persistence of slavery beyond its frontiers. In 1798, a year of disquieting interdependency between slavery and freedom, Burnel revived portions of the Code Noir in legislation that severely restricted the ability of rural workers to change employers, to buy and sell, and even to marry.[45]

To what degree did the Africans' status differ from that of other people in the colony? The civil records of revolutionary Guiana suggest that white officials did not regard African-born people as members of the French nation, whatever their date of arrival. In the Sinnamary town hall on 21 March 1798 a black man called Sans Culotte, whose particulars are unknown, witnessed the marriage of "Citizen Jean-Baptiste, of the Bambara nation, age 37," and "Citizen Marie-Thérèse, around 20 years old, of the Congo nation," before the mayor, Leopold Vogel, a former child bugler in the Hussars from Lorraine.[46] The word "citizen" remained in use as an honorific throughout the 1790s in Guiana. Yet the records of revolutionary Sinnamary resembled Old Regime baptismal records in noting African nations in the same manner that priests had once recorded slave origins.

In the case of Saint-Domingue and Guadeloupe, France's war against a coalition of imperial powers was a boon for black liberty. In August 1793 the revolutionary commissar Sonthonax proclaimed the liberation of slaves in northern Saint-Domingue while awaiting the colony's invasion by Great Britain at a time when Spain supplied black insurgents with arms and supplies. In 1794 the emancipation decree enabled France to retake Guadeloupe from the British by rallying freed slaves to the republican cause. There, as in Saint-Domingue, black soldiers held a privileged status compared with plantation workers throughout the 1790s. No one bothered to invade Guiana during the Revolution, however. The experience of black soldiers in that colony, set beside that of newly arrived Africans, draws attention to the corrosive effect of the war on imperial citizenship in Guiana. The asylum principle, which enabled the delivery of seized slaves to Guiana, also called the black battalion into being. The occupation of Guiana's eastern frontier by Portuguese troops, who aimed to stem the flight of slaves, led the governor to muster 480 black soldiers in April 1795.[47] Those defenders of free soil did not wear the national colors. They lived segregated from the white garrison. They did not hold any rank in the French army.[48] They were also denied French citizenship. Although the 1795 constitution narrowed the citizenry to male proprietors, it made an exception for soldiers that legislators extended overseas to the advantage of colonial troops. The law of 1 January 1798 that restated the asylum principle also enfranchised colonial soldiers as well as freedmen who met a limited property requirement. In Guiana, however, Jeannet-Oudin and Burnel applied the law merely as a license to seize slave ships; they declined to apply the law to empower the colonial citizenry.[49] This policy had the effect of flooding the colony with hijacked Africans called foreigners whom local officials refused to distinguish from everyone else.

Victor Hugues, the former commissar of Guadeloupe, began reenslaving Guiana's people in 1800, when he arrived in the colony.[50] In 1804, reflecting back on his handiwork, he observed: "It is as though this colony had never been revolutionary."[51] In fact the Revolution and the people's memory of their lost liberty structured the process of reenslavement, shaped local styles of resistance, and helped assure the colony's easy conquest by Portugal in 1809. During the Revolution nearly all emancipated people abandoned the property of their former owners and moved elsewhere. Some resettled in town; others regrouped with relatives on other estates or else created family farms. In October 1802, Hugues warned the navy that splitting up families and redistributing slaves to their original owners would produce mass flight to the forest.[52] For that reason, he judged it essential to reenslave people where they were, gradually and by stealth. He crafted a transitional regime for Guiana that stood in ironic relation to the colony's short stint as the soil of liberty. In 1794 Guiana became land that made men free. Under Hugues, the land you lived on absorbed you; the person who owned that land became your master. On Hugues's advice the consular decree of 7 December 1802 "transformed the slave into immovable property [l'immobiliserait] completely and in perpetuity."[53] In simpler terms, the emancipated people became real estate. Soon afterward, however, Hugues chose to ignore his own advice. His decree of 2 Germinal, year 9 (23 March 1803), revived slavery in its original, prerevolutionary form by defining everyone as movable goods.[54] Local people responded to that act by taking to the forest to preserve families intact and to avoid being assigned to old masters. In the woods they joined Maroon bands that predated the Revolution and survived it.

In his correspondence after 1803, Hugues insisted on an eventless transition back to slavery while prosecuting an internal war against forest fugitives that widened as it wore on. In August 1803, the resumption of war with England furnished Hugues with a pretext for raising a new militia.[55] The new force filled a need unconnected to foreign invasion. Its real purpose was to help the garrison to assure "the passage from disorder to slavery of 14,000 blacks."[56]

Writing in 1805, Hugues observed that *marronnage* in Guiana "has existed from time immemorial." There had always been "incursions into plantations to abduct negresses, steal agricultural instruments, arms and powder, &c."[57] That year, fugitives burned plantations at the edge of Cayenne, which led Hugues to create a cordon of military posts around town. The soldiers posted there needed to be replaced continuously as men from both the garrison and the militia succumbed to tropical disease.[58]

Global war shaped the meaning of revolution in French Guiana and structured the local regime of liberty from 1794 to 1799. In this colony at the turn of the nineteenth century, by contrast, local events seemed to direct the character and outcome of international conflict in this region after the collapse of the Peace of Amiens in May 1803. Tumult inside French Guiana resulting from the revival of slavery rendered the colony defenseless against invasion, inspired a cunning military strategy by France's enemies, and made the colony an easy conquest. In January 1809, Hugues capitulated to an expeditionary force comprised of six hundred Brazilian Indians acting with British naval support. The real cause of his surrender lay elsewhere: revolt spread through the colony at the appearance of the enemy as slaves "armed with sabers and agricultural instruments ran through the countryside." Years earlier, Hugues had reconquered Guadeloupe from the British, armed with the emancipation decree. In December 1808 he sent three hundred slave soldiers to defend the eastern frontier of slave soil. The slave soldiers deserted, including one called Apollo, whom the British gave the title of general. Apollo marched westward "burning the properties designated to him." He and his men carried a flag emblazoned with a black man and the word "liberty." Yet the 1809 invasion failed to expand the rights of people in Guiana. The flag was a contrivance of the British, for whom the local memory of emancipation became a tool of conquest. In 1809, by the articles of surrender and at Hugues's insistence, the rebels, including Apollo, were deported to Brazil.[59]

In 1815, at the end of the Napoleonic wars, the American elder statesmen John Adams and Thomas Jefferson exchanged views on the relationship between war and revolution. Of the American Revolution, Adams observed: "What do we mean by the revolution? The war? . . . The revolution was in the Minds of the People, and this was effected . . . before a drop of blood was drawn."[60] In France and its empire, war and revolution were inextricable. The war democratized the Revolution and helped found the republic and fashion France into a transatlantic polity. Yet the war also conferred a despotic character on revolutionary colonial regimes and hence undermined the freedom of emancipated slaves. Through the combined history of privateering, commissarial rule, and the levying of black troops, the case of French Guiana offers an unsettling portrait of war's role in making and destroying what Jefferson called "the age of experiments in government."

10 The French Revolutionary Wars and the Making of American Empire, 1789 – 1796

RAFE BLAUFARB

The small group of historians who have paid particular attention to the impact of the French Revolution on the early American republic have generally concluded that the Revolution and the global war it unleashed exposed the United States to great peril. Popular sentiment in favor of the Revolution tended to nudge the United States toward involvement in the conflict. The activities of Edmond-Charles Genêt, the Girondin minister plenipotentiary sent to America in 1792, threatened to push the United States over the precipice. By organizing Democratic-Republican Societies, arming French privateers in U.S. ports, sending agents and propaganda into British Quebec, and organizing on American territory a military expedition against Spanish Louisiana, Genêt strove to involve the United States in the war.[1] Realizing that even the slightest gesture of aid to revolutionary France could bring potentially fatal British retaliation on the weak new republic, the administration of George Washington clung to a policy of neutrality. Despite bitter differences between Alexander Hamilton and Thomas Jefferson, even these rivals agreed that the United States needed to stay out of the European war. The "struggle for neutrality," as one historian put it, was the dominant theme of American foreign policy during the 1790s. The French Revolution had thrust America "between the two superpowers of that day."[2]

While the international situation was indeed full of danger, domestic quarrels also menaced the integrity of the American republic. Differences of feeling toward revolutionary France and the ideals it was thought to incarnate became entangled with debates over the policies the United States ought to adopt toward France. The resulting "partisan divisions," giving birth first to factions and then to parties, defined the political landscape of the United States for a generation or more.[3] By the late 1790s the struggle between the "French faction" and the "English party" had grown so heated that the rampart between loyal opposition and treason—so necessary to maintain in a democracy—had been deliberately breached by the party in power.[4] Upon leaving office in 1796, President Washington warned the country against the "insidious wiles of foreign influence." Whether or not the Farewell Address was intended as an appeal for isolationism or merely as a cheap shot at the Jeffersonians is the subject of some debate. There can be no question, however, that Washington regarded the internecine divisions provoked by the French Revolution as a grave, even existential, threat.[5]

Marked by fear of war and domestic dissensions, the 1790s are portrayed by historians as a time of danger in which the United States had little to gain but much to lose, as a time when national survival was at stake. To be sure, some scholars have added nuance to this stark picture. They have discerned in "the strife of Europe" a silver lining for America.[6] Some have noted the commercial "profits of neutrality"—although these brought with them increased opportunities for misunderstanding, which twice flared into armed conflict during the Quasi-War with France (1798–1800) and the War of 1812 with Great Britain (1812–15).[7] The closest examination of how the United States benefited from the French Revolutionary Wars is Samuel Flagg Bemis's study of Pinckney's Treaty, a book tellingly subtitled *America's Advantage from Europe's Distress*. In it Bemis examines the diplomacy that fixed the boundary between the United States and Spain (Louisiana and the two Floridas) in 1795, gave Americans access to the Mississippi, and thus ensured the prosperity of the American West.[8] Pinckney's Treaty (also known as the Treaty of San Lorenzo) was not the only North American territorial settlement of the 1790s. Jay's Treaty (1794) demarcated the boundary between British North America and the United States. Moreover, in the Treaty of Greenville (1795) the confederacy of the Northwestern Indians agreed to peace with the United States and renounced its claims to sovereignty over the lands north of the Ohio River.[9] Each of these treaties has been studied in detail, but their relation to one another, their contribution to the growth of American power, and, above all, their connection to the French Revolution have not been made explicit. This article seeks to do this. In it, I argue that the French Revolutionary Wars led Great Britain and Spain, the two European powers that had been opposing the territorial growth of the United States, to abandon their restrictive policies, thus opening the floodgates of America's westward expansion. Perhaps any major European war involving Britain and Spain would have led those two powers to ease their effort at American containment. Even in the absence of European war, perhaps American continental hegemony was inevitable, given the demographic and economic growth of the United States. But it is the French Revolution and the wars it spawned that explains why, when, and how American continental hegemony happened as it did.

During the years 1783–89, the period between American independence and the French Revolution, Great Britain and Spain encouraged Native Americans to counter America's westward expansion. By doing this, the Europeans sought to protect their North American colonies—Canada and the Floridas—by keeping U.S. power well distant from their borders. Their aid to the Indians, however, stopped short of direct involvement in armed hostilities against the Americans, for such an outcome would have undermined, not guaranteed, the security of the Europeans' colonial possessions. The efforts of the Indians, British, and Spanish to discourage American settlement in the Ohio Valley were largely successful and did not provoke war with the United States. During the decade following American independence, relatively few American settlers crossed the mountains, mainly into what became Kentucky and Tennessee.

For its part, the American government failed to respond effectively to the Indian and European efforts against settlement. Hobbled by debt, the Confederation Congress had no interest in compounding its manifold woes by embarking on a costly war with the Indians, the European powers, or all at the same time. The young republic could barely support a military establishment. By mid-1784 the last of the Continental Army had been disbanded. The only military forces remaining were eighty soldiers—twenty-five at Fort Pitt and fifty-five at West Point—and one clerk who alone represented the Department of War. The Confederation Congress realized that such a force could not even guard the nation's arsenals (the one in Springfield, Massachusetts, was undefended and would be seized during Shays's Rebellion!), let alone a territory the size of western Europe.[10] Its response, however, was inadequate: the creation of a seven-hundred-man regiment whose soldiers were described by one of its officers as "the offscourings of large towns and cities—enervated by idleness, debaucheries and every species of vice."[11] One western land speculator bemoaned the lack of protection such men afforded. "Purchased from the prisons . . . and brothels of the nation at two dollars per month, [they] will never answer our purpose for fighting of Indians."[12] The Americans had but this force to assert their sovereignty over the vast territories of the Ohio Valley. It is little wonder that Great Britain and Spain felt confident in pursuing measures to restrain American settlement there.

The most provocative of these was their retention of military posts in areas claimed by the United States. On territory it had ceded to the United States in 1783, Great Britain retained a cordon of eight forts, stretching from Dutchman's Point on Lake Champlain in present-day New York to Mackinac in present-day Michigan.[13] The British foreign minister emphasized their strategic importance in his instructions to George Hammond, Britain's first minister plenipotentiary to the United States:

These posts are of great Service in securing the Fidelity and Attachment of
the Indians, and as they afford to Great Britain the means of commanding the Navigation of the Great Lakes, and the communication of the said
Lakes with the River St. Lawrence, they are certainly of great importance
to the Security of Canada.[14]

Repeated American protests that British retention of the forts was costing
the United States "blood and treasure" were ignored.[15] South of the Tennessee
River, in the present-day states of Tennessee, Mississippi, and Alabama,
the Spanish established posts of their own. These guaranteed the Spanish the
same advantages with the southern Indians that the British enjoyed in the
north. Spain also insisted that the northern boundary of Spanish West Florida
extended to the 32nd parallel, not to the 31st as the Americans claimed. On
the ground the Spanish presence actually extended to the Tennessee River.[16]
In its extensive territorial claims, Spain was on firmer legal footing than Great
Britain. Since the Spanish had not been signatories to the Treaty of Paris, it
was with some justification that they refused to recognize the vast transfer of
territory it had stipulated.

By retaining the posts, the British and Spanish were able to maintain
influence and economic ties with the tribes of the Ohio Valley, which were
necessary to attaining their "great object" of securing "a barrier against
the American states by the intervention of the Indians."[17] To this end, the
European powers provided the Indians with supplies, including arms and
munitions. Although innocuously described as "provisions" or "merchandise,"
careful research has revealed the military nature of these goods. One "list
of merchandize absolutely necessary for the savages depending on Detroit,"
drawn up in 1784, included "10,000 ball and shot," "500 lbs. gunpowder," and
"500 riffle guns."[18] The vigorous commerce in nonmilitary goods carried out
between Europeans and Indians at the posts reinforced their relationship.
European material support, both military and nonmilitary, often ensured the
Indians' logistical superiority in their clashes with the Americans.

The British and Spanish encouraged the Indians to resist the Americans. As
early as July 1783, Sir John Johnson, superintendent general of Indian affairs in
British North America, promised Iroquois leaders that "should the Americans
molest or claim any part of [your] country, we shall then ask assistance of the
King."[19] Johnson's lieutenant, Alexander McKee, offered further assurances
to the more westerly tribes (the Wyandots, Mingos, Delawares, Shawnees,
Ottawas, Potawatomis, and Ojibwas). The king "will continue to promote your
happiness by his protection," McKee promised, and the Americans would
surely recognize Indian sovereignty north of the Ohio River.[20] The Spanish
pursued similar policies. By the end of 1784, they had concluded treaties with

the Creeks, Choctaws, Chickasaws, and Seminoles.[21] In the first of these, signed in Pensacola in June 1784, the Creek leader Alexander McGillivray promised that his people would "expose for the royal service of his Catholic Majesty [its] lives and fortunes."[22] By the agreement, McGillivray explained, "the Crown of Spain will Gain & Secure a powerful barrier in these parts against the ambitious and encroaching Americans."[23] Although current scholarship on European-Native American relations tends to emphasize the ways in which the latter manipulated the rivalries of the former for their own advantage, it is no less true that the European powers sought to enlist the Indians as allies or proxies in their own struggles. Those Indians, perhaps the majority, who viewed the oncoming Americans as the principal threat needed little encouragement. The resulting violence probably did more than anything else to discourage American settlement in the West during the American republic's first decade.

American responses were ineffectual. Caught between settlers (often squatters they were supposed to evict) and Indians—and outnumbered by both—the soldiers were, according to a contemporary, "rather prisoners in [the West] than in possession of it."[24] Casualties were high, but from accident, disease, and murder rather than battle, which the army generally avoided. It was not until 1787 that it suffered its first death at the hands of Indians—a soldier captured and killed by Wyandot warriors, who later flaunted his scalp before Fort Harmer. The garrison did not retaliate.[25] Territorial militias were more aggressive but less discriminating. They had a disturbing tendency to attack neutral villages. Noting this, some Americans worried that the militias were actually fueling frontier violence.[26]

The final factor inhibiting American expansion—and even threatening the integrity of the Union—was European control of the two waterways on which western settlements depended to export their products. The first of these was the St. Lawrence River, controlled by the British through the forts they retained in New York, Pennsylvania, and Michigan. British control of the St. Lawrence even prompted elements in Vermont to seek a free trade agreement with British Canada and contemplate political union with it.[27] The second was the Mississippi River. It was guarded by a string of Spanish posts stretching north to St. Louis, patrolled by gunboats, and easily closed at New Orleans. Americans found on the river were generally arrested. Some were even imprisoned in Cuba. The economic dependence of western settlers on the river was so great that some considered placing themselves under Spanish sovereignty. Separatist sentiment was encouraged by the realization that the feeble United States military presence was incapable of preventing Indian attacks. During the 1780s Spain (and to a lesser extent Britain) tried to exploit these feelings. Prominent westerners, including Judge Sebastian, Colonel Sevier, Revolutionary War veteran George Rogers Clark, and General James

Wilkinson all secretly accepted pensions, gifts, or offices from the Spanish. Even the most iconic westerner of all, Daniel Boone, eventually left Kentucky for a government position in Spanish Louisiana.[28] American statesmen were painfully aware of these separatist currents and feared for the fate of the republic. "The lopping off of Kentucky from the Union is dreadful to contemplate, even if it should not attach itself to some other power," wrote Secretary of State Edmund Randolph in 1794.[29]

In North America, the initial result of the French Revolution was to embolden the British and Spanish in their efforts against American expansion. With French finances in ruins and the country absorbed in its growing revolutionary crisis, chances were slim that it would intervene in a war between America and Britain or Spain. It was not until November 1792 that the British government even considered the possibility of conflict with France.[30] When Britain did enter the war (1 February 1793), it became an ally of Spain. Thus assured of British military assistance, the Spanish adopted an "aggressive anti-American policy."[31] Led by the bellicose governor Carondolet, the Spanish in Louisiana extended their military frontier northward. Fort Nogales was erected in 1792 on a commanding height on the eastern bank of the Mississippi, near the site of present-day Vicksburg. Fort Confederación was established the following year in what is now Alabama.[32] Located between Creek and Choctaw territory, Confederación was intended to reinforce the alliance between the Spanish and the Southeastern Indians.[33]

The British also encouraged the Indians to unite against the Americans. This aim dovetailed with the tribes' own aspirations. Already in 1786, the Mohawk leader Joseph Brant had succeeded in forming a confederation, the "United Indian Nations."[34] The confederation, however, was loose, and the tribes— and even individuals in the same tribe—had different ideas about the best course of action to adopt vis-à-vis the Americans. Would war or negotiations be more effective in halting their advance? How much should be conceded in the event of talks? British agents worked to strengthen Indian unity.[35] According to Richard White, the "confederation had in some ways become indistinguishable from a British alliance" by 1794.[36]

By 1789 war between the Americans and Northwestern Indians seemed inevitable. Although the American governor of the Northwest, Arthur St. Clair, had recently signed the Treaty of Fort Harmar (January 1789) with representatives of the confederation, the chiefs who had undertaken the negotiations were disavowed. Leadership of the confederation passed to the Shawnees, who forged a new coalition determined to use force to prevent Americans from settling north of the Ohio River.[37] Violence flared up on the frontier, and beleaguered American settlers pleaded for help. Even though the

United States had but a tiny standing army, limited resources from which to build a larger one, deep-seated anxieties about the nefarious political influence of permanent military forces, and concerns that war with the Indians might mean war with the British, public pressure for a muscular response proved too strong to resist.

In June 1790 preparations began for an offensive against the Northwestern Indians.[38] According to the plan formulated by Governor St. Clair and General Josiah Harmar, who was to lead the expedition, a force of 1,500 composed primarily of militia from Kentucky and Pennsylvania was to march 150 miles from Cincinnati into the heart of Indian territory. Its destination was Kekionga (called Miami Town by the Americans), a concentration of Indian villages near present-day Fort Wayne, Indiana. Indians who stood to defend their homes would be killed and all crops in the vicinity destroyed, leaving the survivors to starve when winter came. The expedition failed to go as planned. The militia were late to arrive, did not appear in the numbers expected, and lacked military qualities. One observer noted that they included "a great many hardly able to bear arms, such as old, infirm men and young boys."[39] Moreover, the Americans forfeited the advantage of surprise when St. Clair informed the British commander at Detroit of the expedition and its target—a precaution intended to prevent a broader war. The British commander sent messengers throughout the Northwest to alert the tribes. Under the leadership of the war leader Little Turtle, the confederation's warriors mounted a series of devastating ambushes that killed more than a third of the American force, shattered its morale, and sent the survivors fleeing back to Cincinnati.

The following year the Americans raised a new army and sent it against the confederation. Commanded by St. Clair, who had held the rank of general during the Revolutionary War, the force was to number 3,000, a figure considered more than sufficient to overcome Indian resistance. Again, the operation misfired. Although St. Clair employed all means at his disposal—recruiting on the east coast, emergency levies, and appeals to governors to supply militia—the force never exceeded 2,000. Underpaid and ill supplied by a corrupt logistical administration, the troops suffered from disease, drunkenness, and desertion. Their leader, confined to his tent by gout and "rheumatic asthma," suffered as well.[40] The march started out slowly, averaging at first only one and a half miles a day. After plodding eighty-nine miles through the trackless forest, St. Clair finally reached what he thought (erroneously) to be the St. Mary's River and ordered his force to encamp. No security precautions were taken as the troops went to sleep that night. At dawn of the following day, 4 November 1791, they were attacked by more than a thousand well-armed and well-supplied warriors under Little Turtle and Blue Jacket. Alongside them were a number of British officers and Indian department agents, as well as "scores of English and French traders."[41] The result was the worst American defeat at Indian hands. The Americans suffered more than nine hundred casualties (to the Indians' hundred), and the army disintegrated.

The Indians were exultant. So too were the British, who hoped that the Americans would see the hopelessness of military action and resign themselves to "settling all disputes," particularly that of the U.S.-Canada boundary, "in the manner and upon the terms proposed by His Majesty's Government."[42] George Hammond was instructed to propose to the Americans the creation of an independent Indian buffer state from the lands north of the Ohio River and east of the Mississippi.[43] The proposal was rejected by the Americans, who saw it as a ploy to turn the Old Northwest into a "British protectorate."[44] Despite the American rejection, the British sought to extend their influence in the Northwest by encouraging and materially supporting Indian resistance. If the Americans could be excluded from the area, British thinking went, the much-desired buffer state would become a reality even if the United States did not accept it. British officials in Canada continued to urge united resistance to American encroachment and made repeated statements that suggested the possibility of direct support.

Taking the lead was the governor of Canada, Lord Dorchester. Increasingly worried about the "progress of French intrigue" (that is to say, Genêt's propaganda) among the Canadian population and "the influence it seems to have acquired over the councils of the United States and the passions of its people," Dorchester feared that the conflict in Europe would spread to North America.[45] He shared his apprehensions freely with superiors, subordinates, and allies. In a speech to representatives of the Seven Nations of Canada in October 1793, he stated that "war between the United States and Great Britain was inevitable" and "that a new western boundary would be set by the warriors."[46] On 10 February 1794 he told a delegation from the Northwestern confederation much the same thing:

> From the manner in which the people of the States push on, and act, and
> talk on this side, and from what I learn of their conduct towards the Sea,
> I shall not be surprized if we are at war with them in the course of the
> present year; and if so a Line must be drawn by the Warriors. . . . I shall
> acknowledge no Lands to be theirs which have been encroached on by
> them since the year 1783; they then broke the Peace, and as they kept it not
> on their part; it doth not bind on ours. . . . All their approaches towards
> us since that time . . . I consider as an Infringement on the King's Rights;
> and when a Line is drawn between us, be it in Peace or War . . . those
> people must all be gone who do not obtain leave to become the King's
> subjects. . . . Our patience is almost exhausted.[47]

Dorchester backed up his words with action. He increased the provision of supplies and arms to the Indians. More significantly, one week after his speech, upon learning of the advance of yet another American expedition into the Ohio Valley, Dorchester ordered the construction of a new post, Fort Miami, in the heart of the confederation's territory.[48] Located at the foot of the Maumee Rapids, near present-day Toledo, Ohio, it represented a significant extension of the British military presence into territory ceded to the United States in 1783. Although intended by Dorchester as a defensive measure, to cover the strategically critical post of Detroit in case of what he considered to be the "inevitable" outbreak of hostilities with the Americans,[49] his Indian allies interpreted the measure differently. To the Northwestern Indians, the establishment of Fort Miami, with its garrison of redcoats and artillery, could only mean that the British would support them in their struggle against the Americans. The effect of British reassurances, material support, and military preparations was "intoxicating" for the Indians of the Northwest. By mid-1794 the British-Indian alliance "appeared strong and secure."[50]

St. Clair's defeat in late 1791 had come as a rude wake-up call for the Congress of the United States. Belatedly it realized that American sovereignty over the western territories was at stake. Although the lands north of the Ohio were American on paper, it was now clear that they were not American in fact. If the United States could not exert actual control over them, it was now apparent that either the British, or more likely the Northwestern Indians backed by Britain, would eventually replace the United States not merely as the de facto power in the region, but also as its internationally recognized ruler. To impose American authority there, however, required an army, and this the United States no longer possessed. The military establishment would have to be rebuilt from the ground up.

Shortly after the St. Clair disaster, the Washington administration sent Congress a memorandum outlining the kind of force it believed was necessary to take control of the West. It was to be a legion of five thousand long-service, professional soldiers. Swallowing its distaste for standing armies and the expenditures they entailed, Congress granted Washington the army he requested in March 1792.[51] The president promptly appointed another Revolutionary War general, "Mad" Anthony Wayne, to organize and command the new force. In the ensuing campaign Wayne would prove himself an aggressive leader, but he was neither rash nor imprudent. He understood that the raw recruits who came trickling in were in no condition to fight the seasoned warriors of the Northwestern confederacy. He thus spent 1792 and most of 1793 training his army. When he finally ordered it into action in October 1793, it had been transformed into a disciplined fighting force.

There was nothing original in Wayne's campaign plan.[52] His legion was to advance cautiously and methodically toward the heart of the confederacy, building a string of forts along its line of march. It spent the winter of 1793–94 in one of these, Fort Recovery, from which the decisive phase of the operation would be launched. In July 1794 Wayne began his attack. Perceiving the strength of the Americans, worried about rifts in the Indian alliance, and beginning to doubt British trustworthiness,[53] Little Turtle now urged that a peaceful accommodation be sought. But other leaders, encouraged by British Indian Department officials who made clear that they wanted the Americans stopped before they reached Fort Miami, overcame his objections. The confederacy would fight. They chose as their battleground an area two miles south of the British fort, a zone of fallen timber that had been created by a tornado sometime in the distant past. The tangle of tree trunks and branches—which gave the battle its name, Fallen Timbers—formed a natural fortification behind whose protection they would shoot down the oncoming Americans. Wayne and his troops arrived on 20 August 1794. Instead of falling into the trap, he sent forward skirmishers against whom the Indians—supported by a company of Canadian militia—prematurely unleashed their volley.[54] Wayne immediately ordered the main body of his troops to charge. Faced by this disciplined, numerically superior force, the defenders panicked and sought shelter in the nearby British fort. To their dismay, they found its gates shut against them.

The action of the fort's commander was consistent with British policy, whose principal aim was to protect Canada by blocking the American advance (through retention of the forts and aid to the Indians) without provoking a war with the United States.[55] But when viewed in the context of the recent British actions and declarations, the shutting of the fort's gates seemed like a direct betrayal. It marked a turning point in British-Indian relations. The "chain of friendship" that had existed since 1783 had been severed. It would be mended—incompletely—only from 1807 on as tensions again mounted between Britain and the United States. When the War of 1812 began, and Britain incited the Indians to attack the Americans, the Ohio Valley tribes responded tepidly.[56] They had not forgotten what had happened at Fort Miami. According to Jonathan Adler, a young adoptee of the Shawnees, that episode "did more towards making peace betwixt the Indians and Americans than any one thing."[57] British encouragement and promises had proven illusory. The defeated war leader Blue Jacket turned on the British, calling them "nothing." Indian Department agents began to report that rumors were spreading among the tribes that "the French were likely to beat the English in Europe."[58] Abandoned to the tender mercies of the Americans, the leaders of the confederacy were forced to sign the Treaty of Greenville (3 August 1795), renouncing their claims to sovereignty over the lands north of the Ohio River.

Although unaware of the events transpiring in the Ohio Valley, events that threatened to embroil Britain in a North American war, the British government had already resolved to abandon its risky policy of retaining its forts on United States territory and encouraging Indian resistance to American settlement. The War of the French Revolution, which Britain had entered in early 1793 fully expecting to overcome the chaotic republic, had not been going well. At the end of June 1794, word had reached London of General Jourdan's victory at Fleurus (26 June 1794), which opened the way for the French occupation of Belgium and Holland. By January 1795 Belgium was under French control, and Holland, now the Batavian Republic, had switched sides, abandoning the coalition and putting its financial and naval resources at the service of France. Despite the initial, ideological nature of the French Revolutionary Wars, deeply rooted patterns of behavior determined by long-standing geopolitical concerns were beginning to assert themselves. The existential threat posed by the enemy's occupation of the Low Countries now dictated (as it had a century earlier and as it would again a century later) British actions.

Word of Fleurus, moreover, arrived at the Foreign Office at the same moment as a shipment of half a year's backlog of dispatches from North America. These warned of rising tensions with the United States. In particular, they informed foreign minister Grenville of Dorchester's inflammatory speech, the angry responses it had elicited from the Washington administration, Wayne's progress, and the construction of Fort Miami.[59] Faced with an uncertain European war, concluded Grenville, Great Britain could not afford the additional burden of war with the United States. It was urgent to defuse the explosive situation in North America so that Britain could avoid an unnecessary war with the Americans and concentrate its resources on the French threat.

The fortuitous arrival of John Jay five days after the tardy dispatches was the final element prompting the British policy shift. Jay had been appointed envoy extraordinary in April 1794 and had left for England in May. His mission was to halt the slide toward war and negotiate a comprehensive treaty with Great Britain—aims that corresponded exactly to Grenville's desires. As Gouverneur Morris noted upon learning of the battle of Fleurus, "the success of French arms will have secured that of Mr. Jay's mission" to conclude a comprehensive understanding between the United States and Great Britain.[60] Even before Jay and Grenville sat down to discuss the many contentious issues dividing the two countries, they held an informal conversation about the crisis on the American frontier. Jay immediately gave Grenville "the most explicit assurances" that Wayne had no orders to attack the British or invade their territory. They quickly agreed that immediate steps had to be taken to prevent war—or stop it if it had already begun. In consequence, Grenville wrote to Hammond that the two men had agreed that, during the present Negotiation, and until the Conclusion of it, all things ought to remain and be preserved in Statu Quo; that, therefore, both Parties should continue to hold their Possessions, and that all Encroachments on either side should be done away; that all Hostile Measures (if any such should have taken place) shall cease; and that, in case it should unfortunately have happened that Prisoners or Property should have been taken, the Prisoners shall be released, and the Property restored.[61]

Orders were immediately issued to the authorities in Canada to take the greatest precautions to avoid hostilities with the Americans.[62] These were accompanied by a stern dispatch to Dorchester, rebuking him for his speech and his decision to establish Fort Miami. His words and deeds played into the hands of a "considerable" and "most violent party" in the United States and were more likely to "provoke hostilities rather than prevent them."[63] Unapologetic, Dorchester resigned, defending his policy to the last. Given that the feelings of the Americans had been "moving as by French impulse rapidly towards hostilities" in support of "their Jacobin friends," he felt that he had done no more than take necessary precautions against an imminent threat. "Without troops, without authority, amidst a people barely not in arms against the King," and "abandoned to our own feeble efforts for our preservation" because British military resources were being absorbed by the war against France, he had to do whatever he could locally to ready Canada's defenses.[64]

Having calmed the immediate threat of war between their countries, Grenville and Jay began to negotiate a comprehensive treaty.[65] The resulting document, known as Jay's Treaty, was signed on 19 November 1794 and ratified the following year by the Senate, but only by the slimmest of margins. The treaty was deeply unpopular in America, because, on almost every point it contained, the United States had acquiesced to British demands. The only concession won by Jay concerned the controversial posts, from which Great Britain finally agreed to withdraw.[66] Viewed in the light of Grenville's determination to avoid a North American war, this was as much a British as an American victory. By abandoning the posts, Grenville had removed a potential trigger to an unwanted conflict. The French government, however, viewed the treaty as an Anglo-American alliance and a direct violation of the Franco-American Treaty of 1778. French anger at this perceived American betrayal contributed mightily to the outbreak of the Quasi-War several years later. From the British perspective, this was an unexpected benefit of a treaty whose primary purpose had been to reduce the likelihood of war with America so that Britain could concentrate on the struggle with revolutionary France.

The settlement of the boundary dispute between the United States and Great Britain prompted Spain to seek a resolution of its differences with

America. Within less than a year of the signature of Jay's Treaty, Pinckney's Treaty was concluded between Spain and the United States.[67] Treating the issues of America's southwestern border, navigation of the Mississippi, and access to the port of New Orleans, Pinckney's Treaty represented no less of a policy reversal for Spain than Jay's Treaty had been for Great Britain. Ever since American independence in 1783, Spain had rebuffed American overtures. Negotiations in the 1780s between John Jay and the Spanish envoy Diego de Gardoqui had been characterized by Spanish foot-dragging and inflexibility. The draft agreement finally obtained by Jay in 1786 offered so few concessions to the United States that it was rejected by the Senate. There followed a period of deadlock during which, as noted above, Spanish officials in Louisiana built new forts far into the territory claimed by the United States, aided the Southeastern Indians, and encouraged separatism among the American settlers. Spain's entry into the war against France made the Spanish less inclined to negotiate with the Americans. Emboldened by its military alliance with Britain, Spain felt more confident than ever that the Americans would not dare to attack Spanish possessions in North America. By the beginning of 1794, Spanish-American relations were in a "languishing condition."[68]

That year, however, would see an unexpected reversal of Spain's foreign policy, not only toward the United States, but toward the French republic as well. British military policies had begun to trouble Spain. Admiral Hood's decision to destroy the French warships that he had captured at Toulon in 1793 made Spain suspicious of Britain's real war aims. It appeared to many in the Spanish government that Britain's true goal was to secure global hegemony by destroying French naval power—in Spanish eyes, a necessary counterweight to the Royal Navy. Lord Howe's victory over the French Atlantic fleet on 1 June 1794 confirmed Spanish fears. As a colonial power with a relatively weak navy, Spain could not stand idly by while Britain achieved this level of maritime superiority. Within the Spanish government, minds had already been made up to leave the unnatural alliance with Great Britain; all that remained was the precipitant required to convert these feelings into action.

Two events in July 1794, the French political coup of 9 Thermidor and the arrival in Madrid of reports of Jay's mission to England, sparked the Spanish foreign-policy reversal. By making it possible to claim (rightly or wrongly) that the French government had become more moderate, Thermidor opened the door for a Spanish rapprochement with France. In September 1794, Spain's foreign minister, Manuel de Godoy, opened secret talks with French officials. These resulted in the Treaty of Basel (22 July 1795), by which Spain formally renounced its alliance with the British and allied with France.[69] Word of Jay's appointment as envoy extraordinary to England arrived in Spain in early July 1794. The Spanish royal council concluded that the Anglo-American negotiations could have only one purpose—territorial expansion in the Americas at Spain's expense. To preempt this, the Spanish government hastened to neutralize the Americans by granting them substantial concessions. A message was sent to Philadelphia urging the president to send a special representative to Madrid to negotiate a treaty. The man chosen for this mission, Thomas Pinckney, departed in April 1795. By the time he arrived, the Franco-Spanish entente was on the verge of being concluded, prompting Spanish fears of British retaliation. These concerns added urgency to Godoy's talks with Pinckney and led the Spanish minister to make far greater concessions than the Americans had anticipated. In the Treaty of San Lorenzo, the Spanish acknowledged the 31st parallel as the northern boundary of the Floridas, withdrew their military presence accordingly, recognized American navigation rights on the Mississippi, and granted citizens of the United States the right of deposit at New Orleans. The West now had a viable commercial outlet—the necessary precondition for any large-scale American settlement. The shift in Spanish policy did not, however, immediately open the lands of the Southeastern Indians to American occupation. Even without substantial European aid, the Southeastern Indians—more numerous and better organized than their counterparts in the Old Northwest—held off the Americans for another two decades.

With the fixation of America's boundaries and the "comparative peace" achieved with the Indians, the pace of western settlement increased rapidly.[70] South of the Ohio, the principal route into Kentucky and beyond, the Wilderness Road, was opened to wagons in 1796. In the same year Tennessee became a state. North of the Ohio, the end of the war and the Treaty of Greenville made large-scale settlement by Americans possible for the first time. The opening of the West to American expansion was made possible by this "first rapprochement" (with the British, Spanish, and Indians alike), and the rapprochement, in turn, was a consequence of the wars of the French Revolution. Americans at the time were fully aware of the causal link between military events in Europe, the three treaties, and the destiny of their republic. Like Gouverneur Morris, James Monroe, then serving as ambassador to France, believed that French military fortunes were the key determinant of European attitudes toward the United States:

> When Toulon was taken and fortune seemed to frown upon the arms of this republic [France], . . . an order was issued for those spoliations [British orders-in-council] of which we so justly complain. We likewise saw afterwards when the spirit of this nation [France] was roused and victory attended its efforts, that that order was rescinded and some respect shewn to the United States.[71]

Lesser figures than Monroe were equally aware of the impact of French victories on America's standing in the world. Even before the battle of Fleurus, one obscure Georgia congressman, commenting to his constituents on "the almost incredible Success of the French Republicans," perceived that their victories would force Great Britain to respect the United States. "So Long as the Brave Gallicans are prosperous Great Britain will be cautious how she insults us."[72] Although unintentional and unanticipated, a significant outcome of the French Revolution and the global war that ensued was the relative disengagement of the European powers from geopolitical rivalry on the North American continent. Perhaps the most important consequence of this withdrawal was the lifting of barriers to the westward expansion of the United States. This ultimately led to the emergence of the United States as a respected actor on the international stage and was one of the factors that led to its eventual rise to superpower status.

PART IV

11 Every Revolution is a War of Independence

PIERRE SERNA

TRANSLATED BY ALEXIS PERNSTEINER

Anacharsis Cloots, a Francophile Prussian baron who from the very inception of the Revolution had embraced its universalist ideals, was still reeling under the emotional and joyous shock of the events from the previous day, 14 July 1790, the day of the Festival of Federation, when he feverishly wrote Fanny de Beauharnais about his delight. Cloots felt himself reborn and revived by the symbolic celebration ritual of the festival, which both founded French citizenship and promised other revolutions to come, well outside of France, through the simple initiative of freedom-loving men and women federated together. The essence of the Revolution had just been revealed. The height of a successful revolution, the crowning achievement of Enlightenment ideals, had just been reached. This concluded an epic that had begun one year earlier on 14 July 1789, a revolution built on the hope of a new world, the idea of participative citizenship, and the expression of a shared civic and egalitarian political will. This was the basis of a political rebirth. The combination of Enlightenment philosophy with the Revolution reached heights that have not since been surpassed.[1]

The highlight of the day came when an oath was pronounced by all: "We swear to be forever faithful to the Nation, to the Law and to the King, to uphold with all our might the Constitution as decreed by the National Assembly and accepted by the king, and to protect in accordance with the law the safety of people and property, the circulation of grains and food within the kingdom, the collection of taxes under whatever forms might exist, and to stay united with all the French under the indestructible bonds of brotherhood." A new France was born: the Revolution, which had just presented a unique and harmonious performance on the world scene, was now complete. This spectacle served as the emotional source of a new sense of unity among citizens, who were made

French through the political oath. Those who had been unpolitical subjects under the eighteenth century's absolute monarchy were now transformed into citizens of the approaching nineteenth century.[2]

The emotion expressed by Cloots is a historical clue, and the historian cannot dismiss the affective response of history's actors. Though they may be subjective and unstable, collective outpourings of emotion also signal moments of awareness, points in time that everyone understands. Unmediated by history, these moments are like collectively lived turning points. Such was the case on 14 July 1790, a cathartic moment, a moment when everyone could consciously experience a unique event, when the federative ideal and its reality together created a reasoned harmony within the body of citizens.[3] Contemporaries, those actually participating, and, later, some historians singled out this moment as an authentically happy interlude, the quintessence of eighteenth-century hopes: shared reason, collective harmony, communal citizenship. However, this opinion has not gone uncontested. The moment was at once powerful and fragile, for this new hope was soon confronted with the reality of those who refused the new world and were already preparing a formidably effective counterrevolution.[4]

However, the revolution continued. After the Festival of Federation that took place in Strasbourg, Merlin de Douai described the new stakes thus: "The people of Alsace, the people of France could care less about the conventions that, in the time of despotism, sought to unite the people of Alsace with France. The Alsatian people united with the French because they wanted to; thus, only their will, not the Munster Treaty, legitimized the Union." In other places the "diplomatic scrolls" and the "trafficking of peoples" were evoked and declared obsolete. By defining French citizenship, the Festival of Federation paved the way for an infinite revolution, for it widened the circle of citizenship to all humans and traced two paradoxical (at once complementary and mutually exclusive) possibilities for the future: the nation-state *and* the federation of peoples. The terms "union," "incorporation," and "association" came to materialize the idea that, without losing their specificity, wills can aggregate in a complex and flexible exchange that binds the nation with the human community, a frenzied pacifism with an aggressive defense of these principles, and a continuation of ancient struggles with a projection into radically new conflicts.

Today, 1789 is interesting only when considered as an illustration of the revolution of an Atlantic world that seized a civilizational space, which had been engaged, with various nuances, in the same community of thought since the transformations of the sixteenth century, when the seeds of the modern state were planted. Between 1492 and 1750, monarchies of different kinds experienced deep upheavals, which prevent us today from constructing a history based solely on the imperatives of royal state-building. Many different realities may have served to reinforce the power of the princes, and to contribute to the adaptation of central institutions to an ever-changing modernity: demographic shifts, economic structures, social rivalries, geostrategic issues, political reflections, religious reforms, continuous warfare, colonial imperialism. The heads of state and the men who surrounded them had to imagine new forms of governance in order to more effectively apply their decisions to ever-growing spaces. More reliable and effective tools of command (military, police, militias), transportation infrastructure (roads, canals, sea routes), provincial intermediaries, and means of territorial control made the power emanating from the center more visible at the periphery of the kingdoms and beyond, in the colonies.

And here surely lies one of the new, as yet unexplored, keys to understanding the dynamics of the eighteenth-century revolutions. It was once possible to give a narrative of the history of revolutions as something that originated in the metropolitan centers. This was because their colonial expansion was understood as a contagion of emancipation from center to periphery, from capitals to provinces, from mainland to overseas territories. The United States was seen to have immediately established itself as a center, as having escaped its colonial origins. At most, one chapter came to illustrate this wind of freedom that blew from Europe, mainly toward America, in history textbooks.

Recent studies invite us to reconsider this way of reading revolutionary uprisings, and seek to restore the colonial origins of revolution to their proper place in history. Others have obviously noted the wind of freedom that blew from America, but only after the latter had proved itself a victorious nation. Here I intend to develop another aspect: a geopolitical hypothesis that defines the specificity of late eighteenth-century revolutions as the result of a form of contestation typical of "primitive globalization." This "primitive globalization," which took place in peripheral spaces, in places removed from the capitals, developed the modern conditions for the emergence of the era of human rights revolutions.

Revolution Is Not Only a War of Independence, but Above All and Essentially a "Decolonization" in Progress

The European continent can no longer be studied in isolation, as a central place from which would emerge the impetus for action in the New World, which was first submitted to colonization, and then imitated forms of contestation born in the metropoles. This is the crux of a possible history of revolution, which must be defined and constructed through research and hypothesis. Such a task implies avoiding, as I have tried to do, a history of colonial space that would be a history of empire building, a mirror of the construction of states. The following, then, are to be considered as central issues in the building of colonial systems: the history of autochthonous revolt, the insubordination of slave populations, and the sedition of Creole elites and their incessant demands for increased autonomy from the metropole. Similarly, the rebellions of the poor and the revolts of the nobles were at the heart of the construction of the state.

The conditions of colonization in North and South America led to the emergence of societies that, far from the home countries, developed a sense of initiative and at a minimum the capacity to invent civil societies less constrained by European monarchies.[5] Tutelary power was respected, but also quite remote. Worlds with growing autonomy were built, with strong allegiances to Madrid, London, and to a lesser extent, Paris, as long as the capitals did not challenge their development.[6] During the eighteenth century, and particularly after the upheavals of the Seven Years' War (1756–63), freedom, the idea of freedom and all its associated practices, became, on the American side of the Atlantic, eminently positive; it did so not as a cultural manifestation of, for example, the Enlightenment, but as the affirmation of a reality that a minority of colonists, and emancipated slaves where they could be found in these slave societies, had acquired through the prosperity afforded by the exploitation of natural resources in the spaces that they controlled.[7]

Is it not in these overseas spaces that one ought to seek another chronology for a history of revolution on the scale of multiple continents? Is this not essential to understanding the origin of a centuries-long history, that of the "world revolution" that seized the planet from 1770 up to the adventures of decolonization after the Second World War, around 1960, in an almost uninterrupted sequence of uprisings, uprisings that are beginning to arise again in these early years of the twenty-first century in the Maghreb in complex forms of neocolonial disarticulation that are all based—and this is the essential condition of a constructive comparativism—on a conception of freedom and of inherent human rights? In stimulating fashion, Markus Rediker laid the groundwork for such a history in his description of the "hydrarchy" of modern times, a fearsome thousand-headed beast born in the steerage of ships that crisscrossed the seas and harbored multiracial crews of wretched seamen in their holds. In their state of perpetual mutiny, these seamen were always ready to rebel.[8] A maritime proletariat emerged in the seventeenth and eighteenth centuries. These were the future henchmen behind all the coming seditions, the sparks that would ignite the larger rebellions of the second half of the eighteenth century. Both America and Europe were affected, along with Asia, which could not remain indifferent to the political tremors that were spreading the seeds of hatred of order and hierarchy to every harbor in the world.[9]

If such a hypothesis is indeed true, then one must agree to break from a strictly French perspective, a Eurocentric logic, or even simply Atlantic point of view in order to explain the phenomenon of revolution, and to attempt to explain the interest in thus thinking about the origins of the global revolution that began in the eighteenth century.

An unspoken, but both explicit and implicit, historiographical prejudice about the superiority of the French Revolution must then be consciously dismantled. This prejudice is the outcome of an epistemological enterprise that began in the nineteenth century and was unlike any other: a succession of historians, from Michelet to Jaurès and up to Georges Lefebvre, worked to demonstrate this "exceptionality," some by insisting on the construction of a people elevated to a mythical status (Michelet), some by emphasizing a protosocialism with a human face (like the founder of *L'humanité*, Jaurès), some by focusing on its exceptionally rural identity (like Lefebvre, the founder of the Institute of History of the French Revolution at the Sorbonne). While the French Revolution does indeed possess some unique characteristics, these must be taken as the outcome of a history that dates back to the sixteenth century, which was a nodal point in our history because it invented the future of our political systems. The French Revolution featured at least two phenomena that both contained former revolutions and foreshadowed future ones. First was the politicization of the masses and the process of democratization, understood in terms of the effective participation of a number of persons hitherto unimaginable in a country of 28 million persons; all people who had been excluded from the public sphere were now discovering politics.[10] Second, the universalism of the new regime implied, beginning already in the first weeks of the summer of 1789, the obligation to bring *the* revolution to populations likely to adopt it, regardless of state borders and local political systems.[11] The Revolution sought to be, and became, universal. In the case of France, it afforded itself the means to do so through armed force in Europe and the West Indian colonies and became, over the course of the nineteenth century, the matrix for almost all other revolutions. It remained the point of reference until the revolution of 1917 relaunched, with its socialist republics, the policy of geographic dedifferentiation, a policy that set off a new, global civil war.[12] The French Revolution staged an occasionally chaotic and utopian, a sometimes pragmatic and coherent, attempt—in the experiment of sister republics, for example—to internationalize its principles, to include them in coherent political structures, and to form a European whole bound by the republican underpinnings of the Constitution of the Year III [1795], a constitutional construct with a quasi-European dimension. Yet this frame must be further widened, even calmly criticized. The notion of a "Grande Nation" bestowing its Enlightenment and freedoms on the world, a notion symbolized by the Declaration of the Rights of Man of 26 August 1789, must be questioned. The reality of the Directory government is far more complex, from a plundering of populations, which were understandably recalcitrant toward the republic's armies, to a political regeneration based on the discovery of supposedly indigenous republican projects in the Netherlands, Switzerland, and the entire Italian Peninsula.[13]

There is a date that some will find incongruous, but that nevertheless allows for an original interpretation of the revolutionary phenomenon and its modern dynamics: 1962. In this year, an unprecedented trauma shocked the French nation and marked the beginning of a long-term disenchantment with respect to the country's capacity to embody anything but a nation once convinced of spreading its "civilizational" ideas that had progressively lost all of its empire and was now relegated to a secondary status, in spite of its ability to self-narrate a mythologized history.[14] The end of the Algerian War constitutes a paradigm for all the other defeats in wars of decolonization, which are often represented in textbooks reflecting an academic historiography as remote consequences of the French Revolution. After 1945, decolonization shed a cruel light on the contradictions of a France born universal and fraternal in 1789, and turned both colonialist and xenophobic. The country of human rights was drawn into insurmountable difficulties, for, after 1945, it was the rhetoric, the philosophy, and the concepts of the 1789 revolution itself that informed the thinking behind liberation movements aimed at expelling the colonist from the lands that had been usurped. The Empire, which was seen as the last recourse against Nazism, had witnessed the humiliation of 1940 and the ignominy of collaboration. From this point of view, the mainland once again is thought to have inspired the model for liberation, albeit against itself. This demonstrated, if a demonstration was needed, the extraneousness of the revolutionary matrix for colonized peoples. Revolution, it was claimed, was brought to peoples unprepared for modernity. The emancipating revolutions of independence remained founded on an idea from the mainland.

Is it not time, considering modern history as a whole, to upend the dynamics of historiography and consider a logic contrary to the one that has prevailed in history books? What if the revolution of the late eighteenth century was in its very essence based on a political awareness of colonial realities? Was revolution not born in colonized spaces, precisely because they were colonized spaces, that is, because they were decentered, outlying places where questions of rights, freedom, and the status of individuals were brutally and uncompromisingly played out? An investigation into the major revolutions of modern times, which I have purposely left aside until now, shall allow us to consider this proposition.

Consider first the United Provinces, which revolted as a colony against the Spanish crown. The Dutch Beggars, emboldened by a new religion, rejected the oppressive metropole and constructed through rebellion an original political system, a federal and martial republic at the northern borders of the Spanish empire. They prospered from their holdings, which extended from Africa to India and the West Indies, and reaped the benefits for at least two centuries, even if it led them to reproduce the type of colonial project against which they had originally risen.[15]

In the seventeenth century, in order to avoid becoming a spiritual colony of Roman Catholicism, Anglicanism and antiabsolutist parliamentarianism became the most powerful forces at the periphery of European Catholicism. English elites then achieved independence from their Catholic kings, Charles I and James II, through revolution and affirmed their redemptive independence in a civil war that included both the period 1640–60 and the allegedly peaceful revolution of 1688.[16] Revolution began to reveal itself as a war of independence, even before it became a vector of political emancipation or a simple affirmation of rights. These two forms of independence, conquered or invented, were revolutionary and were perceived as such by their contemporaries. They establish the war of independence as a fact ontologically connected to revolutions and also as something associated with the violent and complex dimensions of civil war.[17] The conditions that the symbolic (Rome) or real (Madrid) metropolitan centers imposed on colonized entities inevitably led to revolutionary, foundational wars, which became the marks of identity for new societies, now free and united around a new conception of community, a prototype for future nationalities.[18] For those who made them proper revolutions, these wars were the last line of defense against the imperial powers that had decided to fight their emancipating peripheries. The wars functioned as ruptures that afforded these protorevolutionaries independence in the ontological sense of the word, the freedom to decide for oneself. Is this not what Voltaire finds so fascinating in his *Philosophical Letters*, when he grasps the extent to which the status of freedom is the result of the English uprising?[19]

The situation was the same a few decades later on the other side of the Atlantic and followed a similar trajectory. The American War of Independence, between 1776 and 1781, or the Revolution of the United States of America, is not, contrary to what a conservative tradition has chosen to assert, a war without revolution. Because this was a war of independence, it *was* by definition a revolution. The American Revolution is emblematic because it is both an old-style and a modern revolution. Its seeds had been planted long before, with the successive waves of exiled Protestants who came to the east coast of the American continent from England. Indeed, the territory had become a "dumping ground" for the most dangerous elements of the city of London. It was in this colony, under the inspiration of classical texts, that the memory of the English republic, of the political radicalism of British Protestants, of the spirit of fundamental freedoms inherited from 1688, was to flourish. Over time, this memory gave way to new and revolutionary demands.[20] No taxation without representation, no guarantee of economic support for English state-building without recognition of its sovereignty and, as an extension, of individual rights. The revolution began in a context of chronic sedition after the Seven Years' War. It escalated after the "massacre" of 1770, which led to pervasive acts of subversion, and the Boston Tea Party in December 1773, which flouted the privileges held by the East India Company. The independence of the United States and the war against the mainland were two inseparable events, as together they gave life to a political regime, the republic, which was founded less on cultured and elitist references to the ancient republics of antiquity, and more on the real and material victory against London in a military struggle that forged the nation with blood and iron. The United States was the continuation of the United Provinces.

Continental Europe followed a similar pattern, though the situation was more complex because it was hard to see at first that the colony and the metropole were located in the same space. Yet it was not impossible to think of them that way or to redefine them as such as long as one could get beyond thinking of the colonies as simply exotic. It is essential to consider the political meaning of that common space, that is, the construction of a particular form of spatial domination—including both symbolic power and the real practice of power—of the center over the periphery, the capital over provinces, and the metropole over "internal colonies." This concept was well known in the eighteenth century, moreover, when policies from the highest echelons of the state sought to valorize empty spaces within the territory, as in the case of Spain in the second half of the eighteenth century.

A point of clarification is needed here, before continuing to outline the hypothesis in question: Is a colony to be defined simply by kilometers of distance and separation from the mainland by an ocean or a sea? Can it not also be characterized according to specific forms of domination born from the distinct conquest of a space and the subsequent management of its resources? To what degree and how, in this increasingly globalized world, have colonial realities interfered with the geopolitics of the metropoles? Is it possible to understand the lived experiences of those who, far from the center of power in a world where the colonial reality was essential to the functioning of the world economy, perceived themselves as being subjected to the consequences of a system of power that was imposed, whether metaphorically and in reality, by a remote center? Can the repetition of the word "slave" in thousands of speeches before and during the European revolutions be interpreted otherwise? A contemporary analogy with the socioeconomic realities of any imperial space and of the world economy as a whole, both founded on servitude, functions through rhetorical projection: when people live as real slaves, even when not defined as such officially, such a projection proves subversively effective and legitimizes first rebellion and then revolution.

This enlarged concept of colony reveals new logics of uprising that demand further study according to this new perspective. First, in Russia. The Pugachev rebellion, between 1772 and 1773, which mobilized a portion of the Cossacks between the Urals and Western Siberia in a struggle against the politics of imperial expansion advocated by Catherine II, appears as an archaic revolt against a colonizing power. Here, the stakes have been confused by the dynamics of enlightened despotism, a feature of which was a conservative revolution, which some slightly misguided philosophers, like Diderot, imagined to be a way to extend freedom throughout the vast empire. However, this was not the case. After the battle of Kazan in 1774, when the rebels were defeated, the government reshaped the territory by repressing even the slightest sign of Cossack emancipation.

In their way, the "Belgian" provinces of the Austrian Empire illustrate and corroborate the hypothesis that revolution is a struggle for independence born at the periphery of a space undergoing centralization. Beginning in 1780, the inhabitants of Brabant and Brussels rejected reforms imposed from the outside (Vienna) by Joseph II and rebelled in the name of their ancient liberties. As in the United States, references to ancient and classical models of liberty were blended with a modernity known for its managerial efficiency and the organizational rationality of provinces far removed from the metropole's capital. The result was heavier taxation and a diminution of local freedoms.[21]

Geneva rose up in 1782, and though the French army intervened, tensions remained. I do not mean to suggest that Switzerland and its cantons were colonial outposts. However, the second-rate forms of citizenship granted to the population that arrived after the foundation of the state do indeed recall the kinds of stratification that the creolization of colonial societies both invented and reproduced. Genevan society was built on exclusionary policies of citizenship that referred explicitly to status, in which privilege was a function of one's date of arrival in the territory. The top of society consisted of a tiny minority of "patricians." This was followed by the "bourgeois," who purchased their citizenship and did not participate in political life, though they did dominate "the natives," the powerless descendants of the first settlers. Finally, there were the "inhabitants," who clamored for full integration into the community of artisans.[22] From a geographical point of view, Geneva clearly did not function as a colony. But this was a society in which the free dominated and the less free were subjugated; the first settlers, the descendants of sixteenth-century Protestants, were the most privileged, and two intermediary classes were situated between the two extremes. This kind of classification is typical of colonial societies, in which, over time, the dynamics of commerce eventually lead to tensions and demands by the subjugated for freedom, as was the case in Geneva in 1782.

And in France? The skeptics are undoubtedly doubly reticent to read the Revolution of 1789 as a war of independence and as a kind of war of decolonization. Indeed, in textbooks, generations of historians have worked to represent the long history of France as the story of the construction of a beneficent and centralized state from the monarchic Middle Ages to the Versailles congress of mayors of the republic in the early twentieth century. France is depicted as a country united from time immemorial. It was precisely the power of the royal, encompassing, and centralized state that characterized the Bourbon reign and differentiated it from the majority of European countries. The kingdom's unity concretized its power. And, though new territories were conquered, they were integrated, and they accepted their union with the capital. Given the means by which the monarchy constructed itself, Versailles cannot simply be reduced to an imperial metropole in a private reserve of "colonies" each grafted one upon the other. Later, the hallmark of the republic would be a motto that made it one and indivisible in a struggle to the death against any form of sedition.

Beyond the rhetoric that leads to a number of anachronistic audacities (which are inescapable), how can one represent the France of 1789 as a "metropole with its colonies"? First, we must do away with a Tocquevillian orthodoxy that no one dares question anymore. This democratic aristocrat is upheld as a brilliant thinker because in the midst of the Second Empire he concluded that France had fused the old and new regimes, or rather that the Revolution of 1789 simply continued the work of centralization that had begun, for the most part, during the Old Regime with the development of an efficient state apparatus symbolized by the *intendants*. Within a few decades the deputies who had been freed from their imperative mandates in 1789, representatives-on-mission in 1793–94, and Bonaparte's prefects came to embody modern versions of the medieval *missi dominici* (lord's agents), ensuring the continuity of a state whose centralizing structure would not have been fundamentally affected by the vicissitudes of politics. Moreover, in Tocqueville's view, freedom had already been acquired under the monarchy, and the Revolution was more the result of the sudden reassertion of sovereignty by the king than of a slow degradation of the conditions of this freedom. Tocqueville's luminous analysis has served as the foundation of an entire swath of critical history on the Revolution. The Revolution has been seen as an unconscious continuation of the Old Regime characterized by the construction of a centralized state to the detriment of its provinces. Can this notion, which is most often considered self-evident, not be revisited? Can we not develop an inverse interpretation of this liberal-monarchist refrain, which became the basis of a Tocquevillian, center-left critique, after . . . the decolonization of 1962?[23]

What if, on the eve of the Revolution, France *resembled* "colonies" that were geographically bound and politically united? What if the state apparatus had little local power besides the reports that reached Versailles? Were the peripheries and the center not irremediably separated, and the subjects divided, as in a typical colonial society?[24] France would then have been a country of "small fatherlands" in the literal meaning of the term, which would not have necessarily prevented displays of allegiance to the idea of the kingdom.[25]

In the eighteenth century, at the moment of the first globalization, there existed a strong notion of "empire" that had been based on a dominant discourse in which the science of commerce had become an umbrella concept for all the shifting realities that made the world an integrated space. The intellectual, the political, and, above all, the commercial were now connected. In this context, to be a colony was to a certain extent neither degrading nor a handicap, since logically the colonies were the engine of global prosperity. Only later did a consciousness of the imperial system emerge, which elicited a will for a new contract of association with the metropole, a contract founded on the idea of wealth contributed by the periphery to the center. This was claimed in the name of the original political purity of the colony against the excesses of the center, much as it was defined in the original struggle of American insurgents: (1) no taxation without representation; (2) at first a demand for a share of sovereignty, as in 1688, and then a demand for the political sovereignty of the nation; (3) the whole founded on a science of commerce that encompassed the social, cultural, and civic changes that completely transformed the balance of globalized societies in the second half of the eighteenth century.

Paul Cheney has shown that this imperial model applied not only to the United States but also to eighteenth-century France with its colonies, its center, and also—and this is crucial for the present argument—its liminal spaces, the favored regions on the Atlantic and Mediterranean coasts that during imperial and Atlantic expansion experienced unparalleled prosperity. Everything was transformed by the science of commerce. Suddenly the regions included in the colonial system's prosperity, namely the Atlantic and Mediterranean zones, along with their hinterlands, began to make the same demands that the colonies themselves were making: economic autonomy and self-governance.[26] Recognition of the prosperity and the relative emancipation of the peripheral regions from Versailles provided the first seeds of the revolution that germinated after 1776, conditions characteristic of the logic of a globalized world in which modernity was now seen as originating in "colonized" spaces, either actual colonies or spaces that were becoming aware, through the science of commerce, that they were in a peripheral position of "colonizing" domination. Domination from the metropolitan capital, in this case Versailles, had now become unbearable.

Surely we would benefit from asking whether France should be characterized more as a monarchic empire than as a monarchic nation-state. Historically, the term "monarchic empire" did indeed exist, and there are a number of sources that speak of the king's empire or of France as an empire whether because of its extraordinary size within the European geopolitical sphere, its monarchic constitution, or the heterogeneity of the populations living together in its massive territory.

It is important not to forget that linguistic unity did not exist, which reinforced the feeling of local belonging. One could be a subject of the king without necessarily being conscious of the unity of the country, in which in 1790 only four million people spoke French.[27] Let us recall the indignation of Mirabeau and Sade during their judicial entanglements with the Parlement of Provence: they were indignant that the judges spoke Provençal among themselves, and scandalized, according to Sade, that half of them were the sons of "tuna merchants" and thus foreign to his world of French refinement. Did it not take one hundred years for all to speak the same language, to become aware of a shared geography and community of goods, and to share common lives and values? Did it not take the beginning of a massive national effort at acculturation, a veritable rebirth embodied by the Revolution, its wars, its laws, and its reinvention of the country as an immense homeland?

The lived reality in the territory is largely reminiscent of experiences that, in other spaces, would be described with the terms "metropole" and "colonies." In 1789, the kingdom was not united. Instead, it was full of borders and local particularisms that suggest the kingdom's lack of a rationally unified administration. Michel Antoine often recalls the diffuse nature of power in the so-called French administrative monarchy, which operated with approximately 50,000 agents of the king, whereas the Revolution, in accordance with its laws of autumn 1789 and its democratization of powers, called on 1.2 million citizens in the construction of the state. These citizens were clearly unified around a common project, which at once created equality and uniformity.[28] This was not a continuity, but a rupture. The administrative monarchy did indeed begin to structure itself, as did the offices of Versailles that managed the territorial possessions of the king from afar. Yet, each decentered zone of power traded its docility with the center for constantly renegotiated privileges. Municipal administration was thus one of the true political stakes of the eighteenth century, the site of power for local notables ahead even of the king's emissaries.[29]

Each province followed its own law and tolerated the king's power and men only so long as its own privileges were not put into question. The provinces also accepted a form of exclusivity that structured the local economy with special regulations and marginal arrangements. Edicts were applied in a chaotic fashion; the map of indirect taxes and the anarchic superimposition of regulations varied from region to region, sometimes with a geographical difference of only a few hundred meters. Jean Nicolas has shown how local urban oligarchies deliberately ignored large-scale smuggling and barter operations. The farther from Versailles, the more rampant the tendency. In some areas these oligarchies turned a blind eye to secretly organized warlike battles with veritable armies of smugglers pitted against the soldiers of the royal tax farms. This was the case, for example, in the eastern provinces of the kingdom, even though they were thought to be more disciplined than those of the quarrelsome west or the disobedient south.[30]

The kingdom consisted of an aggregate of zones geographically linked to one another and glued to their own metropoles, even close to Paris. France of 1789 can be characterized as a sum of regions, each with its own distinct local identity that was more or less controlled by the Versailles metropole. France's first turbulent "American colony" was Paris itself! Did not Mercier recall a remark made by the guards of Versailles describing Parisians as "a foreign people"?[31] And if the point were not clear enough, on the king's relationship to his turbulent neighbor the *Observateur de Paris* (Paris Observer) noted in a chapter titled "Emeutes" (Riots) that "if the Parisian, in his moments of effervescence, were to rebel, he would soon be locked in the giant cage that he inhabits; he would be denied grain; and when there was nothing left in the trough, he would have no option but to beg for mercy and forgiveness."[32]

This is not to suggest that the king, or at least the collective person that was the king, surrounded by the best administrators of France, was not aware of this geopolitical patchwork, or that he did not wish to remedy the situation by completing the construction of a modern suzerainty, which would have been a deformed kind of internal colonization of the kingdom. However, Louis XV's reforms, which attempted a kind of enlightened despotism after 1770 with the aim of unifying the justice system and squelching the rebelliousness of provincial parlements, proved ineffective. Nor did the Turgot reforms, which sought to unify the mercantile space and develop a professional world free of barriers and special privileges, amount to much of anything. Together, these failures gave the impression that this complex situation, in which power was shared between a diminishing absolute monarchy and the increasingly rebellious provinces, was inescapable. This is unmistakable evidence of how different realities can be superimposed over one another, and how words invent the real, giving it a new form. A particularly sensitive term in the eighteenth century was the word "slave." An entire world was economically founded on both slavery and the deportation of millions of African men and women. It would be both misplaced and indecent to speak of slavery in France, particularly in light of the living conditions in, for example, the slave plantations in Saint-Domingue. Yet the word was on everyone's lips and indeed began to function as an efficient and subversive mode of representation. It was as though it referred to an objective reality, as though France were an island of slaves to be liberated, as the dream of 14 July 1790 in Cloots's words would make explicit.[33]

This dark vision of a servile society was paralleled by a unifying discourse that began to emerge in the second half of the eighteenth century among the kingdom's elite circles, and the cult of the nation slowly began to take hold.[34] However, this new identity marker grafted itself onto other, older forms. It did not replace them: both the culture of the land and the ambition to organize politically on the local level remained strong. Moreover, what were people talking about in these enlightened milieus? Keith Baker has shown the extent to which the historiographic and polemic debates of the second half of the eighteenth century were built on a hatred of the nobles, who were considered descendants of the thieving, brutal, barbarian warrior Germans who had *colonized* Gallo-Roman civilization.[35] The majority of natives, namely subjugated Gauls colonized by a foreign elite, would band together with renewed vigor to rediscover their forgotten history and expel these herds of noble degenerates from their recaptured land. This historical discussion was contemporaneous with the grand historic narratives of France by Mably, Duclos, and others. It was eminently political in nature, and in 1789, when a symbolic expulsion of the nobles from France was needed, it had important repercussions.[36] If we read beyond the first page of Sieyès's tract *Qu'est-ce que le Tiers-Etat?* (What Is the Third Estate?), it becomes clear that this text is a kind of call to wage a war of independence by destroying the nobles, described as foreign robbers who must be expelled and sent back to their German forests! Some members of the new National Assembly reclaimed the name of Gaul for the newly minted country. The suggestion was as audacious as the one that would lead the men of Saint-Domingue to christen their new country with its precolonization name: Haïti!

The Tiers-Etat, which perceived itself as "colonized," conceived the idea to wage a war of independence in order to create a new political order, one that would not necessarily be based on a notion of a unique and indivisible nation, but rather on an initial demand for local freedom, which would prefigure a federal republic. This, of course, never came to pass. Did not the Revolution in its most glorious moment (14 July 1790) invent a United States of France in the space of a few weeks—when delegations of National Guards from each department gathered together to swear allegiance to the new federation?

The year 1789 saw a radically new kind of Revolution as a war of independence. The year was an important moment in world history, not only because it promulgated universal principles, but also because the French Revolution adopted a form of emancipation directly inspired by regions that had liberated themselves from their respective metropoles. On the periphery of old worlds, these regions invented the conditions for the possibility of a renaissance of a new world, one founded on the legitimacy of the law and freedom within the law. However, this time, the complexities of the model of "mainland-dominated/interlocked spaces" were developed within the context of European centrality, making the visibility of the revolutionary model imported from colonial spaces more difficult to perceive. The Revolution translated this representation and presented itself as breaking with the past, founding a new union, and resolving divisions. Freedom erased borders and made all men and places equal. Camille Desmoulins was thus able to write: "No longer are we from Chartres or Montlhéry, from Picardy or Brittany, from Aix of Arras; we are all French; we are all brothers."[37]

In fact, the country found itself in a perpetual state of passive or active revolt beginning in the 1770s. And it was precisely at the periphery of the kingdom, in Brittany and Provence and then in Dauphiné, that tensions first broke out, and revolts began to arise. These took the form of regional uprisings from dominated spaces that were sufficiently removed from the center to demand their freedoms as if exasperated by the imperial center Versailles. A detailed study of the two seditions in Brittany and Dauphiné would reveal two different political models, both reflecting political aspirations. The noble elites of the west, in solidarity with the rebellion of the Rennes parlement against the king's men, hoped for the progressive autonomy of their province through local management. They found it increasingly difficult to bear the central authority of Versailles and aimed for a conservative secession based on the demand for reinforced privileges (like those that powerful Saint-Domingue plantation owners wished for themselves). The more heterogeneous elites of Dauphiné drafted a proposition for independence in the summer of 1788 that extended beyond their province and invented the idea of a national union that would bring new unity to the space as a whole. The choice was either a revolution through an accepted division of space that recaptured an ancient but conservative form of independence or a revolution as the invention of a modern and emancipatory uniformity of space freed from old forms of authority.[38]

A third, complex form of revolution also existed, which was attempted before being swept aside due to the circumstances of the war. In the summer of

1789, some French territories demanded, beyond a discourse on the nation and on the unity engendered in the homeland's regeneration, that the new country consciously constitute itself as a new and egalitarian federation. The history of decentering the thematics of the Atlantic revolution from the colonies to the metropoles has yet to be developed. First, it must deconstruct the massive tradition of physiocratic inheritance, in which French rurality is made the only truth of the country, of its conservatism, and even of its progressive ideals. Then, it must go beyond the rhetoric of obedience to the National Convention, which was limited to the episode of the Terror but became a paradigm for the whole Revolution, and which Bronislaw Basczko has shown to be eminently difficult to shake off. Subsequent governments under the Directory also got into the habit of using central administrations to lead the country. Finally, it must free itself of its Napoleonic inheritance, which turned the map of France away from its Atlantic front onto the Rhône/Rhine axis, making centralization the French model of the relationship between governors and governed.[39]

Another history of the Revolution is possible, which would reinstate the colonies as such to their fundamental role as the spark that would ignite the entire Atlantic world. This would restore the periphery to its role as the motor behind the overthrow of 1789 and make clear that revolutions of the second half of the eighteenth century can be grasped only within a globalized vision of wars of independence. The period 1789–90 was an epic version of this kind of war of independence, a unique victory of French-style, unitarian federalism. It was later sacrificed to fratricidal quarrels and the local violence prompted by the counterrevolution. The French Revolution, unlike the American rebels in response to the loyalists, was unable to eradicate its counterrevolution. It is true that social domination by the nobles, which was quite ingrained in local customs, quickly turned the experiment of a decentered federalism into a danger for the nation's unity.

Read in this way, the Revolution appears as a war of independence against the Versailles monarchy. Paradoxically, by asserting three contiguous and superimposed levels of overlapping sovereignty this revolution/decolonization established its originality. On the local level, and as early as December 1789, several tens of thousands of municipalities only recently made official conveyed the enormity of the completed task to the world of foreign political observers. The Revolution was not just French, it was municipal![40] Le Comte de Montlosier, one of the most intelligent counterrevolutionaries, understood this immediately. By making the mayor for the first time a police official who guaranteed public order in his own name (a fact that is still exceptional in Europe), the Revolution decentralized executive power to a hitherto unimaginable degree.[41] Indeed, it gave the mayor, through martial law, more power in his municipality than the king himself had in his kingdom.

Before the centralization of space, the Revolution offered political and civic organizational autonomy to the municipalities of France. This had been all but inconceivable in a country engaged in revolution, a country that was so vast on the map of Europe. This autonomy functioned as a vector of politicization that explains the development of political clubs and associations—a sign of the recognition of freedom of expression—as well as the creation of companies of National Guards, proof of a will to inscribe this radical transformation in a public order invented and self-regulated by citizen-soldiers.

Marie-Vic Ozouf-Marignier has ably researched and elucidated a second level, namely the birth of the *département* (region), an inherently revolutionary institution. With its general council, its Directory (executive committee), its president, and its district attorney, it implied the personal investment of a considerable fraction of the "active" citizens (those meeting voting qualifications), who were legitimated by their election to office. The department was a solution to the paradox of, on the one hand, a desire to preserve freedom through a form of local participation in ever-evolving politics, and on the other, the creation of the conditions for national uniformity, with each department following one set of laws.[42]

The radicalization of the revolutionary process and the atmosphere of tension followed by violence and civil war—complex phenomena with multiple causes and responsibility shared by revolutionaries and counterrevolutionaries alike—made impossible the continuing autonomy of the departments in a peaceful process of national unification. The Revolution became a republic and turned its back on the centrifugal dynamics of rebellion on the French periphery. The outline of a federal republic had been vibrantly embodied by Girondism and especially by popular and federalist Jacobinism in the summer of 1793. It took the rigidity of the Montagnard deputies united around the revolutionary government to repress this current in the fall of 1793.[43] There was no longer any interest in developing departmental dynamics or revitalizing the revolutionary movement; instead, the goal became to construct an image of Paris as a lone fighter against counterrevolutionary France and the European coalition. How remote was the time when the Prussian Francophile baron celebrated the Festival of Federation as the hope for a new world.

And yet, one ought not underestimate the major transformations that 1789 engendered, for the Revolution became a mirror for the world, not because it asserted its principles in the form of a proselytizing universality (even the United States did not claim this), but because, far from being radically different from other revolutions, it conflated the situations of all the other revolutions—municipal in the United Provinces and in Switzerland, provincial in Switzerland and Ireland, both national and federated in the United States. It called on all societies dependent on spiritual, geographical, and political metropoles to liberate themselves and conquer their independence, in Europe and the New World, as the painful experience of Saint-Domingue would soon show.

Because France of 1789 revealed an as-yet-unrecognized face of a degenerate and anarchic metropole, because it was in part an effort of poorly connected regions to liberate themselves and invent the conditions of their independence through shared and equal rights, the country can still be of particular interest for the study of revolutions today. It offers an explanatory matrix applicable to many current political tensions. Unfortunately for its detractors, the Revolution is not over. The politics slandered and discredited in one place can be reborn elsewhere. Like the future, revolution shall endure for a long time, not in France but in China, Tunisia, and Egypt. Since the time of May 1789 or since 1776 or 1640 or 1579, it has formed an infinite spiral, a genesis begun again and always different, tirelessly proposing new conditions of access to citizenship, opening an infinite number of possible ideals for reflection, which then get translated into law. Above all, it imagines political action as a form of collective self-realization founded each time on the intrinsic conquest of new freedoms for the majority.

From the United Provinces in the sixteenth century to the banks of the Mediterranean in the twenty-first century, history tirelessly narrates the never-ending story of the construction of freedom, which is never fully acquired, never entirely conquered. Freedom is elusive because it is multiple. It is rebellion's engine, a refusal of the yoke, the quest of peoples for dignity.

Revolution never repeats itself, because it never ends.

Notes

Introduction

1. Georg W. F. Hegel, *The Philosophy of History*, trans. J. Sibree (New York: Dover, 1956), 285.

2. Edmund Burke, *Reflections on the Revolution in France: and on the proceedings in certain societies in London relative to that event* (London: J. Dodsley, 1790), 11.

3. Marx refers to the French Revolution repeatedly in his work but never gathered his various considerations into one single book. On the class struggle, see Karl Marx, Friedrich Engels, and Eric J. Hobsbawm, *The Communist Manifesto: A Modern Edition* (London: Verso, 1998).

4. Alexis de Tocqueville, *The Old Régime and the French Revolution* (New York: Random House, 1955), foreword.

5. Tocqueville, *The Old Régime and the French Revolution*, 253–54. On Tocqueville's involvement with the French colonization of Algeria, see Jennifer Pitts, *A Turn To Empire: The Rise of Imperial Liberalism in Britain and France* (Princeton, NJ: Princeton University Press, 2005), 204–39.

6. Recent approaches have challenged the classic vision of the "Grande Nation" spreading itself from a French center outward, and emphasized indigenous creativity. See Laurent Dubois, *A Colony of Citizens: Revolution and Slave Emancipation in the French Caribbean, 1787–1804* (Chapel Hill: University of North Carolina Press, 2004); Pierre Serna, ed., *Républiques soeurs: Le Directoire et la Révolution atlantique* (Rennes: Presses Universitaires de Rennes, 2009).

7. Quoted in Laurent Dubois and Aurélien Berra, "'Citoyens et Amis!' Esclavage, citoyenneté et République dans les Antilles françaises à l'époque révolutionnaire," *Annales: Histoire, sciences sociales* 58 (2003): 290.

8. Since Michel-Rolph Trouillot rightly complained of the silencing of the past of Saint-Domingue/Haiti in *Silencing the Past* (Boston: Beacon Press, 1997), countless new books have been published on the Caribbean colonies. Among influential works in this area are John D. Garrigus, *Before Haiti: Race and Citizenship in French Saint-Domingue* (New York: Macmillan, 2006); David Patrick Geggus, *Haitian Revolutionary Studies* (Bloomington: Indiana University Press, 2002); and Laurent Dubois, *Avengers of the New World: The Story of the Haitian Revolution* (Cambridge, MA: Harvard University Press, 2005).

9. R. R. Palmer, *The Age of the Democratic Revolution: A Political History of Europe and America, 1760–1800*, 2 vols. (Princeton, NJ: Princeton University Press, 1959 and 1964); Jacques Léon Godechot, *La Grande Nation: L'expansion révolutionnaire de la France dans le monde de 1789 à 1799* (Paris: Aubier, 1956). Palmer and Godechot contributed a joint paper entitled "The Problem of the Atlantic" to the Tenth International Congress of Historical Sciences in Rome in 1955. Godechot focused on the diffusion of French revolutionary influences while Palmer analyzed the parallels in revolutionary experiences.

10. See the discussion of Jacques Godechot by Emmet Kennedy in *French Historians, 1900–2000: New Historical Writing in Twentieth-Century France*, ed. Philip Daileader and Philip Whalen (Chichester, UK: John Wiley and Sons, 2010), 309–12.

11. Jeremy Adelman, "An Age of Imperial Revolutions," *American Historical Review* 113 (2008): 319–40; David Armitage and Sanjay Subrahmanyam, eds., *The Age of Revolutions in Global Context, c. 1760–1840* (New York: Palgrave Macmillan, 2010); Wim Klooster, *Revolutions in the Atlantic World: A Comparative History* (New York: New York University Press, 2009).

12. Maya Jasanoff, "Revolutionary Exiles: The American Loyalist and French Émigré Diasporas," in Armitage and Subrahmanyam, *Age of Revolutions*, 37–58. On the complexity of America's colonial and colonizing status, see Michael Warner, "What's Colonial about Colonial America," in *Possible Pasts: Becoming Colonial in Early America*, ed. Robert Blair St. George (Ithaca, NY: Cornell University Press, 2000), 49–70; Jack P. Greene, "Colonial History and National History: Reflections on a Continuing Problem," *William and Mary Quarterly* 64 (2007): 235–50.

13. Work on "imperial revolutions" counters the older conception of "Atlantic revolutions" developed by Palmer and Godechot. For Godechot's views see also his *France and the Atlantic Revolution of the Eighteenth Century, 1770–1799*, trans. Herbert H. Rowen (New York: Free Press, 1965).

14. Richard Bessel, Nicholas Guyatt, and Jane Rendall, introduction to *War, Empire, and Slavery, 1770–1830*, ed. Bessel, Guyatt, and Rendall (Basingstoke, UK: Palgrave Macmillan, 2010), 6–7. Bessel, Guyatt, and Rendall emphasize that the era 1770–1830 "may be referred to as an 'age of revolution', yet it was also an age of continuing warfare, with associated patterns of social upheaval, enslavement, rebellion and the movement of populations."

15. C. A. Bayly, "The 'Revolutionary Age' in the Wider World, c. 1790–1830," in Bessel, Guyatt, and Rendall, *War, Empire, and Slavery*, 21–43, quote on p. 21; Bayly, "The Age of Revolutions in Global Context: An Afterword," in Armitage and Subrahmanyam, *Age of Revolutions*, 209–17; Bayly, *The Birth of the Modern World, 1780–1914: Global Connections and Comparisons* (Malden, MA: Wiley-Blackwell, 2004).

16. Michael Lang, "Globalization and Its History," *Journal of Modern History* 78, no. 4 (December 2006): 899–931.

17. We prefer "early modern globalization" to Paul Cheney's term "primitive globalization" but follow his lead in talking about globalization in this period. Paul Cheney, *Revolutionary Commerce: Globalization and the French Monarchy* (Cambridge, MA: Harvard University Press, 2010), 1.

18. M. Charon, *Lettre ou Mémoire historique sur les troubles populaires de Paris, en août et septembre 1788, avec des notes* (London[?], 1788), 16–17, as quoted by Walton in this volume.

19. Cheney, *Revolutionary Commerce*; and Sankar Muthu, *Enlightenment against Empire* (Princeton, NJ: Princeton University Press, 2003).

20. Also see William Max Nelson, "Making Men: Enlightenment Ideas of Racial Engineering," *American Historical Review* 115, no. 5 (December 2010): 1364–94.

21. The French, of course, had not lost their interest in having colonies in North America. On this interest and developments during the French Revolution, see Suzanne Desan,

"Transatlantic Spaces of Revolution: The French Revolution, Sciotomanie, and American Lands," *Journal of Early Modern History* 12 (2008): 467–505.

22. For the concept of "provincializing," and its historiographic value, see Dipesh Chakrabarty, *Provincializing Europe: Postcolonial Thought and Historical Difference* (Princeton, NJ: Princeton University Press, 2000).

1 The Global Underground

1. The corpus of literature on the relationship between the British Empire and industrialization is immense, but see the following reassessments: Patrick K. O'Brien, "Inseparable Connections: Trade, Economy, Fiscal State, and the Expansion of Empire, 1688–1815," in *The Oxford History of the British Empire: The Eighteenth Century*, ed. P. J. Marshall (Oxford: Oxford University Press, 1998), 53–77; Kenneth Pomeranz, *The Great Divergence: China, Europe, and the Making of the Modern World Economy* (Princeton, NJ: Princeton University Press, 2000); Maxine Berg, *Luxury and Pleasure in Eighteenth-Century Britain* (Oxford: Oxford University Press, 2005); Ronald Findlay and Kevin H. O'Rourke, *Power and Plenty: Trade, War, and the World Economy in the Second Millennium* (Princeton, NJ: Princeton University Press, 2007), chaps. 5 and 6; Nualu Zahedieh, "Economy," in *The British Atlantic World, 1500–1800*, ed. David Armitage and Michael J. Braddick (New York: Palgrave Macmillan, 2002), chap. 3.

2. Scholarship on the French Revolution has tended to separate the economic and the political. Whereas Marxists once claimed that the Revolution was the work of a dynamic bourgeoisie that supplanted feudalism with capitalism, revisionists parried that no coherent bourgeoisie existed and that industrial capitalism was not sufficiently developed to act as an agent of revolutionary change. The stalemate led to a postrevisionist turn to political culture, which, although remarkably productive, has marginalized fundamental questions about the history and culture of capitalism.

3. Frederick Cooper, "What Is the Concept of Globalization Good For? An African Historian's Perspective," *African Affairs* 100 (2001): 200. For penetrating accounts of globalization in this period, see A. G. Hopkins, ed., *Globalization in World History* (London: Pimlico, 2002); C. A. Bayly, *The Birth of the Modern World, 1780–1914* (Malden, MA: Blackwell, 2004), chaps. 1–3; Pomeranz, *The Great Divergence*; and Findlay and O'Rourke, *Power and Plenty*, chaps. 5 and 6.

4. Adam Smith, *An Inquiry into the Nature and Causes of the Wealth of Nations*, ed. R. H. Campbell and A. S. Skinner (Indianapolis: Liberty Fund, 1981), 429–662.

5. See the studies listed in notes 1 and 3.

6. Bailey Stone, *The Genesis of the French Revolution: A Global-Historical Interpretation* (Cambridge: Cambridge University Press, 1994); C. A. Bayly, *The Birth of the Modern World*, chap. 3; Paul Cheney, *Revolutionary Commerce: Globalization and the French Monarchy* (Cambridge, MA: Harvard University Press, 2010); Annie Jourdan, *Révolution, une exception française?* (Paris: Flammarion, 2004); Lynn Hunt, "The French Revolution in Global Context," in *The Age of Revolutions in Global Context, c. 1760–1840*, ed. David Armitage and Sanjay Subrahmanyam (New York: Palgrave Macmillan, 2010), 20–36; Jeremy D. Popkin, "Saint-Domingue, Slavery, and the Origins of the French Revolution," in *From Deficit to Deluge: The Origins of the French Revolution*, ed. Thomas Kaiser and Dale Van Kley (Stanford, CA: Stanford University Press, 2011), chap. 7; Marcel Dorigny, ed., *Esclavage, résistances et abolitions* (Paris: CTHS, 1999); and Laurent Dubois, *A Colony of Citizens: Revolution and Slave Emancipation in the French Caribbean, 1787–1804* (Chapel Hill: University of North Carolina Press, 2004).

7. Jacob Price, *France and the Chesapeake: A History of the French Tobacco Monopoly, 1674–1791, and of Its Relationship to the British and American Tobacco Trades*, 2 vols. (Ann Arbor: University of Michigan Press, 1973).

8. This slippage from mercantilism to fiscalism was characteristic of French commercial policy, with the exception of the sugar industry, which was geared toward reexportation. Paul Butel, *Les négociants bordelais, l'Europe et les îles au XVIIIe siècle* (Paris: Aubier, 1974).

9. Edgard Depitre, *La toile peinte en France au XVIIe et au XVIIIe siècles: Industrie, commerce, prohibitions* (Paris: M. Rivière, 1912); Serge Chassagne, *La manufacture de toiles imprimées de Tournemine-lès-Angers: Étude d'une entreprise et d'une industrie au XVIIIe siècle* (Paris: Klincksieck, 1971); Chassagne, *Le coton et ses patrons: France, 1760–1840* (Paris: EHESS, 1991).

10. Glenn Ames, *Colbert, Mercantilism, and the French Quest for Asian Trade* (Dekalb: Northern Illinois University Press, 1996). For the later history of the company, see Philippe Haudrère, *La compagnie française des Indes au XVIII siècle*, 2 vols. (Paris: Les Indes Savantes, 2005).

11. The work of Robert Darnton has drawn wide attention to the underground book trade, but books were merely the tip of the illicit iceberg in the eighteenth century. For a broader exploration of the underground, see André Ferrer, *Tabac, sel, indiennes: Douane et contrebande en Franche-Comté au XVIIIe siècle* (Besançon: Presses Universitaires Franc-Comtoises, 2002). For salt smuggling in particular, see Yves Durand, "La contrebande du sel au XVIIIe siècle aux frontières de Bretagne, du Maine et de l'Anjou," *Histoire sociale* 7 (1974): 227–69; and Micheline Huvet-Martinet, "La répression du faux-saunage dans la France de l'Ouest et du Centre à la fin de l'Ancien Régime (1764–1789)," *Annales de Bretagne et des pays de l'ouest* 84 (1977): 423–43.

12. Archives Nationales (hereafter AN), G-1 106, doss. 1, "Fermes générales, 3e division, Tabac."

13. Price, *France and the Chesapeake*, 1:407. Marc Vigié and Muriel Vigié claim that under Colbert the black market provided nearly two-thirds of the tobacco consumed but, despite an absolute rise in contraband tobacco in the eighteenth century, the proportion of illicit tobacco leveled off to around one-third. Marc Vigié and Muriel Vigié, *L'herbe à nicot: Amateurs de tabac, Fermiers Généraux et contrebandiers sous l'Ancien Régime* (Paris, 1989), chap. 11. According to the calculations of Farmer-General Dupin in 1732, 38 percent of the tobacco consumed in the department of Chalons was illicit. AN, 129 AP 29.

14. [François Véron de Forbonnais], *Examen des avantages et des desavantages de la prohibition des toiles peintes* (Marseille, 1755). In 1701, the council of commerce put the figure at 12 million livres. Charles Cole, *French Mercantilism, 1683–1700* (New York: Columbia University Press, 1943), 176.

15. Chassagne, *La manufacture*, 65; Chassagne, *Le coton*.

16. For the predominance of women and children in salt smuggling, see the works in note 11 and Anne Montenach, "Femmes des montagnes dans l'économie informelle: Les 'faux-saunières' en Haut-Dauphiné au XVIIIe siècle," in *Donne e lavoro: Prospettive per una storia delle montagne europee XVIII-XX secc.*, ed. Nelly Valsangiacomo and Luigi Lorenzetti (Milan: Franco Angeli, 2010), 68–82.

17. AN, Y 9512–13 and 10929/b contain many examples of Parisian dealers.

18. Nils Marten Hakansson Liander, "Smuggling Bands in Eighteenth-Century France" (PhD diss., Harvard University, 1981), 291.

19. Bibliothèque Nationale, MSS Fr. 8476 and 8390. The influx into Geneva of 300,000 pounds of tobacco from Strasbourg, he surmised, accounted for the sudden appearance of smuggling bands in his province. A later report numbered the "scoundrels" working in bands in Savoy and Switzerland at "more than 4 to 500." Service Historique de l'Armée de Terre, 1A 3406, no. 181.

20. Foucault's *Discipline and Punish: The Birth of the Prison*, trans. Alan Sheridan (New York: Vintage, 1979) was written before the publication of major studies on the galleys and

thus did not account for the role of smuggling. For the crackdown on the parallel economy, see Michael Kwass, "The First War on Drugs: Tobacco Trafficking, Criminality, and the Fiscal State in Eighteenth-Century France," in *The Hidden History of Crime, Corruption, and States*, ed. Renate Bridenthal (Oxford: Berghahn Books, forthcoming); Ferrer, *Tabac, sel, indiennes*, 245–98; André Zysberg, *Les galériens: Vies et destins de 60,000 forçats sur les galères de France 1680–1748* (Paris: Seuil, 1987); and Marc Vigié, *Le galériens du roi, 1661–1715* (Paris: Fayard, 1985).

21. The classic statement regarding this shift was formulated by Emmanuel Le Roy Ladurie, "Révoltes et contestations rurales en France de 1675 à 1788," *Annales ESC* 29 (1974): 6–22. Disseminated by Roger Chartier, *The Cultural Origins of the French Revolution*, trans. Lydia G. Cochrane (Durham, NC: Duke University Press, 1991), 141–45, Ladurie's thesis was based on the work of Yves-Marie Bercé, *Histoire des Croquants*, 2 vols. (Geneva: Droz, 1974), which failed to consider the persistence of small-scale fiscal rebellions into the eighteenth century.

22. Jean Nicolas, *La rébellion française: Mouvements populaires et conscience sociale 1661–1789* (Paris: Seuil, 2002), annexe 2. From 1661 to 1789, fully 39 percent of all documented cases of rebellion were fiscal in nature, and 65 percent of such rebellions involved contraband. Jean-Claude Hocquet, *Le sel et le pouvoir* (Paris: Albin Michel, 1985), 404, suggested a similar hypothesis that after the failure of the great antifiscal revolts under Richelieu and Mazarin, smuggling constituted "the new form of struggle."

23. Nicolas Schapira, "Contrebande et contrebandiers dans le nord et de l'est de la France, 1740–1789: Les archives de la commission de Reims" (Mémoire de maîtrise, EHESS, 1991), tables III.14 and III.15; and Liander, "Smuggling Bands," table 16.

24. Norbert Elias, *Power and Civility: The Civilizing Process*, trans. Edmund Jephcott (New York: Pantheon Books, 1982), 91–225.

25. AN, Y 9512/B, report of 27 July 1773.

26. AN, G-7 1292.

27. John Markoff, *The Abolition of Feudalism: Peasants, Lords, and Legislators in the French Revolution* (University Park: Pennsylvania State University Press, 1996), 265.

28. The Gournay circle has received much recent attention. See Simone Meyssonnier, *La balance et l'horloge: La genèse de la pensée libérale en France au XVIIIe siècle* (Paris: Passion, 1989); and Loïc Charles, Frédéric Lefebvre, and Christine Théré, eds., *Le Cercle de Vincent de Gournay: Savoirs économiques et pratiques administratives en France au milieu du XVIIIe siècle* (Paris: INED, 2011).

29. Jacques-Claude-Marie Vincent de Gournay, "Observations sur l'examen des avantages et des désavantages de la prohibition des toiles peintes," in *Examen des avantages et des désavantages de la prohibition des toiles peintes* (Marseille, 1755), 75–76.

30. André Morellet, *Réflexions sur les avantages de la libre fabrication et de l'usage des toiles peintes en France* (Geneva, 1758), 36–37.

31. For recent studies that emphasize the radical implications of the physiocratic embrace of natural law, see Cheney, *Revolutionary Commerce*, chap. 5; Dan Edelstein, *The Terror of Natural Right: Republicanism, the Cult of Nature, and the French Revolution* (Chicago: University of Chicago Press, 2009), 101–11; and Bernard E. Harcourt, *The Illusion of Free Markets: Punishment and the Myth of the Natural Order* (Cambridge, MA: Harvard University Press, 2011). In addition to physiocracy, there was also a less public movement for fiscal reform going on inside the royal administration. Here, the main object of reform was to modernize France by ridding it of internal customs duties while maintaining a protectionist external border. See J. F. Bosher, *The Single Duty Project: A Study of the Movement for a French Customs Union in the Eighteenth Century* (London: Athlone Press, 1964).

32. *Théorie de l'impôt* (1760), 141–44 and 151. Similarly, Pierre Samuel Du Pont would write that the real criminals were not the smugglers but the tax farmers who imposed a "fiscal or monopolistic inquisition detrimental to the natural rights of citizens, to their property, to their civil liberty." *Ephémérides du citoyen* 3 (1769): 180–81.

33. *De l'administration provinciale, et de la réforme de l'impôt* (Basel, 1779), 78 and 81.

34. *Les effets de l'impôt indirect, prouvés par les deux exemples de la Gabelle & du Tabac* (1770), 325–27. Physiocrats' sympathy for smugglers contrasted sharply with their hostility to thieves and vagabonds who threatened to disrupt the market. See Harcourt, *The Illusion of Free Markets*, chaps. 1–4.

35. Archives Départementales de l'Isère B 2325, remonstrances of 17 August 1763.

36. David Jacobson, "The Politics of Criminal Law Reform in Pre-Revolutionary France" (PhD diss., Brown University, 1976).

37. "Remontrances relatives aux impôts, 6 mai 1775," in *Les "Remontrances" de Malesherbes, 1771–1775*, ed. Elisabeth Badinter (Paris: Flammarion, 1985), 167–284.

38. The pressure for reform led to piecemeal policy changes at the end of the Old Regime: the customs dues on imported calico were significantly reduced in 1772, a policy confirmed by the Treaty of Eden in 1786; and, during his first tenure as finance minister from 1776 to 1781, Jacques Necker curbed the practice of tax farming and proposed a thoroughgoing reform of the *gabelle*. But the pace of reform would accelerate dramatically in the opening years of the Revolution.

39. Jacques Godechot, *The Taking of the Bastille, July 14th, 1789*, trans. Jean Stewart (New York: Scribner, 1970), 194; George Rudé, *The Crowd in the French Revolution* (Oxford: Oxford University Press, 1967), 49, 180–81, and appendix IV; and Roger Dion, *Histoire de la vigne et du vin en France des origines au XIXe siècle* (Paris: Poisson, 1959), 511–31.

40. Insurgents in the market town of Ham, for example, interrogated Farm agents about their loyalty to the third estate. Liander, "Smuggling Bands," 211.

41. Gilbert Shapiro and John Markoff, *Revolutionary Demands: A Content Analysis of the Cahiers de Doléances of 1789* (Stanford, CA: Stanford University Press, 1998), chap. 20. For the relationship between direct taxation and revolutionary constructions of citizenship, see Michael Kwass, *Privilege and the Politics of Taxation in Eighteenth-Century France: Liberté, Égalité, Fiscalité* (Cambridge: Cambridge University Press, 2000), chap. 6.

42. Quoted in Marcel Marion, *Histoire financière de la France depuis 1715* (Paris: Rousseau et Cie, 1927), 2:227.

43. *Archives parlementaires de 1787 à 1860*, ed. M.J. Mavidal and M.E. Laurent (Paris: P. Dupont, 1862–), 20:411–14.

44. As a result, underground markets contracted in 1791, but they would expand once again under the Empire, when consumption taxes were reestablished, and import prohibitions were strictly enforced.

45. For the colonial dimension, see Willem Klooster, "Inter-Imperial Smuggling in the Americas, 1600–1800," chap. 4 in *Soundings in Atlantic History: Latent Structures and Intellectual Currents, 1500–1825*, ed. Bernard Bailyn and Patricia L. Denault (Cambridge, MA: Harvard University Press, 2009).

46. Tensions mounted in England as well. See William J. Ashworth, *Customs and Excise: Trade, Production, and Consumption in England, 1640–1845* (Oxford: Oxford University Press, 2003); and Cal Winslow, "Sussex Smugglers," in Douglas Hay, Peter Linebaugh, John G. Rule, E. P. Thompson, and Cal Winslow, *Albion's Fatal Tree: Crime and Society in Eighteenth-Century England* (New York: Pantheon Books, 1975), 119–66.

2 The Global Financial Origins of 1789

1. An excellent overview of the domestic financial issues can be found in Gail Bossenga, "Financial Origins of the French Revolution," in *From Deficit to Deluge: The Origins of the French Revolution*, ed. Thomas E. Kaiser and Dale K. Van Kley (Stanford, CA: Stanford

University Press, 2011), 37–66. See also Marie-Laure Legay, Joël Félix, and Eugene White, "Retour sur les origines financières de la Révolution française," *Annales historiques de la Révolution française* 356 (2009): 183–201.

2. Three works provide essential points of departure: Paul Cheney, *Revolutionary Commerce: Globalization and the French Monarchy* (Cambridge, MA: Harvard University Press, 2010); Guillaume Daudin, *Commerce et prospérité: La France au XVIIIe siècle* (Paris: Presses l'Université Paris–Sorbonne, 2005); and James C. Riley, *International Government Finance and the Amsterdam Capital Market, 1740–1815* (Cambridge: Cambridge University Press, 1980).

3. Michel Morineau, "Budgets de l'état et gestion des finances royales en France au dix-huitième siècle," *Revue historique* 536 (Oct.–Dec. 1980): 289–336, esp. 312.

4. David R. Weir, "Tontines, Public Finance, and Revolution in France and England, 1688–1789," *Journal of Economic History* 49, no. 1 (1989): 95–124, esp. 98.

5. David French, *The British Way in Warfare, 1688–2000* (London: Unwin Hyman, 1990), 91.

6. Jonathan R. Dull, *The Age of the Ship of the Line: The British and French Navies, 1650–1815* (Lincoln: University of Nebraska Press, 2009), 119.

7. On interests rates on the debt, see Guillaume Daudin, "Profitability of Slave and Long-Distance Trading in Context: The Case of Eighteenth-Century France," *Journal of Economic History* 64, no. 1 (2004): 144–71, esp. 167.

8. Riley, *International Government Finance*, 15, 119–94.

9. François R. Velde and David R. Weir, "The Financial Market and Government Debt Policy in France, 1746–1793," *Journal of Economic History* 52, no. 1 (1992): 1–39.

10. The best overview of these practices can be found in David D. Bien, "Offices, Corps, and a System of State Credit: The Uses of Privilege under the Ancien Régime," in *The French Revolution and the Creation of Modern Political Culture: The Political Culture of the Old Regime,* ed. Keith Michael Baker (Oxford: Pergamon Press, 1987), 89–114; Gail Bossenga, *The Politics of Privilege: Old Regime and Revolution in Lille* (Cambridge: Cambridge University Press, 1991).

11. For example, *État de situation de nos finances, au mois d'avril 1787, d'après les bases publiées par M. de Calonne, Ministre, et M. Necker* (n.p., 1787); *Mémoire en réponse de M. de Calonne à l'écrit de M. Necker, publié en Avril 1787, contenant l'examen des comptes de la situation des finances redus en 1774, 76, 81, et 1783* (London, 1788). Historians continue to take sides in this debate. See, for example, Robert D. Harris, "Necker's Compte Rendu of 1781: A Reconsideration," *Journal of Modern History* 42, no. 2 (June 1, 1970): 162–83.

12. On the Caisse d'Escompte and the role of foreign bankers, see Herbert Lüthy, *La banque protestante en France, de la révocation de l'Édit de Nantes à la Révolution* (Paris: S.E.V.P.E.N., 1959–61), 2:435–38.

13. J.C. Riley, "Dutch Investment in France, 1781–1787," *Journal of Economic History* 33, no. 4 (December 1, 1973): 732–60. The currency markets were extraordinarily complex because exchange rates varied daily, yet information about them could not be made available daily at any distance (communication by letter or newspaper took days). They also entered into the negotiation of bills of exchange. Jean Bouchary, *Le marché des changes de Paris à la fin du XVIIIe siècle (1778–1800): Avec des graphiques et le relevé des cours* (Paris: P. Hartmann, 1937).

14. For general trends upward of silver production in the Americas, see the chart on p. 227 of Richard L. Garner, "Long-Term Silver Mining Trends in Spanish America: A Comparative Analysis of Peru and Mexico," in *Mines of Silver and Gold in the Americas,* ed. Peter Bakewell (Aldershot, UK: Variorum, 1997). For the importance of silver to the French economy, see Louis Dermigny, "Circuits de l'argent et milieux d'affaires au XVIIIe siècle," *Revue historique* 212 (1954): 239–78.

15. http://www.slavevoyages.org/tast/assessment/estimates.faces (accessed 24 July 2010).

16. Philippe Haudrère, *La compagnie française des Indes au XVIIIe siècle 1719–1795* (Paris: Librairie de l'Inde, 1989), 4:1, 215.

17. Jan de Vries, "Connecting Europe and Asia," in *Global Connections and Monetary History, 1470–1800*, ed. Dennis Owen Flynn, Arturo Giráldez, and Richard Von Glahn (Aldershot, UK: Ashgate, 2003), 46–47. The French ships were, however, smaller on average than those of their competitors.

18. I am using "banker" in a loose way because the term covered a wide variety of largely unregulated activities. Merchant-bankers carried on commerce and banking activities side by side. Bankers might hold money on deposit, negotiate bills of exchange, and/or simply borrow and invest on behalf of others as well as themselves. They might have an actual "house" or just operate out of their own lodgings. On bills of exchange, see Raymond Adrian De Roover, *L'évolution de la lettre de change, XIVe–XVIIIe siècles*, Affaires et gens d'affaires 4 (Paris: A. Colin, 1953); and André Neurrisse, *Histoire du franc*, 3rd ed. (Paris: Presses Universitaires de France, 1974), 28–29.

19. Paul Butel, "France, the Antilles, and Europe in the Seventeenth and Eighteenth Centuries," in *The Rise of Merchant Empires: Long-Distance Trade in the Early Modern World, 1350–1750*, ed. James D. Tracy (Cambridge: Cambridge University Press, 1993), 153–73. On the links between various parts of the French commercial empire, see Richard Drayton, "The Globalisation of France: Provincial Cities and French Expansion c. 1500–1800," *History of European Ideas* 34 (2008): 424–30.

20. Stanley J. Stein and Barbara H. Stein, *Silver, Trade, and War: Spain and America in the Making of Early Modern Europe* (Baltimore: Johns Hopkins University Press, 2000).

21. In 1753–54, French houses in Cadiz brought in nearly three times as much profit as the Spanish houses; in 1762 (the only other date for which evidence is available), they still brought in more than twice as much, despite the war raging. Didier Ozanam, "La colonie française de Cadix au XVIIIe siècle, d'après un document inédit (1777)," *Mélanges de la Casa de Velazquez* 4 (1968): 259–347, esp. 276.

22. Pedro Tedde, *El Banco de San Carlos (1782–1829)* (Madrid: Banco de España, 1988). The key figure was François Cabarrus, a banker from Bayonne. Michel Zylberberg, *Capitalisme et catholicisme dans la France moderne: La dynastie Le Couteulx* (Paris: Publications de la Sorbonne, 2001), 184–86.

23. Louis Dermigny, "La France à la fin de l'ancien régime: Une carte monétaire," *Annales: Économies, sociétés, civilisations* 10, no. 4 (December 1955): 480–93.

24. Pierre Blancard, *Manuel du commerce des Indes orientales et de la Chine* (Paris: Chez Bernard, 1806), 309–10. Most sources lump silver and gold together, making it impossible to judge their relative importance.

25. No mention of cowries appears in Robert Stein's study of the slave trade, but this is surely an oversight given their ubiquity in other sources. He cites spirits, iron bars, and India cloth—and more generally "pièces de cargaison" (pieces of cargo)—in discussing the purchase of slaves. Robert Louis Stein, *The French Slave Trade in the Eighteenth Century: An Old Regime Business* (Madison: University of Wisconsin Press, 1979), 85.

26. Jan S. Hogendorn and Marion Johnson, *The Shell Money of the Slave Trade*, African Studies Series 49 (Cambridge: Cambridge University Press, 1986), 53.

27. See Robert Harms, *The Diligent: Worlds of the Slave Trade* (New York: Basic Books, 2002), 81. Cowries were also used to pay guards, gatekeepers, and washerwomen in West Africa (245, 252). The one example given by Conan of a ship returning from Bengal in 1787 listed 1,200 mans pacca (1 mans pacca=12 kg; hence 14,400 kg) of cowries from the Maldives, the heaviest item in the cargo except perhaps the saltpeter (about which there was some uncertainty on the manifest). Jules Conan, *La dernière compagnie française des Indes (1785–1875)* (Paris: Marcel Rivière, 1942), 104.

28. As a consequence, the reliability of bills of exchange was paramount. Alarms were set off in late 1786 by the report of a large number of falsified bills circulating in Paris.

My thanks to Miranda Spieler for this reference. *Gazette de Leyde*, 15 December 1786, in the section called "Supplement . . . du numéro C," http://www.gazettes18e.fr/gazette-leyde/annee/1786/page/9985/.

29. On the role of credit in Caribbean commerce, see Pierre Gervais, "A Merchant or a French Atlantic? Eighteenth-Century Account Books as Narratives of a Transnational Merchant Political Economy," *French History* 25, no. 1 (2011): 28–47.

30. For the post-1785 French company, see Conan, *La dernière compagnie française des Indes*, 37–40. Calonne's activities in this regard and more generally in relation to French finances are also discussed by Charles Walton in chapter 3 in this volume.

31. Paul Butel, *The Atlantic*, trans. Iain Hamilton Grant (London: Routledge, 1999), 153–54.

32. Javier Cuenca Esteban, "The British Balance of Payments, 1772–1820: India Transfers and War Finance," *Economic History Review* 54, no. 1 (2001): 58–86.

33. For the British balance, see Philippe Haudrère, *Le grand commerce maritime au XVIIIe siècle: Européens et espaces maritimes* (Condé-sur-Noireau: SEDES, 1997), 107. For the French company, see Conan, *La dernière compagnie française des Indes*, esp. 94–96. Between 1785 and 1789, the French Indies company exported 7 million l. in goods and more than 51 million l. in specie and imported in return only 50 million l. in goods.

34. According to Louis Dermigny, the flow of Spanish silver into France diminished after 1785 because the Banco Nacional insisted on stricter border controls over currency in order to maintain its new position in the market. Dermigny, "Circuits de l'argent et milieux d'affaires," 266.

35. Stanley J. Stein and Barbara H. Stein, *Apogee of Empire: Spain and New Spain in the Age of Charles III, 1759–1789* (Baltimore: Johns Hopkins University Press, 2003), 305–37.

36. Overall, the French balance of trade began to move into negative territory after 1770. Daudin has shown that this was due to the negative balance of colonial trade (not intra-European trade). Profits were made in the colonial trade but largely on financing and on the gap between prices in the metropolitan ports and those in the Caribbean. Daudin, *Commerce et prospérité*, 235–37.

37. See, for example, the often daily accounts for early 1781 in Louis Petit de Bachaumont, Mathieu-François Pidansat de Mairobert, and Barthélemy-François-Joseph Moufle d'Angerville, *Mémoires secrets: pour servir à l'histoire de la république des lettres en France, depuis MDCCLXII jusqu'à nos jours, ou Journal d'un observateur [. . .]*, vol. 17 (London: J. Adamson, 1782).

38. Jacques Necker, *Compte rendu au roi* (Paris: De l'Imprimerie du Cabinet du Roi, 1781), 2–3.

39. On the growth of credit markets, see Mark Potter and Jean-Laurent Rosenthal, "The Development of Intermediation in French Credit Markets: Evidence from the Estates of Burgundy," *Journal of Economic History* 62, no. 4 (2002): 1024–49. On the explosion of private borrowing in the eighteenth century, see Philip T. Hoffman, Gilles Postel-Vinay, and Jean-Laurent Rosenthal, *Priceless Markets: The Political Economy of Credit in Paris, 1660–1870* (Chicago: University of Chicago Press, 2000), 96–113. See also Legay, Félix and White, "Retour sur les origines financières," 195.

40. The new East India Company was set up in April–May 1785. Already by 7 August 1785 Calonne was forced to act with a decree outlawing "marchés à terme" (short selling and other forms of market manipulation without the actual exchange of securities). When the decree's publication induced a rapid decline in market values, the government pulled back from enforcing it. G. Susane, *La tactique financière de Calonne* (New York: B. Franklin, 1972), 257–58.

41. For the machinations concerning stock prices, see George V. Taylor, "The Paris Bourse on the Eve of the Revolution, 1781–1789," *American Historical Review* 67, no. 4 (1962): 951–77; Honoré Gabriel Riquetti de Mirabeau (comte), *Dénonciation de l'agiotage au roi et à*

l'Assemblée des Notables (n.p., 1787). Mirabeau's role and its significance for wider discussions of speculation is covered in detail in John Shovlin, *The Political Economy of Virtue: Luxury, Patriotism, and the Origins of the French Revolution* (Ithaca, NY: Cornell University Press, 2006), 158–73. Charles Walton has found letters from Mirabeau to Calonne written in February 1787 in which Mirabeau expresses his hope that Calonne will help his friends buy shares in the Caisse d'Escompte. Apparently Mirabeau had some kind of falling out with Calonne just about this time. Public Record Office PC 1 Carton 125, #50 and 51.

42. The essential starting point is Jean Bouchary, *Les manieurs d'argent à Paris à la fin du XVIIIe siècle*, 3 vols., Bibliothèque d'histoire économique (Paris: Librairie des Sciences Politiques et Sociales, M. Rivière et Cie, 1939–43). Stock market manipulation was not the only form of financial chicanery. Bankers often got special access to the best rates on French government loans, and insiders hoped for information that would enable them to pick the best loans in which to invest (highest rates, lowest likelihood that the loans would be absorbed into new, lower-rate instruments).

43. Archives Nationales (hereafter AN) T* 646, Papiers d'Étienne Clavière, part 5, Registre. The figures given in this paragraph are my calculations based on his entries into this register. I chose to focus on April 1786 because he seemed to lose interest in complete recording over time. My figures cannot possibly capture the complexity of Clavière's financial dealings; his one entry on 1 April 1786 for "Lettres et billets à payer" (328,883 l.) listed fifty-three different *traites*, *billets*, and *bons au porteur*, all forms of commercial paper, with more than twenty different bankers.

44. Clavière's name does not appear in any of the government registers established to restrain short selling. They were all set up in the last half of 1785. AN, F12 797 B has registers of stock liquidations in the East India Company, the Caisse d'Escompte, and the water company. He may have purchased his shares later or dealt through third parties.

45. Not surprisingly, given the size of his investments, Clavière kept up a frenetic pace of correspondence. Between 28 January 1785 and 10 July 1786 he wrote 526 letters to eighty-three correspondents in twenty-five different European cities. AN, T* 646/2, Copie de lettres.

46. Honoré-Gabriel de Riquetti, comte de Mirabeau, *De la banque de l'Espagne, dite de Saint-Charles* (n.p., 1785); Mirabeau, *Sur les actions de la Compagnie des Eaux de Paris* (London, 1785); Jacques-Pierre Brissot de Warville, *Dénonciation au public d'un nouveau projet d'agiotage; ou, Lettre à M. le comte de S*** . sur un nouveau projet de compagnie d'assurance contre les incendies à Paris, sur ses inconvéniens, & en général sur les inconvéniens des compagnies par actions* (London, 1786); Brissot, *Seconde lettre contre la compagnie d'assurance, pour les incendies à Paris, & contre l'agiotage en général. Adressée à MM. Perrier & compagnie* [the water company] (London, 1786). Bouchary discusses Clavière's manipulations in detail in *Les manieurs d'argent*, 1:11–101. Clavière remained a close ally of Brissot. Jean Marc Rivier, *Étienne Clavière (1735–1793): Un révolutionnaire, ami des noirs* (Paris: Panormitis, 2006).

47. Letter to Pierre Stadnitski, 31 March 1786, cited in Bouchary, *Les manieurs d'argent*, 1:87–88.

48. AN, T* 646/5, entry for 1 April 1786. On Stadnitski and the U.S. debt, see the advertisement in no. 49 of *Nouvelles extraordinaires de divers endroits* (Luzac, 1791). Stadnitski was on the patriot side in the Dutch revolt according to Riley, "Dutch Investment in France," 734.

49. AN, T* 646/4, Livre de Caisse, folios 1 and 11. The opening page (folio 1 left side) gives the date January 1780, but this seems to be an error, as the facing page (folio 1 right side) is dated January 1781, and folio 2 left side begins 16 January 1781 when folio 1 left side had ended 12 January 1780. It is difficult to speak in terms of credit and debit for this account book, as Clavière enters under money coming in commercial paper that sometimes constitutes loans (as well as gold coins), and under money going out everything from household expenses to loan repayments (sometimes with other loans). Therefore my account emphasizes the amounts of money involved rather than their exact status.

50. It should not be assumed from the gap in the account book that Clavière had stopped investing between March 1784 and August 1785. From his letters in this period, it is clear that he was closely following and investing in shares of the Caisse d'Escompte and in the various state loans. See, for example, AN, T*646/1, Journal de lettres, letter to Delessert & Cie in Paris of 25 April 1784. Large sums begin to appear in November 1784 (letter to Baroud, 2 November 1784, concerning nearly 1 million l. in investments, though consisting in part of exchanges between commercial houses with Clavière as intermediary).

51. All the folio pages are those in AN, T* 646/4, Livre de Caisse. The *livre de caisse* and the "*registre*" do not report the same amounts; the first tracks money coming in and out, and the second lists actual holdings and obligations.

52. See table 2 on p. 20 of Velde and Weir, "The Financial Market and Government Debt Policy."

53. Maurice Tourneux, ed., *Correspondance littéraire, philosophique et critique*, vol. 15 (Paris: Garnier Frères, 1877), 33 (entry dated April 1787). It is, however, questionable whether Clavière and Panchaud were allied.

54. Brissot published pamphlets even earlier against the prospect of bankruptcy, no doubt with arguments supplied by Clavière. Jacques-Pierre Brissot de Warville, *Point de banqueroute; ou, Lettres à un créancier de l'état, sur l'impossibilité de la Banqueroute Nationale, & sur les moyens de ramener le crédit & la paix* (London, 1787); Étienne Clavière, *Opinions d'un créancier de l'état: sur quelques matières de finance importantes dans le moment actuel* (Paris: Chez Buisson, 1789). On Clavière's fascinating life story, surprisingly little has been published. Rivier's biography, *Etienne Clavière (1735–1793)*, is heavily dependent on Bouchary's groundbreaking work.

55. For an introduction to the life cycles of capital at the time, see George V. Taylor, "Types of Capitalism in Eighteenth-Century France," *English Historical Review* 79, no. 312 (1964): 478–97.

3 The Fall from Eden

1. *Considerations on the Political and Commercial Circumstances of Great Britain and Ireland . . .* (London: Debrett, 1787), 1.

2. The phrase belongs to the Marquess of Carmarthen, the British foreign secretary, in 1786; see John Ehrman, *The British Government and Commercial Negotiations with Europe, 1783–1793* (Cambridge: Cambridge University Press, 1962), 185.

3. Albert Hirschman, *The Passions and the Interests: Political Arguments for Capitalism before Its Triumph* (Princeton, NJ: Princeton University Press, 1977); David A. Bell, *The First Total War: Napoleon's Europe and the Birth of Warfare as We Know It* (Boston: Houghton Mifflin, 2007), 73; Daniel Gordon, *Citizens without Sovereignty: Equality and Sociability in French Thought, 1670–1789* (Princeton, NJ: Princeton University Press, 1994), esp. 129–75. Not all political economists subscribed to the *doux commerce* thesis: Paul Cheney, *Revolutionary Commerce: Globalization and the French Monarchy* (Cambridge, MA: Harvard University Press, 2010), esp. 156–58.

4. William Petty, Marquis of Lansdowne, *The Speech of the Right Honourable the Earl of Shelburne, in the House of Lords, on Monday, February 13, 1783, on the articles of peace* (Ipswich, [1783]), 4.

5. British National Archives (Kew), Public Records Office (hereafter PRO), FO (Foreign Office) 4, "General Correspondence before 1906: United States," carton 2, "David Hartley Papers," doc. 39, letter, Hartley to the foreign secretary, May 1783.

6. Paul Cheney, "A False Dawn for Enlightenment Cosmopolitanism? Franco-American Trade during the American War of Independence," *William and Mary Quarterly*, 3rd ser., 63, no. 3 (July 2006): 485.

7. Marie Donaghay, "The Ghosts of Ruined Ships: The Commercial Treaty of 1786 and the Lessons of the Past," in *The Consortium on Revolutionary Europe Proceedings*, ed. Harold T. Parker, Louise S. Parker, and John C. White (Athens, GA: Consortium on Revolutionary Europe, 1981), 112.

8. In 1783, Vergennes asked the controller general of finances to relax the wartime trade restrictions on British goods, in part to use this renewed trade as leverage with Britain; Marie Donaghay, "The Anglo-French Negotiations of 1786–1787" (PhD diss., University of Virginia, 1970), 42. For France's return to prohibitions in 1785: *Arrêt du Conseil d'État du Roi, qui renouvelle les anciennes défenses d'introduire dans le Royaume, aucunes Toiles de coton et Mousselines venant de l'Étranger . . . du 10 juillet 1785* (Paris: Imprimerie Royale, 1785) and *Arrêt du Conseil d'État du Roi, concernant les marchandises étrangères, prohibées dans le Royaume, 17 juillet 1785* (Paris: Imprimerie Royale, 1785).

9. A French spy operating in England reported on the great number of petitions drafted for the upcoming session of Parliament; PRO, PC (Privy Council) 1 "Miscellaneous Unbound Papers," carton 123, letter, Joseph Anselme to the French administration, London, 8 November 1785.

10. British Library (hereafter BL), Auckland Papers, carton 34421, docs. 121–22, William Eden to Gilbert Elliot, 19 April 1786.

11. PRO, PC 1, carton 123, "Observations sur la Note concernant la Base du Traité de commerce, communiquées par Monsieur le comte de Vergennes à Monsieur le Contrôleur Général," included in "Troisième mémoire sur le Traité de commerce entre la France et l'Angleterre."

12. Donaghay, "The Ghosts of Ruined Ships," 111–18; Donaghay, "The Anglo-French Negotiations," 33–57. For Vergennes's diplomatic strategy, see John Hardman and Munro Price, eds., *Louis XVI and the Comte de Vergennes: Correspondence, 1774–1787* (Oxford: Voltaire Foundation, 1998), esp. 105.

13. Donaghay, "The Ghosts of Ruined Ships," 115.

14. Ibid.

15. Philippe Haudrère, *La Compagnie française des Indes au XVIIIe siècle, 1719–1795*, 2nd ed. (Paris: Les Indes Savantes, 2005), 2:751–815.

16. Frederick L. Nussbaum, "The Formation of the New East India Company of Calonne," *American Historical Review* 38, no. 3 (April 1933): 475–97.

17. Ibid., 490.

18. Ibid.

19. Ibid., 494–96.

20. PRO, PC 1, carton 123, doc. 22, "Troisième mémoire sur le Traité de commerce entre la France et l'Angleterre," p. 259.

21. BL, Auckland Papers, carton 34420, docs. 142–44, "A Few General Observations on the Trade between Great Britain and France," 25 October 1785.

22. PRO, PC 1, carton 123, doc. 15, "Observations."

23. *Observations de la Chambre du Commerce de Normandie sur le Traité de Commerce entre la France et l'Angleterre. Suivi du Plan d'une Banque nationale de France* (Rouen, [1788]), 28.

24. Pierre-Samuel Dupont de Nemours, *Lettre à la chambre du commerce de Normandie, sur le mémoire qu'elle a publié relativement au traité de commerce avec l'Angleterre* (Paris: Moutard, 1788), 7.

25. Ibid., 102–4, for bureaucratic obstacles; 170–71, for the undervaluing of imports by French customs.

26. Dupont de Nemours, *Lettre à la chambre du commerce de Normandie*, 104. See also Georges Weulersse, *La physiocratie à l'aube de la Révolution, 1781–1792* (Paris: EHESS, 1985), 263–64.

27. Philippe Minard, *La fortune du colbertisme: État et industrie dans la France des Lumières* (Paris: Fayard, 1998), 218; Wilma J. Pugh, "Calonne's 'New Deal'," *Journal of Modern History* 11, no. 3 (September 1939): 301.

28. Caroline Weber, *Queen of Fashion: What Marie-Antoinette Wore to the Revolution* (New York: Hold, 2006), 175; Nussbaum, "The Formation of the New East India Company," 494–96; Loïc Charles and Guillaume Daudin, "Le Bureau de la balance du commerce au XVIIIe siècle," *Revue d'histoire moderne et contemporaine* 58, no. 1 (January–March 2009): 143.

29. Minard, *La fortune du colbertisme*, 440 n. 20. Earmarking subsidies for other uses was common: Herbert Lüthy, *La banque protestante en France de la révocation de l'Édit de Nantes à la Révolution (1730–1794)* (Paris: SEVPEN, 1961), 2:690.

30. Dupont de Nemours, *Lettre à la chambre du commerce de Normandie*, 77. See Léon Cahen, "Une nouvelle interprétation du Traité franco-anglais de 1786–1787," *Revue historique* 185, no. 1 (January–June 1939): 273; Cahen looked in ministerial papers for complaints against the treaty, but many circulated at the local level; see Matthieu de Oliveira, "Le négoce nordiste d'un traité franco-anglais à l'autre: Attentes, réceptions et aménagements (1786–1802)," in *Le négoce de la paix: Les nations et les traités franco-britanniques (1713–1802); Actes de la journée d'étude de Rouen du 6 juin 2003*, ed. Jean-Pierre Jesenne, Renaud Morieux, and Pascal Dupuy (Paris: Société des Études Robespierristes, 2008), 174–75. Censored newspapers found roundabout ways to criticize the treaty through book reviews; see Colin Jones, "The Great Chain of Buying: Medical Advertisement, the Bourgeois Public Sphere, and the Origins of the French Revolution," *American Historical Review* 101, no. 1 (1996): 38 n. 104.

31. Already in October 1787, the Norman town of Elbeuf saw half its workers lose their jobs. Between 1786 and the end of 1787, Troyes saw its workshops drop from 3,000 to 1,157. In Sedan, 1,000 workshops employing 15,000 workers in 1786 were reduced to 200, leaving 9,000 unemployed. Charles Schmidt, "La crise industrielle de 1788 en France," *Revue historique* 97 (1908): 79–80, 83.

32. For the earthenware industry, see Pierre Dardel, *Commerce, industrie et navigation à Rouen et au Havre au XVIIIème siècle: Rivalité croissante entre ces deux ports, la conjuncture* (Rouen: Société Libre d'Émulation de la Seine-Maritime, 1966), 64. For rising emigration rates, see Jean-Pierre Bardet, *Rouen aux XVIIe et XVIIIe siècles: Les mutations d'un espace social; Documents* (Paris: SEDES-Paris, 1983), p. 111, table 87 ("Quotient d'emigration pour 1000 familles"); for bankruptcies, p. 113, table 90 ("Faillites enregistrées par les Consuls"). The most dramatic spike in bankruptcies corresponded to the period when the administration was tacitly allowing British goods into France; it began dropping around 1787 but remained high through 1789.

33. Oliveira, "Le négoce nordiste d'un traité franco-anglais," 174.

34. Archives municipales de Lille, carton 17.998, "Commerce et industrie, 1790–1819," report of 28 January 1791, *Observations des fabricants des fils retords du Département du Nord, sur le Projet de permettre l'importation en France des fils retords étrangers moyennant un droit de Traite* (Douai: Derbaix, [1791]), 5.

35. Cahen, "Une nouvelle interprétation du Traité franco-anglais"; W.O. Henderson, "The Anglo-French Commercial Treaty of 1786," *Economic History Review*, new ser., 10, no. 1 (1957).

36. French customs were already tolerating fraudulent declarations, as the administration explained in one of its memoirs during the treaty negotiations: PRO, PC 1, carton 123, doc. 22, "Troisième mémoire sur le Traité de commerce entre la France et l'Angleterre," pp. 263–64.

37. BL, Auckland Papers, carton 34421, fols. 92–94, letter, William Eden to Lord Carmarthen, 13 April 1786. Ambroise-Marie Arnould, director of the Balance of Trade Office

in the early Revolution noted that trade between France and Britain had begun booming with the Peace of Paris in 1783: *De la balance du commerce et des relations commerciales extérieures de la France dans toutes les parties du globe, particulièrement à la fin du règne de Louis XIV et au moment de la Révolution* (Paris: Buisson, 1791; Geneva: Slatkine, 1983), 1:173.

38. Insurance rates for smuggling goods from Birmingham and Manchester to France went from 6 to 10 percent after France declared prohibitive tariffs in 1785. BL, Auckland Papers, carton 34421, docs. 48–49.

39. Richard Munthe Brace, "The Anglo-French Treaty of Commerce of 1786: A Reappraisal," *The Historian* 47, no. 2 (March 1947): 160.

40. See the chart on wine exports from the port of Bordeaux in Philippe Gardey, *Négociants et marchands de Bordeaux, de la guerre d'Amérique à la Restauration (1780–1830)* (Paris: Presses de l'Université Paris-Sorbonne, 2009), 223. For taxes on French wines in Britain, including a new consumption tax, see François Dumas, *Étude sur le Traité de commerce de 1786 entre la France et l'Angleterre* (Toulouse: Privat, 1904), 147.

41. Charles Ludington, "'Claret is the liquor for boys; port for men': How Port Became the 'Englishman's Wine,' 1750s to 1800," *Journal of British Studies* 48, no. 2 (2009): 364–90.

42. Henderson, "The Anglo-French Commercial Treaty of 1786," 110.

43. Alan Forrest, *Society and Politics in Revolutionary Bordeaux* (London: Oxford University Press, 1975), 51. Cahen, a revisionist of the treaty, argues that Bordeaux was already overproducing glass before the treaty was implemented. Cahen, "Une nouvelle interprétation du Traité franco-anglais," 279. The assertion begs the very question that was so contentious at the time: obviously, Bordeaux glassworks were overproducing in the face of an influx of cheaper British glass.

44. Judith A. Miller, *Mastering the Market: The State and the Grain Trade in Northern France, 1700–1860* (Cambridge: Cambridge University Press, 1999), 110–11.

45. Jean-François de Tolozan [or Tolosan], *Mémoire sur le commerce de la France et de ses colonies* (Paris: Moutard, 1789), 5.

46. Miller, *Mastering the Market*, 117–19.

47. Schmidt, "La crise industrielle," 88.

48. Ibid., 91; Oliveira, "Le négoce nordiste d'un traité franco-anglais," 175.

49. Schmidt, "La crise industrielle," 82.

50. Dardel, *Commerce, industrie et navigation*, 65.

51. Quoted in Oliveira, "Le négoce nordiste d'un traité franco-anglais," 175.

52. Jérome Mavidal and Émile Laurent, eds., *Archives parlementaires de 1787 à 1860*, 1st ser. (hereafter *AP*) (Paris: Dupont, 1875–1913), 6:431.

53. *AP* 2:402.

54. *AP* 5:516.

55. Tolozan, *Mémoire sur le commerce de la France et de ses colonies*, 47, 105.

56. Edouard Boyetet, *Recueil de divers mémoires, relatifs au traité de commerce avec l'Angleterre, faits avant, pendant et après cette négociation* (Versailles: Baudouin, 1789), 1.

57. *Observations sur la lettre [de Dupont de Nemours] à la Chambre du commerce de Normandie . . .* (1788); balance-of-trade data for 1787 appears on p. 95; estimations for the first six months of 1788 on p. 109.

58. Arnould, *De la balance du commerce*, 1:181.

59. Renaud Morieux, "Les nations et les intérêts: Les manufacturiers, les institutions représentatives et le langage des intérêts dans le traité de commerce franco-anglais de 1786–1787," in *La concurrence des saviors: France–Grande-Bretagne, XVIIIe-XIXe siècles*, ed. Christophe Charle and Julien Vincent (Rennes: Presses Universitaires de Rennes, 2011), 39–74.

60. Orville T. Murphy, "DuPont de Nemours and the Anglo-French Commercial Treaty of 1786," *Economic History Review* 19, no. 3 (1966): 573.

61. Quoted in Auguste Arnauné, *Le commerce extérieur et les tarifs de douane* (Paris: Alcan, 1911), 99.

62. Archives Nationales, F12 "Commerce et industrie," carton 652, "Mémoire adressé aux députés du bailliage de Rouen par les entrepreneurs des manufactures de Louviers," mentioned in Fernand Gerbaux and Charles Schmidt, eds., *Procès-verbaux des Comités d'agriculture et de commerce* (Paris: Imprimerie nationale, 1906), 1:49 n. 1.

63. Arthur Young, *Travels, during the years 1787, 1788, and 1789* (Bury St. Edmunds: J. Rackham for W. Richardson, 1792), 73.

64. M. Charon, *Lettre ou Mémoire historique sur les troubles populaires de Paris, en août et septembre 1788, avec des notes* (London[?], 1788), 16–17.

65. *Aux Français, sur le 14 juillet* [no author or publication information], Bibliothèque historique de la ville de Paris, call number 12029, 1–2.

66. *Observations de la Chambre du Commerce de Normandie sur le Traité de Commerce*, 115–16.

67. *AP* 1:720.

68. J.-J. Vernier, *Les cahiers de doléances du bailliage de Troyes et du bailliage du Bar-sur-Seine* (Troyes: Nouel, 1909), 3:197–98.

69. Jean Tarrade, "Le groupe de pression du commerce à la fin de l'Ancien Régime et sous l'Assemblée constituante," *Bulletin de la Société d'histoire moderne* (1970): 25.

70. Ibid., 24–25.

71. See Gerbaux and Schmidt, *Procès-verbaux des Comités d'agriculture et de commerce*, passim.

72. *AP* 21:135.

73. Ibid., 138, 143.

74. Jean Clinquart, "Les avatars de la 'Police du commerce extérieur' (1789–1799)," in *État, finances et économie pendant la Révolution française: Colloque tenu à Bercy les 12, 13, 14 octobre 1989 . . . [organisé par le] Comité pour l'histoire économique et financière de la France* (Paris: Imprimerie Nationale, 1991), 538.

75. Jean Clinquart, *L'administration des douanes en France sous la Révolution* (Paris: Association pour l'Histoire des Douanes, 1978), esp. 71, 91, 164.

76. Minard, *La fortune du colbertisme*, 350–72.

77. Steven L. Kaplan, *La fin des corporations* (Paris: Fayard, 2001), 615.

78. PRO, PC 1, carton 124, doc. 148, "Articles proposés par l'évêque d'Autun [Talleyrand] au ministère anglais et réponses du cabinet de St. James (de la main de Christin)."

79. Ehrman, *The British Government and Commercial Negotiations with Europe*, 194 n. 4.

80. Ibid., 220–21. Trade statistics generated by the French administration, which are less reliable, nevertheless show a similar trend; Dumas, *Étude sur le Traité de commerce*, 146.

81. Edna Hindie Lemay, ed., *Dictionnaire des constituants, 1789–1791* (Paris: Universitas, 1991), 1:415.

82. Jeff Horn, *The Path Not Taken: French Industrialization in the Age of Revolution* (Cambridge, MA: MIT Press, 2006).

4 1685 and the French Revolution

I would like to thank the volume's editors, the Press's anonymous reader, Jeffrey Collins, and Rebecca Manley for their helpful comments on earlier versions of this chapter.

1. See Elisabeth Labrousse, *La révocation de l'Édit de Nantes: Une foi, une loi, un roi?* (Paris: Payot, 1990).

2. John Marshall, *John Locke, Toleration, and Early Enlightenment Culture: Religious Intolerance and Arguments for Religious Toleration in Early Modern and "Early Enlightenment" Europe* (Cambridge: Cambridge University Press, 2006), 18.

3. Eckart Birnstiel and Chrystel Bernat, eds., *La diaspora des Huguenots: Les réfugiés protestants de France et leur dispersion dans le monde (XVIe-XVIIIe siècles)* (Paris: Champion, 2001).

4. Myriam Yardeni, *Le refuge huguenot: Assimilation et culture* (Paris: Champion, 2002), 33–34.

5. Historians have, however, revised an older view that the revocation of the Edict of Nantes severely damaged France's economy. See Myriam Yardeni, "Naissance et essor d'un mythe: La révocation de l'Édit de Nantes et le déclin économique de la France," in *Repenser l'histoire: Aspects de l'historiographie huguenote des Guerres de religion à la Révolution française* (Paris: H. Champion, 2000), 191–206.

6. Dale Van Kley, *The Religious Origins of the French Revolution: From Calvin to the Civil Constitution, 1560–1791* (New Haven, CT: Yale University Press, 1996); Catherine-Laurence Maire, *De la cause de Dieu à la cause de la Nation: Le Jansénisme au XVIIIe siècle* (Paris: Gallimard, 1998).

7. Jules Michelet, *Histoire de France, nouvelle édition revue et augmentée* (Paris: Marpon, 1879), 15:4.

8. Paul Hazard, *La crise de la conscience européenne (1680–1715)*, 3 vols. (Paris: Boivin, 1935).

9. On "intellectual origins," see Denis Richet, "Autour des origines idéologiques lointaines de la Révolution française: Élites et despotisme," *Annales: Histoire, sciences sociales* 24 (1969): 1–23; and Keith Michael Baker, "On the Problem of the Ideological Origins of the French Revolution," in *Inventing the French Revolution: Essays on French Political Culture in the Eighteenth Century* (Cambridge: Cambridge University Press, 1990), 12–27.

10. Van Kley, *The Religious Origins of the French Revolution*, 8.

11. On the role of France's domestic Protestant population in the desacralization of the monarchy, see Jeffrey Merrick, *The Desacralization of the French Monarchy in the Eighteenth Century* (Baton Rouge: Louisiana State University Press, 1990), chap. 6.

12. Bayle and Jurieu disagreed themselves, however, about such fundamental issues as whether absolutism was a legitimate form of government and whether states should practice religious toleration. See Elisabeth Labrousse, "The Political Ideas of the Huguenot Diaspora (Bayle and Jurieu)," in *Church, State, and Society under the Bourbon Kings of France*, ed. Richard M. Golden (Lawrence, KS: Coronado Press, 1982).

13. Hazard, *La crise de la conscience européenne*; E.S. de Beer, "The Huguenots and the Enlightenment," *Proceedings of the Huguenot Society of London* 21 (1967): 179–95; Marshall, *John Locke, Toleration, and Early Enlightenment Culture*; and, in a different form, Jonathan Israel, *Radical Enlightenment: Philosophy and the Making of Modernity, 1650–1750* (Oxford: Oxford University Press, 2001).

14. On Bayle, see above all Elisabeth Labrousse, *Pierre Bayle*, 2 vols. (The Hague: M. Nijhoff, 1963).

15. Gustave Leopold Van Roosbroeck, *Persian Letters before Montesquieu* (New York: Publications of the Institute of French Studies, 1932).

16. Lynn Hunt, Margaret C. Jacob, and Wijnand Mijnhardt, *The Book That Changed Europe: Picart & Bernard's Religious Ceremonies of the World* (Cambridge, MA: Belknap Press of Harvard University Press, 2010).

17. Hugh Trevor-Roper, "A Huguenot Historian: Paul Rapin," in *Huguenots in Britain and Their French Background, 1550–1800*, ed. Irene Scouloudi (Basingstoke, UK: Macmillan Press, 1987); M.G. Sullivan, "Rapin, Hume, and the Identity of the Historian in Eighteenth-Century England," *History of European Ideas* 28 (2002): 145–62.

18. Yardeni, *Le refuge huguenot*, 29, 35; Geoffrey Adams, *The Huguenots and French Opinion, 1685–1787: The Enlightenment Debate on Toleration* (Waterloo, Ont.: Wilfred Laurier University Press, 1991); Marshall, *John Locke, Toleration, and Early Enlightenment Culture*.

19. Jurieu in particular was skeptical of religious toleration. Labrousse, "The Political Ideas of the Huguenot Diaspora (Bayle and Jurieu);" Marshall, *John Locke, Toleration, and Early Enlightenment Culture*.

20. J.G.A. Pocock, *The Machiavellian Moment: Florentine Political Thought and the Atlantic Republican Tradition* (Princeton, NJ: Princeton University Press, 1975); Martin van Gelderen and Quentin Skinner, eds., *Republicanism: A Shared European Heritage*, vol. 1, *Republicanism and Constitutionalism in Early Modern Europe* (Cambridge: Cambridge University Press, 2002), pt. 3.

21. David Lieberman, "The Mixed Constitution and the Common Law," in *The Cambridge History of Eighteenth-Century Political Thought*, ed. Mark Goldie and Robert Wokler (Cambridge: Cambridge University Press, 2006), 318.

22. "Revive" because the Huguenot writers of the late sixteenth century, notably Hotman in *Francogallia*, had argued for a version of mixed government.

23. Quoted in Lieberman, "The Mixed Constitution and the Common Law," 337. Delolme in particular strayed quite far from the traditional notion of mixed government. On the broader developments in this discourse in the eighteenth century, see Lieberman; and David Wootton, "Liberty, Metaphor, and Mechanism: 'Checks and Balances' and the Origins of Modern Constitutionalism," in *Liberty and American Experience in the Eighteenth Century*, ed. David Womersley (Indianapolis: Liberty Fund, 2006).

24. François Furet and Mona Ozouf, *Terminer la révolution: Mounier et Barnave dans la Révolution française* (Grenoble: Presses Universitaires de Grenoble, 1990), intro. and pt. 1; Aurelian Craiutu, *A Virtue for Courageous Minds: Moderation in French Political Thought, 1748–1830* (Princeton, NJ: Princeton University Press, 2012), chap. 3.

25. Baker, *Inventing the French Revolution*, chap. 11; Timothy Tackett, *Becoming a Revolutionary: The Deputies of the French National Assembly and the Emergence of a Revolutionary Culture (1789–1790)* (Princeton, NJ: Princeton University Press, 1996), 188–94.

26. François Furet, "Concepts juridiques et conjoncture révolutionnaire," *Annales: Histoire, sciences sociales* 47 (1992): 1187.

27. For a suggestive account of the intellectual origins of this unitary conception of sovereignty and the rejection of mixed government, see Jean-Fabien Spitz, "Une archéologie du jacobinisme: Quelques remarques sur la 'thèse royale' dans la seconde moitié du 18e siècle," *Dix-huitième siècle* 39 (2007): 385–414.

28. See my *Reimagining Politics after the Terror: The Republican Origins of French Liberalism* (Ithaca, NY: Cornell University Press, 2008), chap. 1, esp. 35–42.

29. René-Louis de Voyer, marquis d'Argenson, *Mémoires et journal inédit du marquis d'Argenson, ministre des affaires étrangères sous Louis XV* (Paris: Jannet, 1857), 5:346.

30. Rachel Hammersley has likewise recently emphasized the role of the Huguenot exiles in transmitting English republicanism to France, but she places substantially less emphasis on the ideal of mixed government. See Hammersley, *The English Republican Tradition and Eighteenth-Century France: Between the Ancients and the Moderns* (Manchester: Manchester University Press, 2010), chap. 2.

31. *Nouvelles de la République des Lettres*, March 1700, 243–69; April 1700, 426–56; May 1700, 553–79; September 1700, 243–63.

32. Ibid., September 1700, 244, 252.

33. Ibid., 258.

34. Hammersley, *The English Republican Tradition*, 36.

35. Ibid.

36. *Bibliothèque britannique*, vol. 9 (1737), 408–30; ibid., vol. 16 (1740), 48–86.

37. Ibid., vol. 16 (1740), 50.

38. Samson, translator's preface to Algernon Sidney, *Discours sur le gouvernement*, trans. P.A. Samson (The Hague: L. et H. Van Dole, 1717), 6recto.

39. Ibid., 381, 389; English from the original, Algernon Sidney, *Discourses Concerning Government*, ed. Thomas G. West (Indianapolis: Liberty Classics, 1990), 166, 169.

40. Edouard Tillet, *La constitution anglaise, un modèle politique et institutionnel dans la France des Lumières* (Aix-en-Provence: Presses Universitaires d'Aix-Marseille, 2001), 149.

41. D'Argenson, *Mémoires et journal inédit*, 5:271.

42. Hammersley, *The English Republican Tradition*, 34, 39–40.

43. Margaret Jacob, *The Radical Enlightenment: Pantheists, Freemasons, and Republicans* (London: Allen & Unwin, 1981), 20–21; Hammersley, *The English Republican Tradition*, 35.

44. Labrousse, "The Political Ideas of the Huguenot Diaspora," 222–27; Guy Howard Dodge, *The Political Theory of the Huguenots of the Dispersion, with Special Reference to the Thought and Influence of Pierre Jurieu* (New York: Octagon Books, 1972), 6–7. See also Jean Marie Goulemot, *Le règne de l'histoire: Discours historiques et révolutions, XVIIe–XVIIIe siècle* (Paris: A. Michel, 1996), 53–57; and Éric Gojosso, *Le concept de République en France (XVIe–XVIIIe siècle)* (Aix-en-Provence: Presses Universitaires d'Aix-Marseille, 1998), 237–45.

45. Charles-Louis de Secondat, baron de Montesquieu, *De l'esprit des lois* [1748], in *Oeuvres complètes*, ed. Roger Caillois (Paris: Gallimard, 1949–51), 2:304.

46. Edmond Dziembowski, "The English Political Model in Eighteenth-Century France," *Historical Research* 74, no. 184 (May 2001): 151–71; Richard Whatmore, "French Perspectives on British Politics, 1688–1734," in *Les idées passent-elles la Manche? Savoirs, représentations, pratiques (France-Angleterre, Xe–XXe siècles)*, ed. Jean-Philippe Genêt and François-Joseph Ruggiu (Paris: PUPS, 2007). In a different vein, Paul Cheney has recently emphasized the interest in English and also Dutch political models among those who sought to improve France's trade and economy, many of whom wrote in the service of the monarchy. See Cheney, *Revolutionary Commerce: Globalization and the French Monarchy* (Cambridge, MA: Harvard University Press, 2010).

47. On the emergent French discussion, see Elie Carcassonne, *Montesquieu et le problème de la constitution française au XVIIIe siècle* (Paris: Presses Universitaires de France, 1927), chap. 1.

48. Tillet, *La constitution anglaise*, 26–27.

49. Quoted in Tillet, *La constitution anglaise*, 60.

50. Tillet, *La constitution anglaise*, 60. See also, Dodge, *The Political Theory of the Huguenots*, 232–33.

51. Whether Calvinism contained an internal disposition to republicanism is disputed. For a classic statement that it did, see Hans Baron, "Calvinist Republicanism and Its Historical Roots," *Church History* 8 (1939): 30–42.

52. This paragraph is based on Trevor-Roper, "A Huguenot Historian"; M.G. Sullivan, "Rapin de Thoyras, Paul de (1661–1725)," *Oxford Dictionary of National Biography*, online ed. (Oxford: Oxford University Press, 2004–), http://www.oxforddnb.com/view/article/23145.

53. Joseph Dedieu, *Montesquieu et la tradition politique anglaise en France: Les sources anglaise de l'"Esprit des lois"* (Paris: J. Gabalda, 1909); Nelly Girard d'Albissin, *Un précurseur de Montesquieu: Rapin-Thoyras, premier historien français des institutions anglaises* (Paris: Klincksieck, 1969); Tillet, *La constitution anglaise*.

54. Trevor-Roper, "A Huguenot Historian," 13; Sullivan, "Rapin de Thoyras, Paul de."

55. Paul de Rapin de Thoyras, *Dissertation sur les Whigs et les Torys* (The Hague: Charles Le Vier, 1717), 1, 3.

56. Paul de Rapin de Thoyras, *Histoire d'Angleterre* (The Hague: Alexandre de Rogissart, 1724), 7:8, 264–67; 9:2.

57. J.G. A Pocock, *The Ancient Constitution and the Feudal Law: A Study of English Historical Thought in the Seventeenth Century*, reissue with a retrospect (Cambridge: Cambridge University Press, 1987), 364; Trevor-Roper, "A Huguenot Historian," 5, 15.

58. On the distinction between political and juridical or technical constitutional balance, see Charles Eisenmann, "La pensée constitutionnelle de Montesquieu," *Cahiers de philosophie politique* 2–3 (1984–85): 35–66 (originally published in 1952).

59. Girard d'Albissin, *Un précurseur de Montesquieu*, 46–47; Rapin de Thoyras, *Histoire*, 1:xiv.

60. Patrick Collinson, *De Republica Anglorum: Or History with the Politics Put Back* (Cambridge: Cambridge University Press, 1990), 23.

61. René-Louis de Voyer, marquis d'Argenson, *Considérations sur le gouvernement ancien et présent de la France* (Amsterdam: Marc Michel Rey, 1764), 3. D'Argenson's *Considérations* was not published until 1764, but it circulated in manuscript and was read by, among others, Voltaire and Rousseau.

62. Rapin de Thoyras, *Histoire*, 1:475.

63. Rapin de Thoyras, *Dissertation*, 1–4; Rapin de Thoyras, *Histoire*, 1:iv.

64. Catherine Larrère, review of *La constitution anglaise, un modèle politique et institutionnel dans la France des Lumières*, by Edouard Tillet, *Revue Montesquieu* 5 (2001): 205.

65. Rapin de Thoyras, *Histoire*, 1:477.

66. Rapin de Thoyras, *Dissertation*, 183–84.

67. Quoted in Tillet, *La constitution anglaise*, 247.

68. Dedieu, *Montesquieu et la tradition politique anglaise*, 84, 91.

69. Carroll Joynes, "The Gazette De Leyde: The Opposition Press and French Politics, 1759–1757," in *Press and Politics in Pre-Revolutionary France*, ed. Jack Censer and Jeremy Popkin (Berkeley: University of California Press, 1987); Jeremy Popkin, *News and Politics in the Age of Revolution: Jean Luzac's "Gazette De Leyde"* (Ithaca, NY: Cornell University Press, 1989).

70. Popkin, *News and Politics in the Age of Revolution*, x.

71. Elizabeth L. Eisenstein, *Grub Street Abroad: Aspects of the French Cosmopolitan Press from the Age of Louis XIV to the French Revolution* (Oxford: Clarendon Press, 1992), 111.

72. Ibid., 118–28.

73. The decree of 15 December 1790, which stood until 1945, has been the subject of surprisingly little scholarship. See Eckart Birnstiel, "Le retour des Huguenots du Refuge en France: De la Révocation à la Révolution," *Bulletin de la Société de l'histoire du protestantisme français* 4 (1989): 785–87.

74. See my *Reimagining Politics after the Terror*. On Théremin's return, see Alain Ruiz, "Le retour au 'pays des ancêtres' en 1795 du huguenot Charles-Guillaume Théremin, diplomate prussien puis citoyen français," *Cahiers d'études germaniques* 13 (1987): 73–83.

75. Charles-Guillaume Théremin, *De la Situation intérieure de la République* (Paris, 1797); Théremin to Sieyès, 12 Fructidor, Year 3 (29 August 1795), Archives Nationales, 284 AP 17–8/10.

76. Germaine de Staël, another key liberal thinker of the post-Terror period, was a Protestant who was born in France but was not of French Protestant descent (her father, Jacques Necker, France's director general of finance in 1776–81 and 1788–89, had moved from Geneva to Paris in 1747). On Staël and the origins of French liberalism, see my *Reimagining Politics after the Terror*, chap. 3. I do not wish to suggest that Protestantism informed liberalism in a philosophical sense. For an important argument that Constant's Protestantism informed his liberalism in just such a sense, however, see Helena Rosenblatt, *Liberal Values: Benjamin Constant and the Politics of Religion* (Cambridge: Cambridge University Press, 2008).

5 Colonizing France

For comments on previous drafts, I would like to thank my coeditors and Charles Walton. This paper was written while I was a fellow at the Institute for Historical Studies at the University of Texas at Austin. I would like to extend a special thanks to the Institute and its director, Julie Hardwick.

1. François-René de Chateaubriand, *Memoires d'outre-tombe* (Paris: Gallimard, 1997), 1:428.

2. Arthur Young, *Travels in France, during the Years 1787, 1788, 1789*, ed. M. Betham-Edwards, 3rd ed. (London, 1890), 123.

3. See Michèle Duchet, *Anthropologie et histoire au siècle des Lumières* (Paris: Albin Michel, 1995).

4. Seigneur de Montbrun, quoted in Mona Ozouf, *Festivals and the French Revolution*, trans. Alan Sheridan (Cambridge, MA: Harvard University Press, 1988), 236. For the letter to Paris, see A. Gazier, ed., *Lettres à Grégoire sur les patois de France, 1790–1794* (Paris, 1880; repr., Geneva: Slatkine, 1969), 84–85.

5. On literary silences and material culture, see Madeleine Dobie, *Trading Places: Colonization and Slavery in Eighteenth-Century French Culture* (Ithaca, NY: Cornell University Press, 2010); on internal colonization, see Christopher Hodson, "Colonizing the *Patrie*: An Experiment Gone Wrong in Old Regime France," *French Historical Studies* 32, no. 2 (Spring 2009): 193–222; and on colonialism and the sciences, see James E. McClellan III and François Regourd, "The Colonial Machine: French Science and Colonization in the Ancien Régime," in "Nature and Empire: Science and the Colonial Enterprise," ed. R. MacLeod, special issue, *Osiris* 15 (2001): 31–50.

6. Pierre Rosanvallon, *Democracy Past and Future*, ed. Samuel Moyn (New York, 2006), 82.

7. On the different ideas of regeneration and their transformations over the course of the Revolution, see Mona Ozouf, *L'homme régénéré: Essais sur la Révolution française* (Paris: Gallimard, 1989); and Antoine de Baecque, *The Body Politic: Corporeal Metaphor in Revolutionary France, 1770–1800*, trans. Charlotte Mandell (Stanford, CA: Stanford University Press, 1997), 131–56; David A. Bell, *The Cult of the Nation in France: Inventing Nationalism, 1680–1800* (Cambridge, MA: Harvard University Press, 2001); and Andrew Jainchill, *Reimagining Politics after the Terror: The Republican Origins of French Liberalism* (Ithaca, NY: Cornell University Press, 2008), 62–107.

8. Ruth F. Necheles, *The Abbé Grégoire, 1787–1831: The Odyssey of an Egalitarian* (Westport, CT: Greenwood Publishing, 1971), 53–54; and Alyssa Goldstein Sepinwall, *The Abbé Grégoire and the French Revolution: The Making of Modern Universalism* (Berkeley: University of California Press, 2005), 92–93.

9. Scholars like Ozouf and Bourguet have brilliantly traced the development of internal ethnography and statistics in the revolutionary and Napoleonic eras, but the connection to earlier colonial history has been generally overlooked. Mona Ozouf, *L'école de la France: Essais sur la Révolution, l'utopie et l'enseignement* (Paris: Gallimard, 1984), 27–54, 351–79; Ozouf, *Festivals and the French Revolution*, 217–23; and Marie-Noëlle Bourguet, *Déchiffrer la France: La statistique départementale à l'époque napoléonienne* (Paris: Éditions des archives contemporaines, 1989). For an exception, acknowledging earlier colonization, see the short paragraph in André Burguière, "Monarchical Centralization and the Birth of Social Sciences: Voyagers and Statisticians in Search of France at the End of the Eighteenth Century," in *Tocqueville and Beyond: Essays in Honor of David D. Bien*, ed. Robert M. Schwartz and Robert A. Schneider (Newark, DE: University of Delaware Press, 2003), 229.

10. Joseph-Marie Lequinio, *Voyage dans le Jura* (Paris, Year IX [1800]), 1:10–12. On Buffon and his position within the field of natural history, see Jacques Roger, *Buffon: A Life in Natural History*, trans. Sarah Lucille Bonnefoi, ed. L. Pearce Williams (Ithaca, NY: Cornell University Press, 1997); and E.C. Spary, *Utopia's Garden: French Natural History from Old Regime to Revolution* (Chicago: University of Chicago Press, 2000).

11. Michel Vovelle, *De la cave au grenier: Un itinéraire en Provence au XVIIIe siècle* (Quebec: S. Fleury, 1980), 407–35; Bourguet, *Déchiffrer la France*, 21–46; Daniel Roche, *France in the Enlightenment*, trans. Arthur Goldhammer (Cambridge, MA: Harvard University Press, 1998), 11–40; and Amy S. Wyngaard, *From Savage to Citizen: The Invention of the Peasant in the French Enlightenment* (Newark, DE: University of Delaware Press, 2004), 151–71.

On the vague and clichéd nature of much of the earlier information, see Bourguet, *Déchiffrer la France*, 27–28; and Burguière, "Monarchical Centralization," 228–29.

12. Wyngaard, *From Savage to Citizen*, 162.

13. C. Dralet, *Plan détaillé topographique, suivi de la topographie du département du Gers* (Paris, year IX [1800–1801]), 19.

14. See Constantin-François Volney, *Questions de statistique à l'usage des voyageurs* [1795], in *Œuvres* (Paris: Fayard, 1989), 1:673; and the works of Degérando and Cuvier in *Aux origines de l'anthropologie française: Les mémoires de la Société des Observateurs de l'Homme en l'an VIII*, ed. Jean Copans and Jean Jamin (Paris: Le Sycomore, 1978), 129–69, 173–76.

15. Sergio Moravia, "The Enlightenment and the Science of Man," *History of Science* 18, no. 4 (December 1980): 247–68; Michèle Duchet, *Anthropologie et histoire au siècle des Lumières* (Paris, 1995); and Christopher Fox, Roy Porter, and Robert Wokler, eds., *Inventing Human Science: Eighteenth-Century Domains* (Berkeley: University of California Press, 1995).

16. Jacques Roger, *The Life Sciences in Eighteenth-Century French Thought*, ed. Keith R. Benson, trans. Robert Ellrich (Stanford, CA: Stanford University Press, 1997); Phillip R. Sloan, "The Gaze of Natural History," in Fox, Porter, and Wokler, *Inventing Human Science*, 126–41; Sloan, "Natural History," in *The Cambridge History of Eighteenth-Century Philosophy*, ed. Knud Haakonssen (New York: Cambridge University Press, 2005), 2:911–24; and Peter Hanns Reill, *Vitalizing Nature in the Enlightenment* (Berkeley: University of California Press, 2005).

17. Georges-Louis Leclerc, comte de Buffon, *Les époques de la nature* (1778), ed. Jacques Roger (Paris: Éditions du Muséum, 1988), 220.

18. Ozouf, *L'homme régénéré*; Baecque, *The Body Politic*; Bell, *The Cult of the Nation*; and Jainchill, *Reimagining Politics*.

19. The connections between colonialism and the anthropological perspective of Enlightenment natural history is thoroughly analyzed by Duchet, *Anthropologie et histoire*.

20. Duchet, *Anthropologie et histoire*, 116.

21. Roger, *Buffon*, 382.

22. Duchet, *Anthropologie et histoire*, 260.

23. On colonial networks, global travelers, bio-prospecting, and acclimatization in the development of Enlightenment natural history, see also Spary, *Utopia's Garden*; Lisbet Koerner, *Linnaeus: Nature and Nation* (Cambridge, MA: Harvard University Press, 1999); Londa Schiebinger and Claudia Swan, eds., *Colonial Botany: Science, Commerce, and Politics in the Early Modern World* (Philadelphia: University of Pennsylvania Press, 2005); and James E. McClellan III, *Colonialism and Science: Saint Domingue in the Old Regime* (Baltimore: Johns Hopkins University Press, 1992).

24. For a sophisticated approach to Grégoire's eccletic beliefs, and their transformation over time, see Sepinwall, *The Abbé Grégoire*.

25. Abbé Henri Grégoire, *Rapport sur les destructions opérées par le vandalisme, et sur les moyens de le réprimer: Séance du 14 fructidor, l'an second de la République une et indivisible* (Paris, 1794), 22.

26. Abbé Henri Grégoire, *Rapport sur l'ouverture d'un concours pour les livres élémentaires de la première éducation: Séance du 3 pluviôse, l'an second de la République une et indivisible*, in *Procès-verbaux du Comité d'Instruction Publique de la Convention Nationale*, ed. J. Guillaume (Paris, 1894), 3:365. On the distance between what the people are and what they could be, see also Grégoire, *Sur les moyens d'améliorer l'agriculture en France*, in *Procès-verbaux du Comité d'Instruction Publique*, 2:472; and Grégoire, "Réflexions extraites d'un ouvrage du citoyen Grégoire sur les moyens de perfectionner les sciences politiques," in *Mémoires de l'Institut national des sciences et des arts: Sciences morales et politiques* 1 (1798): 554.

27. On the importance of his relationship with the Société des Philantropes of Strasbourg, see Sepinwall, *The Abbé Grégoire*, 25–34.

28. *Statuts généraux de la Société des Philantropes* [of Nancy], *rédigés dans les comices de 1776* (n.p., n.d.; repr., n.p. 1932), 3, 43, 45.

29. Ibid., 46–47.

30. He refers to Linnaeus, Bexon (a collaborator of Buffon), Lavater, Legrand d'Aussy, Cambry, and Papon, among others; Abbé Henri Grégoire, "Promenade dans les Vosges," ed. A. Benoît, *Annales de société d'émulation du département des Vosges* 71 (1895): 227–30, 270, 273. Also see the reprinted excerpt recounting another trip, "Voyages de l'abbé Grégoire dans les Vosges," in *Voyages anciens et modernes dans les Vosges: Promenades, descriptions, souvenirs, lettres, etc, 1500–1870*, ed. Louis Jouve (Épinal, 1881), 87–99.

31. Charles-Augustin Vandermonde, *Essai sur la manière de perfectionner l'espèce humaine*, 2 vols. (Paris, 1756).

32. William Max Nelson, "Making Men: Enlightenment Ideas of Racial Engineering," *American Historical Review* 115, no. 5 (December 2010): 1364–94.

33. Michael E. Winston, *From Perfectibility to Perversion: Meliorism in Eighteenth-Century France* (New York: Peter Lang, 2005), 120–50; Sean M. Quinlan, *The Great Nation in Decline: Sex, Modernity, and Health Crises in Revolutionary France, c. 1750–1850* (Aldershot, UK: Ashgate, 2007), 111–44; and Xavier Martin, *Human Nature and the French Revolution: From Enlightenment to the Napoleonic Code* (New York: Berghahn Books, 2001), 164.

34. Abbé Henri Grégoire, *Essai sur la régénération physique, morale et politique des Juifs: Ouvrage couronné par la Société Royale des Sciences et des Arts de Metz, le 23 août 1788* (1788; Paris: Flammarion, 1988), 75. On Grégoire's *Essai* in general, see Sepinwall, *The Abbé Grégoire*, 56–77.

35. Sepinwall, *The Abbé Grégoire*, 95–96, 193.

36. Ibid., 193.

37. Abbé Henri Grégoire, "Sur la nécessité et les moyens d'anéantir les patois et d'universaliser l'usage de la française," presented to the Convention Nationale on 16 prairial Year II [4 June 1794], in *Une politique de la langue: La Révolution française et les patois; L'enquête de Grégoire*, ed. Michel de Certeau, Dominique Julia, and Jacques Revel (Paris: Gallimard, 1975), 303.

38. Grégoire, *Sur les moyens d'améliorer l'agriculture en France*, 469.

39. On Grégoire's collaboration with André Thouin, see Spary, *Utopia's Garden*, 227.

40. Grégoire, *Sur les moyens d'améliorer l'agriculture en France*, 469–70.

41. Ibid., 470.

42. Grégoire, "Sur la nécessité et les moyens d'anéantir les patois."

43. On the ways that François de Neufchâteau was radicalized as a magistrate in Saint-Domingue, see James Livesey, "A Revolutionary Career? François de Neufchâteau Does Well by Doing Good, 1774–1794," *French History* 18, no. 2 (2004): 186–92. On his life and career more generally, see Livesey, "An Agent of Enlightenment in the French Revolution: Nicolas-Louis François de Neufchâteau, 1752–1800" (PhD diss., Harvard University 1994); and Dominique Margairaz, *François de Neufchâteau: Biographie intellectuelle* (Paris: Publications de la Sorbonne, 2005).

44. De Marbois to François de Neufchâteau, Port-au-Prince, 15 February 1787, Archives Nationales, 27 AP 11 (2); quoted in Livesey, "A Revolutionary Career?" 191.

45. On the colonies and the 286 censuses, see J. Dupâquier and E. Vilquin, "Le pouvoir royal et la statistique démographique," in *Pour une histoire de la statistique* (Paris: Institut National de la Statistique et des Études Économiques, 1978), 1:83–101. On the colonies and the nominative census, see Robert Bradley Scafe, "The Measure of Greatness: Population and the Census under Louis XIV" (PhD diss., Stanford University, 2005), 116–52.

46. See the tables appended to Nicolas-Louis François de Neufchâteau, *Mémoire en forme de discours sur la disette du numéraire à Saint-Domingue, et sur les moyens d'y remédier* (Cap François, 1788), n.p.

47. Neufchâteau, *Mémoire en forme de discours*.

48. On the grand statistical project and its significance, see Jean-Claude Perrot and Stuart J. Woolf, *State and Statistics in France, 1789–1815* (New York: Harwood, 1984); and Bourguet, *Déchiffrer la France*.

49. Nicolas-Louis François de Neufchâteau, *Recueil des lettres circulaires, instructions, programmes, discours, et autres actes publics, émanés du Cen François (de Neufchâteau), pendant ses deux exercices du Ministère de l'intérieur* (1799–1802), 2:166.

50. On the Observers of Man, see Jean-Luc Chappey, *La Société des Observateurs de l'Homme: Des anthropologues au temps de Bonaparte* (Paris: Société des études robespierristes, 2002).

51. Joseph-Marie Degérando, "Considérations sur les diverses méthods à suivre dans l'observation des peuples sauvages" (1800), in Copans and Jamin, *Aux origines de l'anthropologie française*, 128.

52. On Degérando and the Observers of Man in the history of anthropology, see George W. Stocking, Jr., *Race, Culture, and Evolution: Essays in the History of Anthropology* (Chicago: University of Chicago Press, 1982), 13–41; and Chappey, *La Société des Observateurs de l'Homme*.

53. Louis-François Jauffret, "Introduction aux mémoires de la Société des Observateurs de l'Homme," in Copans and Jamin, *Aux origines de l'anthropologie française*, 74.

54. Jauffret, "Introduction," 78.

55. On "internal colonization" during the Revolution and the nineteenth century, see Eugen Weber, *Peasants into Frenchmen: The Modernity of Rural France, 1870–1914* (Stanford, CA: Stanford University Press, 1976), 3–23, 485–96; and Certeau, Julia, and Revel, *Une politique de la langue.*

56. Susan Buck-Morss, *Hegel, Haiti, and Universal History* (Pittsburgh: University of Pittsburgh Press, 2009).

6 Foreigners, Cosmopolitanism, and French Revolutionary Universalism

For their helpful suggestions and questions, I would like to thank Paul Hanson, Lynn Hunt, Katie Jarvis, William Nelson, and Timothy Tackett.

1. *Archives parlementaires de 1787 à 1860: Recueil complet des débats législatifs et politiques des chambres françaises*, 1st ser. (hereafter *AP*) (Paris: Librairie administrative de Paul Dupont, 1879–), 48:688–89, 24 Aug. 1792; Projet de décret, *AP* 49:40, 26 Aug. 1792.

2. Chénier, Basire, Lasource, *AP* 48:688–91, 24 Aug. 1792.

3. Robert Palmer, *The Age of Democratic Revolution* (Princeton, NJ: Princeton University Press, 1959–64), 2:54–55, quote p. 54; Michael Rapport, *Nationality and Citizenship in Revolutionary France: The Treatment of Foreigners 1789–1799* (Oxford: Clarendon Press, 2000), 137–38; Thomas J. Schlereth, *The Cosmopolitan Ideal in Enlightenment Thought* (Notre Dame, IN: University of Notre Dame Press, 1977), 132–33; Albert Mathiez, *La Révolution et les étrangers* (Paris: La Renaissance du livre, 1918), 75–78; Patrick Weil, *How to Be French: Nationality in the Making since 1789*, trans. Catherine Porter (Durham, NC: Duke University Press, 2008), 14–16; Peter Sahlins, *Unnaturally French: Foreign Citizens in the Old Regime and After* (Ithaca, NY: Cornell University Press, 2004), 276–78; Sophie Wahnich, *L'impossible citoyen: L'étranger dans le discours de la Révolution française* (Paris: Albin Michel, 1997), 175–81.

4. For an introduction, see Naomi Schor, "Universalism," in *The Columbia History of Twentieth-Century French Thought*, ed. Lawrence D. Kritzman (New York: Columbia University Press, 2006), 344–48. Historians and theorists have disagreed on at least two questions: Was universalism inherently and discursively exclusionary? To what extent did potential citizens have to surrender their particular cultural practices and identities and assimilate to French categories in order to qualify as citizens? Influential approaches include Laurent Dubois, *A Colony of Citizens: Revolution and Slave Emancipation in the French Caribbean,*

1787–1804 (Chapel Hill, NC: University of North Carolina Press, 2004); Lynn Hunt, *Inventing Human Rights* (New York: W. W. Norton, 2007); Joan Scott, *The Politics of the Veil* (Princeton, NJ: Princeton University Press, 2007); Wahnich, *L'impossible citoyen*.

5. Recent work on globalization emphasizes that although universalism makes global claims, its language and practices are always hybrid, continually constructed in negotiation with local and contingent forces. Anna Lowenhaupt Tsing, *Friction: An Ethnography of Global Connection* (Princeton, NJ: Princeton University Press, 2005), esp. introduction; A.G. Hopkins, ed., *Global History: Interactions between the Universal and the Local* (Houndsmill, UK: Palgrave Macmillan, 2006); Michael Lang, "Globalization and Its History," *Journal of Modern History* 78 (2006): 899–931.

6. Marc Belissa, *Fraternité universelle et intérêt national (1713–1795): Les cosmopolitiques du droit des gens* (Paris: Éditions Kimé, 1998).

7. *Révolutions de Paris*, quoted in Mona Ozouf, *Festivals and the French Revolution*, trans. Alan Sheridan (Cambridge, MA: Harvard University Press, 1988), 66–69; Sophie Wahnich, *La longue patience du peuple: 1792, Naissance de la République* (Paris, 2008: Éditions Payot & Rivages), 221–30.

8. F. Braesch, *La Commune du dix août 1792: Étude sur l'histoire de Paris du 20 juin au 2 décembre 1792* (Paris: Hachette et cie, 1911); Paul R. Hanson, *Contesting the French Revolution* (Oxford: Wiley-Blackwell, 2009), 87–96; and Hanson, *The Jacobin Republic under Fire: The Federalist Revolt and the French Revolution* (University Park: Pennsylvania State University Press, 2003), 33–44.

9. *AP* 48:688–91, 24 Aug. 1792; Projet de décret, *AP* 49:40, 26 Aug. 1792.

10. Belissa, *Fraternité universelle*, esp. 50–119; Gonthier-Louis Fink, "Cosmopolitisme," in *Dictionnaire européen des Lumières*, ed. Michel Delon (Paris: Presses universitaires de France, 1997), 277–79; Paul Hazard, "Cosmopolite," in *Mélanges d'histoire littéraire, générale et comparée, offerts à Fernand Baldensperger* (Paris: H. Champion, 1930), 1:353–64; Margaret C. Jacob, *Strangers Nowhere in the World: The Rise of Cosmopolitanism in Early Modern Europe* (Philadelphia: University of Pennsylvania Press, 2006); Elise Lipkowitz, "'The Sciences Are Never at War?': The Scientific Republic of Letters in the Era of the French Revolution, 1789–1815" (PhD diss., Northwestern University, 2009); Sophia Rosenfeld, "Citizens of Nowhere in Particular: Cosmopolitanism, Writing, and Political Engagement in Eighteenth-Century Europe," *National Identities* 4 (2002): 25–43.

11. Chénier, Lamourette, Vergniaud, *AP* 48:688–91; Projet de décret, *AP* 49:40, 26 Aug. 1792.

12. Joachim-Heinrich Campe, *Briefe aus Paris zur Zeit der Revolution*, quoted in Louis Kientz, *J. H. Campe et la Révolution française* (Paris: H. Didier, 1939), 22, (see also pp. 6–13 on the duke); Gonthier-Louis Fink, "The French Revolution as Reflected in German Literature and Political Journals from 1789 to 1800," in *The Internalized Revolution: German Reactions to the French Revolution, 1789–1989*, ed. Ehrhard Bahr and Thomas P. Saine (New York: Garland Publishing, 1992), 11–31.

13. Guadet, Hérault de Séchelles (not named, except as president of the Assembly), *AP* 48:689–91, 24 Aug. 1792; Rosenfeld, "Citizens of Nowhere in Particular."

14. *Journal des débats et des décrets*, no. 332, quoted in James Guillaume, *Études révolutionnaires* (Paris: Stock, 1908–9), 2:432; Lamourette, *AP* 48:689, 24 Aug. 1792.

15. *Courrier des 83 départements*, no. 26, 26 Aug. 1792; Chénier, *AP* 48:689, 24 Aug 1792. E. Puccinelli, "Gorani, Giuseppi," in *Dizionario biografico degli Italiani* (Rome: Istituto della Enciclopedia italiana, 2002), 58:4–8.

16. Chabot, *AP* 48:690; Barère, *AP* 52:577, 19 Oct. 1792.

17. *Courrier des 83 départements*, no. 26, 26 Aug. 1792; *Annales patriotiques et littéraires de la France, et Affaires politiques de l'Europe*, no. 239, 26 Aug. 1792.

18. *AP* 48:690.

19. Lamourette, *AP* 48:689, 24 Aug. 1792; Philippe Roger, *L'ennemi américain: Généalogie de l'antiaméricanisme français* (Paris: Seuil, 2002), 38–49; Durand Echeverria, *Mirage in the West: A History of the French Image of American Society to 1815* (Princeton, NJ: Princeton University Press, 1957), 7–14.

20. James Mackintosh, *Vindiciae Gallicae: Defence of the French Revolution and Its English Admirers against the Accusation of the Right Honourable Edmund Burke* (London: G. G. J. and J. Robinson, 1791), 220; Anacharsis Cloots, *La République universelle, ou adresse aux tyrannicides* (Paris: Chez les marchands de nouveautés, an IV de la liberté [1792]), 3, 12, 155. On regeneration, see chapter 5 by William Nelson in this volume.

21. Thuriot, Lasource, *AP* 48:689–91, 24 Aug. 1792.

22. Basire, *AP* 48:689–91, 24 Aug. 1792.

23. To categorize the deputies' political allegiances, I used Alison Patrick, *The Men of the First French Republic: Political Alignments in the National Convention of 1792* (Baltimore: Johns Hopkins University Press, 1972). Factional lines were not yet clearly drawn in August 1792, but I follow the conventional practice of using "Girondins" and "Montagnards" to identify these groups. Far Left journalists ignored the debate while the major Girondin papers covered it.

24. *AP* 48:690.

25. Projet de décret, *AP* 49:10, 26 Aug. 1792.

26. Belissa, *Fraternité universelle*; Rosenfeld, "Citizens of Nowhere in Particular." David A. Bell argues controversially that this decree also carried the commitment to wage "total war," if necessary, against nations that did not embrace revolutionary ideology. Bell, *The First Total War: Napoleon's Europe and the Birth of Warfare as We Know It* (Boston: Houghton Mifflin Harcourt, 2007), chap. 3, esp. 108–9.

27. *Courrier des 83 départements*, no. 26, 26 Aug. 1792.

28. Chénier, *AP* 48:689, 24 Aug.1792; Friedrich Klopstock, "Sie und nicht Wir," quoted in R. Vieux, "La Révolution française jugée par un poète allemand: Essai sur les odes révolutionnaires de Klopstock," in *Mélanges Henri Lichtenberger* (Paris: Stock, 1934), 225. Klopstock's poem, "Der Freiheitskrieg," in the summer of 1792 chastised the Germans for wanting the "blood of this people" who had banished wars of conquest. Jean Murat, *Klopstock: Les thèmes principaux de son oeuvre* (Paris: Les Belles Lettres, 1959), 266–77. Belissa, *Fraternité universelle*, 47–49, 196. Between 1786 and 1789, Bentham circulated writings privately that were published after his death as *Plan for Universal and Perpetual Peace*. See Benjamin Sacks, *Peace Plans of the Seventeenth and Eighteenth Centuries* (Sandoval, NM: Coronado Press, 1962), 12, 100–104.

29. *Chronique de Paris* no. 230, 26 Aug. 1792.

30. Vergniaud, *AP* 48:689, 24 Aug. 1792; *Le Patriote français*, no. 1112, 26 Aug. 1792.

31. *Courrier des 83 départements*, no. 26, 26 Aug. 1792.

32. Chénier, *AP* 48:689, 24 Aug.1792; David Williams, *Leçons à un jeune prince, sur la disposition actuelle de l'Europe à une Révolution générale* (1790). Damian Walford Davies, "David Williams (1738–1816)," in *Oxford Dictionary of National Biography*, online ed. (Oxford: Oxford University Press, 2004–); Jerzy Lukowski, *The Partitions of Poland: 1772, 1793, 1795* (London: Longman, 1999), chap. 6.

33. *AP* 48:688, 24 Aug. 1792. Hamilton also may have been misread as favorable to the Revolution because in 1790 he had initiated payments of interest on the Americans' debt to France. Palmer suggests that the French associated Jefferson (the more obvious choice) with Lafayette and assumed that, at this moment, Hamilton as an author of the *Federalist* was more sympathetic to the Revolution than Jefferson was. Palmer, *Age of Democratic Revolution*, 2:55.

34. Peter Onuf and Nicholas Onuf, *Federal Union, Modern World: The Law of Nations in an Age of Revolutions, 1776–1814* (Madison, WI: Madison House, 1993); Belissa, *Fraternité*

universelle, 147–64. My thanks to John Kaminski and Kenneth Bowling for their aid with American politics.

35. Anacharsis Cloots, *Bases constitutionelles du genre humain* (Paris: Imprimerie natio-nale, 1793), 21; Jeremy Bentham, *Emancipate Your Colonies! Addressed to the National Conven-tion of France, Anno 1793*, in *The Works of Jeremy Bentham, Published under the Superintendence of his Executor, John Bowring* (Edinburgh: W. Tait, 1838–43), 4:407–18. Given to Talleyrand's secretary in 1793, this work was not published until 1830. Bentham's defense of colonial liberty and "the rights of men" omitted slaves' freedom.

36. To give but one example, in the name of "liberty and the free exercise of sovereignty so solemnly promised to the Belgians," representatives of Belgium in January 1793 exhorted their French occupiers to recognize that sovereignty and demonstrate "before the universe" that the French renunciation of conquest had not been an empty lie. Quoted in Belissa, *Fraternité universelle*, 336–37.

7 Feminism and Abolitionism

I am grateful to Charles Walton for commenting on an earlier version of this chapter, which I presented at the Consortium on the Revolutionary Era, 1750–1850 conference in Tallahassee in March 2011. In addition to the editors of this volume, whose advice helped me refine my argument, Doris Kadish, Jann Matlock, Karen Offen, Jared Poley, Cynthia Radding, and Anne Verjus read earlier versions and offered valuable suggestions. The re-search and writing of this chapter took place at the National Humanities Center, where I had the good fortune to spend the 2010–2011 academic year as a resident fellow, funded by a Burkhardt Fellowship from the American Council of Learned Societies. I appreciate the feedback I received from fellows in the writing group there.

1. "The Declaration of the Rights of Man and Citizen," in *The French Revolution and Human Rights: A Brief Documentary History*, ed. and trans. Lynn Hunt (Boston: Bedford St. Martins, 1996), 78. On the contradictions inherent in the Declaration's commitment to "universal" rights, see Christine Fauré, "From the Rights of Man to Women's Rights: A Difficult Intellectual Conversion," in *Political and Historical Encyclopedia of Women*, ed. Christine Fauré, trans. Richard Dubois et. al. (New York: Routledge, 2003), 109–20.

2. True feminist movements, with the necessary organizations and publications to as-sert such views, date from the 1830s, while the term "feminism" did not appear until the 1870s. Michèle Riot-Sarcey, *Histoire du féminisme*, 2nd ed. (Paris: La Découverte, 2008); Ka-ren M. Offen, *European Feminisms, 1750–1950: A Political History* (Stanford, CA: Stanford University Press, 2000); and Claire Goldberg Moses, *French Feminism in the Nineteenth Century* (Albany: State University of New York Press, 1984).

3. Offen, *European Feminisms*, 21.

4. In making this case for the parallel developments of feminism, abolitionism, and ear-ly liberalism, I am building on work that underlines the anticolonial stance of Enlighten-ment and early liberal thinkers. See Sankar Muthu, *Enlightenment against Empire* (Prince-ton, NJ: Princeton University Press, 2003); and Jennifer Pitts, *A Turn to Empire: The Rise of Imperial Liberalism in Britain and France* (Princeton, NJ: Princeton University Press, 2005).

5. Christine Stansell, *The Feminist Promise, 1792 to the Present* (New York: Modern Li-brary, 2010), chap. 2. See also Clare Midgley, *Women against Slavery: The British Campaigns, 1780–1870* (New York: Routledge, 1992).

6. Karen Offen, "How (and Why) the Analogy of Marriage with Slavery Provided the Springboard for Women's Rights Demands in France, 1640–1848," in *Women's Rights*

and *Transatlantic Antislavery in the Era of Emancipation*, ed. Kathryn Kish Sklar and James Brewer Stewart (New Haven, CT: Yale University Press, 2007), 57–81; and Doris Y. Kadish and Françoise Massardier-Kenney, eds., *Translating Slavery*, vol. 1: *Gender and Race in French Abolitionist Writing, 1780–1830*, 2nd ed. (Kent, OH: Kent State University Press, 2009). Kadish describes the years between 1780 and 1830 as "an especially active period during which French women resisted the joint oppression of slaves and women" (viii).

7. Joan B. Landes, *Women and the Public Sphere in the Age of the French Revolution* (Ithaca, NY: Cornell University Press, 1988); Lynn Hunt, *The Family Romance of the French Revolution* (Berkeley: University of California Press, 1992); and Dena Goodman, *The Republic of Letters: A Cultural History of the French Enlightenment* (Ithaca, NY: Cornell University Press, 1994).

8. Suzanne Desan, *The Family on Trial in Revolutionary France* (Berkeley: University of California Press, 2004); Jennifer Heuer, *The Family and the Nation: Gender and Citizenship in Revolutionary France, 1789–1830* (Ithaca, NY: Cornell University Press, 2005); Patrick Weil, *How to Be French: Nationality in the Making since 1789*, trans. Catherine Porter (Durham, NC: Duke University Press, 2008); and Denise Z. Davidson, *France after Revolution: Urban Life, Gender, and the New Social Order* (Cambridge, MA: Harvard University Press, 2007).

9. Dominique Godineau, *The Women of Paris and Their French Revolution*, trans. Katherine Streip (Berkeley: University of California Press, 1998); and Jacques Guilhaumou and Martine Lapied, "Women's Political Action during the French Revolution," in Fauré, *Political and Historical Encyclopedia of Women*, 71–87.

10. In a path-breaking study, Joan Wallach Scott draws attention to the dilemma faced by French feminists who needed to argue for women's rights while denying women's difference. Scott, *Only Paradoxes to Offer: French Feminists and the Rights of Man* (Cambridge, MA: Harvard University Press, 1996). See also Christine Fauré, *Democracy without Women: Feminism and the Rise of Liberal Individualism in France*, trans. Claudia Gorbman and John Berks (Bloomington: Indiana University Press, 1991); Geneviève Fraisse, *Reason's Muse: Sexual Difference and the Birth of Democracy*, trans. Jane Marie Todd (Chicago: University of Chicago Press, 1994); and Lisa Beckstrand, *Deviant Women of the French Revolution and the Rise of Feminism* (Madison, NJ: Fairleigh Dickinson University Press, 2009).

11. Jean-Pierre Barlier, *La Société des Amis des Noirs 1788–1791: Aux origines de la première abolition de l'esclavage (4 février 1794)* (Paris: l'Amandier, 2010); Marcel Dorigny and Bernard Gainot, *La Société des Amis des Noirs: Contribution à l'histoire de l'abolition et de l'esclavage* (Paris: UNESCO, 1998); and Erick Noël, *Être noir en France au XVIIIe siècle* (Paris: Tallandier, 2006), chap. 11. The literature on British and American abolitionism is very large. One overview is David Brion Davis, *The Problem of Slavery in the Age of Revolution, 1770–1823*, 2nd ed. (Oxford: Oxford University Press, 1999).

12. Lawrence C. Jennings, *French Anti-Slavery: The Movement for the Abolition of Slavery in France, 1802–1848* (Cambridge: Cambridge University Press, 2000); and Christopher L. Miller, *The French Atlantic Triangle: Literature and Culture of the Slave Trade* (Durham, NC: Duke University Press, 2008).

13. *Requête des Dames à l'Assemblée Nationale*, quoted in Offen, *European Feminisms*, 54–55.

14. Jeremy D. Popkin, *You Are All Free: The Haitian Revolution and the Abolition of Slavery* (Cambridge: Cambridge University Press, 2010), 33–38. Debates about "race" may have served as a way to skirt the bigger issue of slavery. Darcy Grimaldo Grigsby, *Extremities: Painting Empire in Post-Revolutionary France* (New Haven, CT: Yale University Press, 2002), 17–20.

15. It was of course inherently contradictory to define human beings as "unfree," a paradox similar to those traced by Scott in *Only Paradoxes to Offer*.

16. Anne Verjus, *Le cens de la famille: Les femmes et le vote, 1789–1848* (Paris: Belin, 2002); and Karen M. Offen, "Women and the Question of 'Universal' Suffrage in 1848: A Transat-

lantic Comparison of Suffragist Rhetoric," *NWSA Journal* 11 (1999): 150–77. French women did not receive the right to vote until 1944, in part because many secular republicans feared women's supposed religiosity and monarchism and voted against their enfranchisement during the Third Republic.

17. Leonore Loft, *Passion, Politics, and Philosophie: Rediscovering J.-P. Brissot* (Westport, CT: Greenwood Press, 2002), 123–25.

18. Sieyès, quoted in Jean-Clément Martin, *La révolte brisée: Femmes dans la Révolution française et l'Empire* (Paris: Armand Colin, 2008), 79.

19. Elisabeth Liris, "Le droit à l'instruction: Prises de paroles et projets pédagogiques des femmes, 1789–1799," in *Femmes éducatrices au siècle des Lumières*, ed. Isabelle Brouard-Arends and Marie-Emmanuelle Plagnol-Diéval (Rennes: Presses Universitaires de Rennes, 2007), 103–18.

20. Concorcet, *Sur l'Admission des femmes aux droits de cité* (July 1790). A late nineteenth-century translation by John Morley appears in *Women, the Family, and Freedom: The Debate in Documents*, ed. Susan Groag Bell and Karen M. Offen (Stanford, CA: Stanford University Press, 1983), 1:99–103, quotation p. 99. See Offen, *European Feminisms*, 57; and Lynn Hunt, *Inventing Human Rights: A History* (New York: Norton, 2007), 170–72.

21. Olympe de Gouges, *L'esclavage des nègres, ou l'heureux naufrage*, ed. Sylvie Chalaye and Jacqueline Razgonnikoff (Paris: Harmattan, 2006). See also Miller, *French Atlantic Triangle*, chap. 6; Beckstrand, *Deviant Women*, chap. 6; and Scott, *Only Paradoxes to Offer*, chap 2.

22. Olivier Blanc, *Marie-Olympe de Gouges: Une humaniste à la fin du XVIIIe siècle* (Paris: René Viénet, 2003), 129–31.

23. On the influence of revolutionary events on women elsewhere, see Annie Jourdan, *La révolution batave entre la France et l'Amérique (1795–1806)* (Rennes: Presses Universitaires de Rennes, 2008); and Susan Branson, *These Fiery Frenchified Dames: Women and Political Culture in Early National Philadelphia* (Philadelphia: University of Pennsylvania Press, 2001), chap 2.

24. Charles-Maurice de Talleyrand-Périgord, *Rapport sur l'instruction publique, fait au nom du Comité de constitution* (1791) quoted in Offen, *European Feminisms*, 59–60. See Tom Furniss, "Mary Wollstonecraft's French Revolution," in *The Cambridge Companion to Mary Wollstonecraft*, ed. Claudia L. Johnson (Cambridge: Cambridge University Press, 2002), 60–68.

25. Moira Ferguson, *Colonialism and Gender Relations from Mary Wollstonecraft to Jamaica Kincaid: East Caribbean Connections* (New York: Columbia University Press, 1993), chap. 2.

26. Etta Palm d'Aelders, *Appel aux françaises sur le régénération des mœurs et la nécessité de l'influence des femmes dans un gouvernement libre* (1791), quoted in Gary Kates, *The Cercle Social, the Girondins, and the French Revolution* (Princeton, NJ: Princeton University Press, 1985), 123. See also Judith Vega, "Feminist Republicanism: Etta Palm-Aelders on Justice, Virtue, and Men," *History of European Ideas* 10 (1989): 333–51.

27. Theodor Gottlieb von Hippel, *On Improving the Status of Women*, ed. and trans. Timothy F. Sellner (Detroit: Wayne State University Press, 1979), 188. Bonnie S. Anderson, "*Frauenemancipation* and Beyond: The Use of the Concept of Emancipation by Early European Feminists," in Sklar and Stewart, *Women's Rights and Transatlantic Antislavery in the Era of Emancipation*, 82–83; and Offen, *European Feminisms*, 72.

28. Pierre Guyomar, *Le Partisan de l'égalité politique entre les individus* (1793) quoted in Offen, "Analogy of Marriage," 68.

29. Reactions to Guyomar's arguments are discussed in Martin, *La révolte brisée*, 133.

30. Riot-Sarcey, *Histoire du féminisme*, 17–19. Amar's speech and the decree of 30 October 1793 appear in translation at http://chnm.gmu.edu/revolution/d/294/ (accessed 30 August 2012).

31. Noël, *Être noir en France*, 202–3.

32. Popkin, *You Are All Free*, chap. 8.

33. Godineau, *The Women of Paris*, 170–74.

34. Bronislaw Baczko, *Ending the Terror: The French Revolution after Robespierre*, trans. Michel Petheram (Cambridge: Cambridge University Press, 1994), 78–114. See also James Livesey, *Making Democracy in the French Revolution* (Cambridge, MA: Harvard University Press, 2001); and Pierre Serna, *La République des girouettes, 1789–1815 et au-delà: Une anomalie politique; La France de l'extrême centre* (Seyssel: Champ Vallon, 2005). On women's involvement in intellectual and scientific societies, see Jann Matlock, "Anatomy in Beauty's Empire: Teaching Women the Body in Late Eighteenth- and Early Nineteenth-Century France" (paper presented at the Society for French Historical Studies Conference, Washington University, Saint Louis, MO, March 2009). I appreciate Professor Matlock's willingness to send me this paper, which will be appearing in her forthcoming book, *The Invisible Woman and Her Secrets: Bodies, Vision, and Aesthetics in Nineteenth-Century France*.

35. Martin, *La révolte brisée*, 212–14.

36. Jennifer J. Popiel, *Rousseau's Daughters: Domesticity, Education, and Autonomy in Modern France* (Durham: University of New Hampshire Press, 2008); and Lesley H. Walker, *A Mother's Love: Crafting Feminine Virtue in Enlightenment France* (Lewisburg, PA: Bucknell University Press, 2009).

37. Carla Hesse, *The Other Enlightenment: How French Women Became Modern* (Ithaca, NY: Cornell University Press, 2001).

38. Andrew Jainchill, *Reimagining Politics after the Terror: The Republican Origins of French Liberalism* (Ithaca, NY: Cornell University Press, 2008); and Jeremy D. Popkin, "The French Revolution's Other Island," in *The World of the Haitian Revolution*, ed. David Geggus and Norman Fiering (Bloomington: Indiana University Press, 2009), 199–222.

39. Emma Rothschild, *Economic Sentiments: Adam Smith, Condorcet, and the Enlightenment* (Cambridge, MA: Harvard University Press, 2001), chap. 7; and Pitts, *A Turn to Empire*, 173–90.

40. K. Steven Vincent, *Benjamin Constant and the Birth of French Liberalism* (New York: Palgrave Macmillan, 2011), 132–33; and Deborah Jenson, *Trauma and Its Representations: The Social Life of Mimesis in Post-Revolutionary France* (Baltimore: Johns Hopkins University Press, 2001), 63–64. See also Biancamaria Fontana, *Benjamin Constant and the Post-Revolutionary Mind* (New Haven, CT: Yale University Press, 1991); and Renee Winegarten, *Germaine de Staël and Benjamin Constant: A Dual Biography* (New Haven, CT: Yale University Press, 2008). On "pleasure" as it was conceived in the late 1790s, see Rebecca L. Spang, "The Frivolous French: 'Liberty of Pleasure' and the End of Luxury," in *Taking Liberties: Problems of a New Order from the French Revolution to Napoleon*, ed. Howard G. Brown and Judith A. Miller (Manchester: Manchester University Press, 2002), 110–25.

41. "Epître aux femmes," quoted in Offen, *European Feminisms*, 67. On Pipelet/de Salm, see Elizabeth Colwill, "Laws of Nature/Rights of Genius: The *Drame* of Constance de Salm," in *Going Public: Women and Publishing in Early Modern France*, ed. Elizabeth C. Goldsmith and Dena Goodman (Ithaca, NY: Cornell University Press, 1995), 224–42.

42. The speech, which Pipelet delivered on 30 Vendémiaire, Year 7 (21 October 1798), appeared as a pamphlet: "Rapport sur les fleurs artificielles de la citoyenne Roux-Montagnat par Constance de Th[éis] Pipelet de la Société du Lycée des Arts."

43. "Rapport sur un ouvrage du Cit. Théremin intitulé *De la Condition des femmes dans une république* par Constance D.T. Pipelet" (Year VIII [1800]). See Hunt, *Inventing Human Rights*, 173–74, Jainchill, *Reimagining Politics*, 123–29; and Carla Hesse, "The Cultural Contradictions of Feminism in the French Revolution," in *The Age of Cultural Revolutions: Britain and France, 1750–1820*, ed. Colin Jones and Dror Wahrman (Berkeley: University of California Press, 2002), 194–95.

44. Frédéric Régent, "Le rétablissement de l'esclavage et du préjugé de couleur en Guadeloupe (1802–1803)," and Carolyn Fick, "La résistance populaire au corps expéditionnaire du général Leclerc et au rétablissement de l'esclavage à Saint-Domingue," in *Rétablissement de l'esclavage dans les colonies françaises, 1802 aux origines de Haïti: Ruptures et continuités de la*

politique coloniale française (1800–1830), ed. Yves Bénot and Marcel Dorigny (Paris: Maison-neuve et Larose, 2003), 283–96 and 127–48 respectively.

45. Offen draws attention to the fact that "colonial slavery and marital obedience were both reinstated in the early 1800s," but insists that this "does not deprive the earlier developments of their immense historical significance." "Analogy of Marriage," 72.

46. Steven Kale, *French Salons: High Society and Political Sociability from the Old Regime to the Revolution of 1848* (Baltimore: Johns Hopkins University Press, 2004); and Hesse, *The Other Enlightenment.*

47. Martin, *La révolte brisée*, 204; James Smalls, "Slavery Is a Woman: 'Race,' Gender, and Visuality in Marie Benoist's *Portrait d'une négresse* (1800)," *Nineteenth-Century Art Worldwide* 3, no. 1 (Spring 2004) (accessed 30 August 2012); and Margaret Fields Denton, "A Woman's Place: The Gendering of Genres in Post-Revolutionary French Painting," *Art History* 21 (June 1998): 219–46.

48. Jennings, *French Anti-Slavery*, 5; and Miller, *The French Atlantic Triangle*, pt. 2.

49. Philippe R. Girard, *The Slaves Who Defeated Napoléon: Toussaint Louverture and the Haitian War of Independence, 1801–1804* (Tuscaloosa: University of Alabama Press, 2011). I appreciate Professor Girard's willingness to share excerpts from his book with me before its publication. See also Pierre Branda and Thierry Lentz, *Napoléon, l'esclavage et les colonies* (Paris: Fayard, 2006).

50. Henri Grégoire, *Da la littérature des nègres* (Paris: Maradan, 1808), v–vi. See Alyssa Goldstein Sepinwall, *The Abbé Grégoire and the French Revolution: The Making of Modern Universalism* (Berkeley: University of California Press, 2005), chaps. 7 and 8.

51. See Jennifer Pitts, "Republicanism, Liberalism, and Empire in Post-Revolutionary France" (paper presented at Yale University, April 2009), in *Empire and Modern Political Thought*, ed. Sankar Muthu (Cambridge: Cambridge University Press, 2012). I thank Professor Pitts for allowing me to cite this paper, which I read before its publication.

52. Jennings, *French Anti-Slavery*, 8–18; and Miller, *The French Atlantic Triangle*, 195–98.

53. France granted official recognition in 1825 in exchange for large indemnities from Haiti to reimburse the former colonists. Jean-François Brière, *Haïti et la France, 1804–1848: Le rêve brisé* (Paris: Karthala, 2008).

54. Jean-Jacques Goblot, *La jeune France libérale: "Le Globe" et son groupe littéraire 1824–1830* (Paris: Plon, 1995); Alan B. Spitzer, *The French Generation of 1820* (Princeton, NJ: Princeton University Press, 1987), chap. 4; and Pierre Rosanvallon, *Le moment Guizot* (Paris: Gallimard, 1985).

55. Charles de Rémusat, *The Saint-Domingue Plantation; or The Insurrection*, ed. Doris Y. Kadish, trans. Norman R. Shapiro (Baton Rouge: Louisiana State University Press, 2008).

56. Kadish, introduction to Rémusat, *Saint-Domingue Plantation*, xv; and Mona Ozouf, *Women's Words: Essay on French Singularity,* trans. Jane Marie Todd (Chicago: University of Chicago Press, 1997), 88.

8 Egypt in the French Revolution

1. In English: J. Christopher Herold, *Bonaparte in Egypt* (New York: Harper & Row, 1962); Juan Cole, *Napoleon's Egypt: Invading the Middle East* (New York: Palgrave Macmillan, 2007). Several key works remain untranslated; in French: Henry Laurens, *L'expédition d'Égypte: 1798–1801* (Paris: Colin, 1989); Allain Bernède and Gérard-Pierre Chaduc, eds., *La campagne d'Égypte, 1798–1801: Mythes et réalités* (Paris: Musée de l'Armée, 1999); "L'expédition d'Égypte vue d'Égypte," special issue, *Égypte/Monde Arabe* 1 (1999); in Arabic: Nasser Ahmed Ibrahim, ed., *Mi'ata 'am 'ala-l-hamlat al-faransiyya: Ru'iyya masriyya* (Two Hundred Years after the French Occupation of Egypt: Egyptian Reflections) (Cairo: Maktabat al-Dar al-'Arabiyya lil-Kitab, 2008).

2. André Raymond, *Égyptiens et français au Caire, 1798–1801* (Cairo: Institut Français d'Archéologie Orientale, 1998); Lars Bjorneboe, *In Search of the True Political Position of the 'Ulama: An Analysis of the Aims and Perspectives of the Chronicles of 'Abd Al-Rahman Al-Jabarti* (Damascus: Danish Institute in Damascus, 2006).

3. Nicole Dhombres and Jean Dhombres, *Naissance d'un pouvoir: Sciences et savants en France, 1793–1824* (Paris: Payot, 1989), 104. See also Marie-Noëlle Bourguet, "Science and Memory: The Stakes of the Expedition to Egypt (1798–1801)," in *Taking Liberties: Problems of a New Order from the French Revolution to Napoleon*, ed. Howard G. Brown and Judith A. Miller (Manchester: Manchester University Press, 2003), 103.

4. Louis Bergeron, *France under Napoleon*, trans. R. R. Palmer (Princeton, NJ: Princeton University Press, 1981), 53–56.

5. R. R. Palmer, *The Age of the Democratic Revolution* (Princeton, NJ: Princeton University Press, 1959); for the intellectual revival in eighteenth-century Egypt, see Peter Gran, *Islamic Roots of Capitalism: Egypt, 1760–1840* (Austin: University of Texas Press, 1979).

6. Christopher Bayly, "The 'Revolutionary Age' in the Wider World, c. 1790–1830," in *War, Empire, and Slavery, 1770–1830*, ed. Richard Bessel, Nicholas Guyatt, and Jane Rendall (London: Palgrave Macmillan), 21–43.

7. Bruce Masters, *Christians and Jews in the Ottoman Arab World: The Roots of Sectarianism* (New York: Cambridge University Press, 2001).

8. See Marc Belissa, *Repenser l'ordre européen (1795–1802): De la société des rois aux droits des nations* (Paris: Éditions Klimé, 2006).

9. Bernard Gainot, "Révolution, Liberté=Europe des nations? Sororité conflictuelle," in *Mélanges Michel Vovelle sur la Révolution, approches plurielles* (Paris: Société des études robespierristes, 1997), 457–68.

10. Andrew Jainchill, *Reimagining Politics after the Terror: The Republican Origins of French Liberalism* (Ithaca, NY: Cornell University Press, 2008), 146–47.

11. See Michel Vovelle, *Les Républiques Soeurs sous le regard de la Grande Nation* (Paris: L'Harmattan, 2007).

12. Stuart Woolf, *A History of Italy, 1700–1860: The Social Constraints of Political Change* (London: Methuen, 1979), 177.

13. Vovelle, *Les Républiques Soeurs*, 23.

14. See Gabriele Turi, *Viva Maria: Riforme, rivoluzione e insorgenze in Toscana (1790–1799)* (Bologna: Soc. Ed. Il Mulino, 1999).

15. See Emmanuel Rodocanachi, "Bonaparte et les îles Ioniennes: Un épisode des conquêtes de la République et du premier Empire (1797–1816)," *La nouvelle revue* 5–6 (1898): 447.

16. To the Directory, 29 Thermidor, Year V (16 August, 1797), in Napoleon, *Correspondance inédite officielle et confidentielle de Napoléon Bonaparte avec les cours étrangers, les princes, les ministres et les généraux français et étrangèrs, en Italie, en Allemagne, et en Égypte* (Paris: C. L. F. Panckoucke, 1819), 77.

17. Jean-Yves Guiomar, "Histoire et signification de la 'grande nation' (août 1797-automne 1799)," in *Du directoire au consulat*, vol. 1, *Le lien politique local dans la Grande Nation*, ed. Jacques Bernet (Villeneuve d'Ascq: Centre de Recherche sur l'Histoire de l'Europe du Nord-Ouest Univ. Charles de Gaulle Lille III, 1999), 319 (emphasis mine).

18. Henry Laurens, "Bonaparte, l'Orient et la 'Grande Nation,'" *Annales historiques de la Révolution française* 273 (1988): 291 (emphasis mine).

19. Jeremy Black, *British Foreign Policy in an Age of Revolutions, 1783–1793* (Cambridge: Cambridge University Press, 1994), 48–49.

20. See Irfan Habib, "The Diplomatic Vision of Tipu Sultan: Briefs for Embassies to Turkey and France, 1785–6," in *State and Diplomacy under Tipu Sultan: Documents and Essays* (New Delhi: Tulika, 2001), 19–66.

21. See Maurits H. van den Boogert, *The Capitulations and the Ottoman Legal System: Qadis, Consuls and Beratlıs in the 18th Century* (Leiden: Brill, 2005); André Raymond, *Artisans et commerçants au Caire au XVIIIe siècle* (Damascus: Inst. Français de Damas, 1973), 451–503.

22. Raoul Clément, *Les français d'Égypte aux XVIIe et XVIIIe siècles* (Cairo: Impr. de l'Institut Français d'Archéologie Orientale, 1960), 67.

23. See Paul Masson, *Histoire du commerce française dans le Levant au XVIIIe siècle* (Paris: Hachette, 1911); Ian Coller, "East of Enlightenment: Provincializing Europeans in Eighteenth-Century Paris and Istanbul," *Journal of World History* 21 (2010): 447–70.

24. Merlijn Olnon, "Towards Classifying Avanias: A Study of Two Cases Involving the English and Dutch Nations in Seventeenth-Century Izmir," in *Friends and Rivals in the East: Studies in Anglo-Dutch Relations in the Levant from the Seventeenth to the Early Nineteenth Century*, ed. Alastair Hamilton, Alexander H. de Groot, and Maurits H. van den Boogert (Leiden: Brill, 2000), 185.

25. See Claude Étienne Savary, *Lettres sur l'Égypte* (Paris, 1786), 2:135–38; Pierre Étienne Herbin de Halle, *Conquêtes des Français en Égypte* (Paris: C. Pougens/ Malherbe, An VII [1799]), 266.

26. Ibid., 230; François-Charles Roux, *Les origines de l'expédition d'Égypte* (Paris: Plon-Nourrit et Cie, 1910), 224–25.

27. Clément, *Les français d'Égypte*, 274.

28. Roux, *Les origines*, 246.

29. G. Olivier, *Voyage dans l'Empire othoman, l'Égypte et la Perse: Fait par ordre du Gouvernement, pendant les six premières années de la République* (Paris: Chez H. Agasse, 1801), 3:202.

30. Roux, *Les origines*, 248.

31. Olivier, *Voyage,* 209.

32. Roux, *Les origines*, 327.

33. Archives Diplomatiques, Paris, MD Turquie 15.

34. Ibid.

35. "Rapport de Talleyrand sur la situation extérieure de la France, 8 Messidor, An VII [26 Juin 1799]," *Revue d'histoire diplomatique* 3 (1889).

36. *Pièces diverses et correspondance relatives aux opérations de l'Armée d'Orient en Égypte* (Paris: Baudouin, impr. du Corps législatif et du Tribunat, messidor, an IX [1801]), 1:156.

37. Ibid., 157.

38. *Le Courier de l'Égypte* 9 (10 Vendémiaire, Year 7), 3.

39. Kléber added: "We will rub them in his face."

40. Henry Laurens, *Kléber en Égypte:1798–1800* (Damascus: IFAO, 1988), 1:46.

41. *Traité entre Mourad-Bey et le général Kléber au Kaire an 8* (Cairo: Impr. Nationale, 1800).

42. These documents were first discovered by Shafiq Ghurbal, *Al-jiniral Ya'qub wa al-faris Lascaris wa mashru' istiqlal Misr fi sanat 1801* (Cairo: Matbaat al-Maarif, 1932), and translated by Georges Douin, *L'Égypte indépendante: Projet de 1801* (Cairo: Société Royale de Géographie d'Égypte, 1924).

43. George A. Haddad, "A Project for the Independence of Egypt, 1801," *Journal of the American Oriental Society* 90 (1970): 180.

44. Ibid., 181. Sheikh Hummam was a governor of Upper Egypt in the time of 'Ali Bey al-Kabir; see Michael Winter, *Egyptian Society under Ottoman Rule* (New York: Routledge, 1992), 105.

45. Haddad, "A Project," 181.

46. I have followed the story of these Egyptian expatriates at length in my book *Arab France: Islam and the Making of Modern Europe, 1798–1831* (Berkeley: University of California Press, 2010).

9   Abolition and Reenslavement in the Caribbean

1. Soc. pop. Loudun, 19 Apr. 1794, pièce 7a, *Archives parlementaires de 1787 à 1860: Recueil complet des débats législatifs et politiques des chambres françaises*, 1st ser. (hereafter *AP*) (Paris, 1879–), 89:45.

2. Soc. pop. La Rochelle, 14 Apr. 1794, pièce 20, *AP* 88:569.

3. Arthur Girault, *Principes de colonisation et de législation coloniale*, 2nd ed. (Paris: L. Larose, 1904), 1:196.

4. Bernard Gainot, "The Constitutionalization of General Freedvom under the Directory," in *The Abolitions of Slavery from L. F. Sonthonax to Victor Schoelcher: 1793, 1794, 1848*, ed. Marcel Dorigny (New York: Berghahn/UNESCO, 2003), 182.

5. Laurent Dubois, *A Colony of Citizens: Revolution and Slave Emancipation in the French Caribbean, 1787–1804* (Chapel Hill: University of North Carolina Press, 2004), 172.

6. Laurent Dubois, "Citizen Soldiers: Emancipation and Military Service in the Revolutionary French Caribbean," in *Arming Slaves: From Classical Times to the Modern Age*, ed. Christopher Leslie Brown and Philip D. Morgan (New Haven, CT: Yale University Press, 2006), 234.

7. On war's role in promoting imperial disunity, see Trevor Burnard, "The British Atlantic," in *Atlantic History: A Critical Appraisal*, ed. Jack P. Greene and Philip D. Morgan (New York: Oxford University Press, 2009), 111–36. On fissures in the French empire during the Seven Years' War, see John Garrigus, *Before Haiti: Race and Citizenship in French Saint-Domingue* (New York: Palgrave-Macmillan, 2006), 111–15; see also Kenneth Banks, *Chasing Empire across the Sea* (Montreal and Kingston: McGill-Queen's University Press, 2002), 202–16. On war and imperial constitutional crisis in the Spanish context, see Jeremy Adelman, *Sovereignty and Revolution in the Iberian Atlantic* (Princeton, NJ: Princeton University Press, 2006).

8. Ciro Flammarion Cardoso, *La Guyane française (1715–1817): Aspects économiques et sociaux* (Petit-Bourg, Guadeloupe: Ibis Rouge, 1999), 335.

9. On late eighteenth-century development efforts, see Pierre-Victor Malouet, *Collection de mémoires et correspondances officielles sur les colonies et notamment sur la Guiane française et hollandaise* (Paris: Baudouin, year 10 [1801-2]), 2:340–46 and 368–74; see also Joseph-Samuel Guisan, *Traité sur les terres noyées de la Guiane* (Cayenne: Imprimerie du Roi, 1788); Charles Eynard, *Le chevalier Guisan, sa vie et ses travaux à la Guyane* (Paris: A. Cherbuliez, 1844). On an earlier physiocratic development scheme for French Guiana and its malignant consequences, see Emma Rothschild, "A Horrible Tragedy in the French Atlantic," *Past & Present* 192 (August 2006): 67–108.

10. Charles-Guillaume Vial, Chevalier d'Alais, governor of Guiana, to minister of the navy, Compte rendu des habitations du Roy, 27 Jan. 1789, C14 63, fol. 8. Microfilm of the C14 series, which gathers the "correspondance à l'arrivée de la Guyane" (1651–1848) with an emphasis on the period from 1651 to 1809, is available at both the Archives Nationales (Paris) and the Centre des Archives d'Outre Mer (Aix-en-Provence).

11. Lettres Patentes du Roi, Qui accordent à l'Isle de Cayenne & la Guyane françoise, la liberté de commerce avec toute les Nations pendant douze ans, No. 1778, May 1768, in *Acts of French Royal Administration Concerning Canada, Guiana, the West Indies, and Louisiana, Prior to 1791*, ed. Lawrence C. Wroth and Gertrude L. Annan (New York: New York Public Library, 1930), 126.

12. Jeremy Popkin, *You Are All Free: The Haitian Revolution and the Abolition of Slavery* (New York: Cambridge University Press, 2010).

13. *AP* 84:284 (4 Feb. 1794).

14. Arts. 155–56, Constitution of 22 Aug. 1795, in *Constitutions de la France depuis 1789*, ed. Jacques Godechot (Paris: Garnier-Flammarion, 1970), 119.

15. On the evolving extraconstitutional principles of colonial rule, see *AP* 40:577 (28 March 1792); Décret additionnel à la loi relative à l'envoi des commissaires civils à Saint-Domingue (Décret du 28 Mars 1792), 15 June 1792, in Jules-François Saintoyant, *La colonisation française pendant la Révolution (1789-1799)* (Paris: Renaissance du Livre, 1930), 1:411; Décret concernant la mise en état de défense des colonies, 5–6 March 1793, ibid., 1:427–28.

16. For a detailed discussion of this problem, see Miranda Spieler, "The Legal Structure of Colonial Rule during the French Revolution," *William and Mary Quarterly*, 3rd ser., 66, no. 2 (2009): 365–408.

17. Art. 1, Decree of 10 Oct. 1793, *AP* 76:312.

18. On Armand de Kersaint's effort to abolish privateering, see *AP* 42:225 (22 Apr. 1792) and *AP* 42:587–89 (1 May 1792). For the retort of Pierre Vergniaud, see *AP* 44:347 (31 May 1792). On letters of marque, see *AP* 58:104 (31 Jan. 1793).

19. Jacques Godechot, *La grande nation: L'expansion révolutionnaire de la France dans le monde de 1789 à 1799*, 2nd ed. (Paris: Aubier Montaigne, 1983), esp. 331–56.

20. On Dutch patriots and the slavery question, see Simon Schama, *Patriots and Liberators: Revolution in the Netherlands, 1780–1813* (New York: Knopf, 1977), 249 and 261.

21. Yves Bénot, "Comment Santo Domingo n'a pas été occupé par la République française en 1795–1796," *Annales historiques de la Révolution française* 311 (January-March 1998): 79–87.

22. See Flávio Gomes, "Other Black Atlantic Borders: Escape Routes, *Mocambos*, and Fears of Sedition in Brazil in French Guiana (Eighteenth and Nineteenth Centuries)," *New West Indian Guide/Niewe West-Indische Guids* 77, nos. 3–4 (2003): 253–87.

23. Extrait des registres de délibérations du conseil de guerre, 25–27 Oct. 1794, C14 73, fol. 36-fol. 37.

24. François-Maurice de Cointet, governor of French Guiana, to Commission de Marine et des Colonies, Cayenne, 18 August 1795, C14 73, fol. 8-fol. 10.

25. Yves Bénot, *La Guyane sous la Révolution française, ou l'impasse de la révolution pacifique* (Kourou: Ibis Rouge, 1997), 82–85.

26. "Extrait d'une lettre écrite de la Pointe-à-Pitre, le 5 novembre 1795," *Gazette française et américaine*, 8 Jan. 1796, no. 81, p. 3.

27. Ulane Bonnel, *La France, les États Unis, et la guerre de course (1797–1815)* (Paris: Nouvelles Éditions Latines, 1961), 101.

28. Étienne-Laurent-Pierre Burnel, agent du Directoire, to minister of the navy, 13 August 1799, C14 77, fol. 67; Nicolas-Georges Jeannet-Oudin, Mémoire sur les colonies en général et sur la Guyane en particulier présenté au Premier Consul Bonaparte, [24 Oct. 1801], C14 79, fol. 104v.

29. Jeannet-Oudin, agent du Directoire, to governor-general of Surinam, 12 Sept. 1798, C14 76, fol. 62-fol. 63.

30. Dubois, *A Colony of Citizens*, 298–99.

31. Jeannet-Oudin to minister of the navy, 3 Oct. 1796, C14 74, fol. 119-fol. 123.

32. Burnel to minister of the navy, 13 Aug. 1799, C14 77, fol. 67.

33. "Mémores et projets par le Capitaine de Vaisseau J[acques] J[oseph] Eyriès. Guyane française. (1795)," C14 73, fol. 213.

34. Zachary Macaulay, *Life and Letters of Zachary Macaulay, by His Granddaughter Viscountess Knutsford* (London: Edward Arnold, 1900), 82.

35. Adam Afzelius, *Sierra Leone Journal, 1795–1796*, ed. Alexander Peter Kup, Studia Ethnographica Upsaliensia 27 (Uppsala: Almqvist and Wiksells, 1967), 14.

36. Claude Wanquet, "La première abolition française de l'esclavage fut-elle une mystification? Le cas Daniel Lescallier," in *Esclavage, résistances, et abolitions*, ed. Marcel Dorigny (Paris: Comité des Travaux Historiques et Scientifiques, 1999), 253–68.

37. On the question of whether to indemnify (or reward) captors of the English slave ship *The Swallow*, see Rapport (unsigned), Paris, 17 July 1800, C14 78, fol. 184.

38. Jeannet-Oudin, Mémoire sur les colonies en général et sur la Guyane en particulier présenté au Premier Consul Bonaparte, [24 Oct. 1801], C14 79, fol. 104v.

39. Title 3, art. 18, Loi concernant l'organisation constitutionnelle des colonies, No. 1659 of 12 nivôse year 6 (1 Jan. 1798), in *Bulletin des lois de la République française*, no. 177, p. 4.

40. Pierre-Samuel du Dupont de Nemours, "Exposé des motifs des décrets des 13 et 15 mai 1791 sur l'état des personnes aux colonies, 29 May 1791," in Saintoyant, *La colonisation française*, 1:392–93.

41. Bénot, *La Guyane sous la Révolution*, 89–102 and 107.

42. Voyages Database, 2009, *The Trans-Atlantic Slave Trade Database*, http://slavevoyages. org/tast/database/search.faces?yearFrom=1796&yearTo=1800&mjslptimp=36300 (accessed 23 April 2012).

43. Voyages Database, 2009, *The Trans-Atlantic Slave Trade Database*, http://slavevoyages. org/tast/database/search.faces?yearFrom=1795&yearTo=1800&mjslptimp=36200 (accessed 23 April 2012).

44. Charles Malenfant, chef de bataillon, to minister of the navy, Paris, 9 February 1800, C14 78, fol. 233.

45. Bénot, *La Guyane sous la Révolution*, 164–65.

46. Sinnamary: Naissances, Mariages et Décès (an 4–an 6), ANSOM 119, Centre des Archives d'Outre Mer (Aix-en-Provence).

47. On the creation of the battalion, see Cointet to Commission de Marine et des Colonies, 23 Sept. 1795, C14 73, fol. 12-fol. 14.

48. Jeannet-Oudin to minister of the navy, 30 Aug. 1796, C14 76, fol. 113-fol. 118.

49. Burnel to minister of the navy, 7 Dec. 1798, C14 76, fol. 101v.

50. On the appointment of Victor Hugues as Agent des Consuls, see Rapport aux Consuls de la République, 4 Dec. 1799, C14 77, fol. 188. On reenslavement in French Guiana, see Monique Pouliquen, "L'esclavage subi, aboli, rétabli en Guyane de 1789 à 1809," *L'esclavage et les plantations: De l'établissement de la servitude à son abolition; un hommage à Pierre Pluchon* (Presses Universitaires de Rennes, 2008), 241–64.

51. Hugues to minister of the navy, 15 Oct. 1804, C14 83, fol. 86v.

52. Hugues to minister of the navy, 12 Oct. 1802, C14 80, fol. 124-fol. 134.

53. Hugues to minister of the navy, 12 Oct. 1802, C14 80, fol. 130; Observations sur le projet d'arrêté tendant à établir à Cayenne et dans la Guyane française un esclavage plein pour certains noirs et une simple conscription rurale pour les autres [30 Nov. 1802], C14 80, fol. 26v.

54. Proclamation de Hugues concernant l'arrêté des Consuls du 16 frimaire an 11 [7 décembre 1802] fixant l'organisation intérieure de la colonie, C14 82, fol. 149.

55. Hugues, Arrêté, 24 August 1803, C14 82, fol. 143.

56. Hugues to minister of the navy, 8 Dec. 1803, C14 82, fol. 105.

57. Hugues to minister of the navy, 11 Nov. 1805, C14 83, fol. 165.

58. For a firsthand account of the postrevolutionary hunt for maroons under Hugues, see Gabriel Debien, "Un nantais à la chasse aux marrons en Guyane (octobre-décembre 1808), in *Enquêtes et documents* (Nantes: Centre de Recherche sur l'Histoire de la France Atlantique), 1:163–72. For an eighteenth-century primary source describing a Maroon settlement, see "Rebel Village in French Guiana: A Captive's Description," in *Maroon Societies*, ed. Richard Price, 3rd ed. (Baltimore: Johns Hopkins University Press, 1996), 312–19; first published in Sylvie Mirot, "Un document inédit sur le marronnage à la Guyane française au XVIIIe siècle," *Revue de l'histoire des colonies françaises* 41 (1954): 245–56.

59. Victor Hugues, à son excellence Monsieur le Comte de Cessac, C14 87, (80p), esp. fol. 13v and fol. 23; Baron Carra de Vaux, "Documents sur la perte et la retrocession de la Guyane française (1809–1817)," *Revue de l'histoire des colonies francaises* (3rd trim. 1913): 333–68.

60. Adams to Jefferson, 24 Aug. 1815, in *Correspondence of John Adams and Thomas Jefferson*, ed. Paul Wilstach (Indianapolis: Bobbs-Merrill, 1925), 116.

10 The French Revolutionary Wars
and the Making of American Empire

I wish to thank Suzanne Desan, Andrew Frank, Lynn Hunt, John Parmenter, and the anonymous reader for their suggestions.

1. On Genêt, see Harry Ammon, *The Genet Mission* (New York: Norton, 1973); and Eugene P. Link, *Democratic-Republican Societies, 1790–1800* (New York: Columbia University Press, 1942). On Genêt's most effective collaborator, see Robert J. Alderson, Jr., *This Bright Era of Happy Revolutions: French Consul Michel-Ange-Bernard Mangourit and International Republicanism in Charleston, 1792–1794* (Columbia: University of South Carolina Press, 2008).

2. Albert Hall Bowman, *The Struggle for Neutrality: Franco-American Diplomacy during the Federalist Era* (Knoxville: University of Tennessee Press, 1974), vii.

3. Marie-Jeanne Rossignol, *The Nationalist Ferment: The Origins of U.S. Foreign Policy, 1789–1812*, trans. Lillian A. Parrott (Columbus: Ohio State University Press, 2004), 37.

4. Through the Alien and Sedition Acts of 1798.

5. Felix Gilbert, *To the Farewell Address: Ideas of Early American Foreign Policy* (Princeton, NJ: Princeton University Press, 1961).

6. The phrase is from the title of J. Fred Rippy's *America and the Strife of Europe* (Chicago: University of Chicago Press, 1938).

7. Bradford Perkins, *The Cambridge History of American Foreign Relations*, vol. 1, *The Creation of a Republican Empire, 1776–1865* (Cambridge: Cambridge University Press, 1993), 91.

8. Samuel Flagg Bemis, *Pinckney's Treaty: America's Advantage from Europe's Distress, 1783–1800* (New Haven, CT: Yale University Press, 1960).

9. On the Treaty of Greenville, see Andrew R.L. Cayton, "Radicals in the 'Western World': The Federalist Conquest of Trans-Appalachian North America," in *Federalists Reconsidered*, ed. Doron Ben-Atar and Barbara B. Oberg (Charlottesville, VA and London: University Press of Virginia, 1998), 77–96; and Barbara Alice Mann, "The Greenville Treaty of 1795: Pen-and-Ink Witchcraft in the Struggle for the Old Northwest," in *Enduring Legacies: Native American Treaties and Contemporary Controversies*, ed. Bruce E. Johansen (Westport, CT: Praeger, 2004), 135–201.

10. Dave R. Palmer, *1794: America, Its Army, and the Birth of the Nation* (Novato, CA: Presidio, 1994), 42.

11. Ibid., 60.

12. Ibid., 61.

13. The other British forts were at Detroit, Erie, Niagara, Oswego, Oswegatchie, and Point-au-Fer. Thomas Jefferson, secretary of state of the United States, to George Hammond, British minister to the United States, Philadelphia, 15 December 1791, in *Diplomatic Correspondence of the United States: Canadian Relations, 1784–1860*, vol. 1, ed. William R. Manning (Washington D.C.: n.p., 1940), 47.

14. Lord Hawkesbury's Draft of Instructions to Hammond, 4 July 1791, in *Instructions to the British Ministers to the United States, 1791–1812*, vol. 3 of the *Annual Report of the American Historical Association for the Year 1936*, ed. Bernard Mayo (Washington, D.C.: n.p., 1941), 6.

15. George Hammond to Thomas Jefferson, Philadelphia, 20 June 1793, in Manning, *Diplomatic Correspondence*, 403.

16. David J. Weber, *The Spanish Frontier in North America* (New Haven, CT: Yale University Press, 1992).

17. British National Archives (hereafter BNA), Colonial Office (hereafter CO), 43/10, Colonial Office to Lieutenant-Governor Clarke, London, 5 May 1792.

18. Cited in Samuel Flagg Bemis, *Jay's Treaty: A Study in Commerce and Diplomacy*, 2nd ed. (New Haven, CT: Yale University Press, 1962), 21.

19. Quoted in Timothy D. Willig, *Restoring the Chain of Friendship: British Policy and the Indians of the Great Lakes, 1783–1815* (Lincoln: University of Nebraska Press, 2008), 13.

20. Willig, *Restoring the Chain of Friendship*, 14. Willig notes that such commitments did not always reflect official British policy. Men like Johnson and McKee had substantial personal and financial connections to the tribes and did not necessarily act as neutral agents of their government's policy (Willig, 22). On this point, see also Richard White, *The Middle Ground: Indians, Empires, and Republics in the Great Lakes Region, 1650–1815* (Cambridge: Cambridge University Press, 1991), 456.

21. Weber, *The Spanish Frontier*, 282.

22. Hubert Bruce Fuller, *The Purchase of Florida: Its History and Diplomacy* (Gainesville: University of Florida Press, 1964), 35.

23. Quoted in Weber, *The Spanish Frontier*, 282.

24. Quoted in Palmer, *1794*, 63.

25. Palmer, *1794*, 63.

26. Reginald Horsman, *The Frontier in the Formative Years, 1783–1815* (New York: Rinehart and Winston, 1970), 39. For a detailed discussion of the "bizarre pattern of American aggression against the most moderate of Indians," see Gregory Evans Dowd, *A Spirited Resistance: The North American Indian Struggle for Unity, 1745–1815* (Baltimore: Johns Hopkins University Press, 1992), 95–99; quote from p. 96.

27. Jerald A. Combs, *The Jay Treaty: Political Battleground of the Founding Fathers* (Berkeley: University of California Press, 1970), 92–93. The British also considered taking steps to prevent "Kentucky, and all other Settlements now forming in the Interior parts of the Great Continent of North America, from becoming dependent on the Government of the United States . . . and to induce them to form Treaties of Commerce and Friendship with Great Britain" (Combs, 93).

28. Fuller, *The Purchase of Florida*, 48.

29. Quoted in French Ensor Chadwick, *The Relations of the United States and Spain: Diplomacy* (New York: C. Scribner's Sons, 1909), 36–37. On concern for the Union's integrity, see James E. Lewis, Jr., *The American Union and the Problem of Neighborhood: The United States and the Collapse of the Spanish Empire, 1783–1829* (Chapel Hill: University of North Carolina Press, 1998).

30. Bemis, *Jay's Treaty*, 183.

31. Kent L. Steckmesser, *The Westward Movement: A Short History* (New York: McGraw-Hill, 1968), 111.

32. Rossignol, *The Nationalist Ferment*, 7–8.

33. The alliance, concluded by the Treaty of Nogales (October 1793), committed the Cherokees, Chickasaws, Choctaws, and Creeks to "contribute . . . to the preservation of [Spain's] Dominion." Weber, *The Spanish Frontier*, 284.

34. Robert S. Allen, *His Majesty's Indian Allies; British Indian Policy in the Defence of Canada, 1774–1815* (Toronto: Dundurn, 1992), 68.

35. On these efforts, see Willig, *Restoring the Chain of Friendship*.

36. White, *The Middle Ground*, 448.

37. Rossignol, *The Nationalist Ferment*, 11.

38. Unless otherwise indicated, this and the following paragraph are based on Richard H. Kohn, *Eagle and Sword: The Federalists and the Creation of the Military Establishment in America, 1783–1802* (New York: Free Press, 1975), 91–127; Palmer, *1794*, 164–201; and Francis

Paul Prucha, *The Sword of the Republic: The United States Army on the Frontier, 1783–1846* (New York: Macmillan, 1969), 1–42.

39. Quoted in Palmer, *1794*, 172.

40. Palmer, *1794*, 195.

41. Dale Van Every, *Ark of Empire: The American Frontier, 1784–1803* (New York: Morrow, 1963), 234.

42. BNA, CO, 43/10, Colonial Office to Lord Dorchester, London, 8 January 1794.

43. The British foreign minister, Lord Grenville, instructed Hammond to "endeavour to negotiate such an accommodation . . . securing to the different Indian Nations along the British and American Frontiers, their Lands and hunting Grounds, as an independent Country." Grenville to Hammond, Whitehall, 17 March 1792, in Mayo, *Instructions to the British Ministers to the United States*, 25.

44. Samuel Flagg Bemis, *The American Secretaries of State and Their Diplomacy* (New York: Knopf, 1927–29), 2:30, quoted in Rossignol, *The Nationalist Ferment*, 13.

45. BNA, CO, 42/98, Lord Dorchester to Lieutenant-Governor Simcoe, Quebec, 26 April 1794.

46. White, *The Middle Ground*, 464–65.

47. Quoted in Van Every, *Ark of Empire*, 297–98. The speech was printed in American newspapers on 24 March 1794. Bowman, *The Struggle for Neutrality*, 145.

48. BNA, CO, 42/98, Lord Dorchester to Lieutenant-Governor Simcoe, 17 February 1794.

49. Ibid., 14 April 1794. The full quote warns of "the appearance of hostilities with our neighbours, which the intrigues and influence of France seem to render inevitable."

50. Allen, *His Majesty's Indian Allies*, 82.

51. Palmer, *1794*, 204–6.

52. This paragraph is based on Alan D. Gaff, *Bayonets in the Wilderness: Anthony Wayne's Legion in the Old Northwest* (Norman: University of Oklahoma Press, 2004); Kohn, *Eagle and Sword*, 139–57; Palmer, *1794*, 249–59; and Prucha, *The Sword of the Republic*, 18–42.

53. By this time, news of French military successes in Europe had begun to spread among Native Americans. This may have raised doubts in their minds about the extent to which Britain would commit to a conflict in North America. See note 58.

54. One historian estimates that the militia numbered two hundred. Dowd, *A Spirited Resistance*, 113.

55. This policy is laid out repeatedly in the various dispatches from the Colonial Office to the governor of Canada from 1791 through 1794. See BNA, CO, 43/10.

56. Willig, *Restoring the Chain of Friendship*, 243.

57. Quoted in Willig, *Restoring the Chain of Friendship*, 56.

58. White, *The Middle Ground*, 468.

59. Charles Marion Thomas, *American Neutrality in 1793: A Study in Cabinet Government* (New York: Columbia University Press, 1931), 49. The acrimonious exchanges over Dorchester's comments have been published in Manning, *Diplomatic Correspondence*.

60. Gouverneur Morris to Edmund Randolph, Sainport, 23 July 1794, in Manning, *Diplomatic Correspondence*, 421.

61. BNA, Foreign Office, 5/5, Grenville to Hammond, London, 15 July 1794.

62. BNA, CO, 43/10, Colonial Office to Lord Dorchester, 15 July 1794.

63. Ibid., Colonial Office to Lord Dorchester, 5 July 1794.

64. BNA, War Office, 1/14, Dorchester to Henry Dundas, Quebec, 4 September 1794. On Dorchester's resignation, see Bemis, *Jay's Treaty*, 320.

65. There are a number of comprehensive accounts of Jay's Treaty. The best are Bemis, *Jay's Treaty*, and Combs, *The Jay Treaty*.

66. The ease with which this concession was obtained surprised the American government. Even as it was being offered by Grenville in London, the secretary of state in Philadelphia was sadly admitting that he did "not entertain the most distant hope of the

surrender of the Western Posts." Edmund Randolph to James Monroe, United States minister to France, Philadelphia, 25 September 1794, in Manning, *Diplomatic Correspondence*, 84–85.

67. Unless otherwise indicated, the following discussion is based on Bemis, *Pinckney's Treaty*.

68. Bemis, *Pinckney's Treaty*, 194.

69. By the same treaty, Prussia withdrew from the war. By 1795, therefore, the war had come to resemble a replay of the American War of Independence in that the three second-tier naval powers of Europe—France, Holland, and Spain—had joined forces against the dominant maritime empire of the time—Great Britain. Realpolitik considerations of the most traditional sort, not just ideology, had clearly emerged as a major influence in the French Revolutionary War.

70. Horsman, *The Frontier*, 11.

71. James Monroe to Edmund Randolph, Paris, 12 February 1795, in Manning, *Diplomatic Correspondence*, 457.

72. Thomas P. Carnes (Georgia) to his constituents, Philadelphia, 2 May 1794, in *Circular Letters of Congressmen to Their Constituents, 1789–1829*, vol. 1, *First Congress–Ninth Congress, 1789–1807*, ed. Noble E. Cunningham, Jr. (Williamsburg, VA and Chapel Hill: University of North Carolina Press, 1978), 25–26.

11　Every Revolution Is a War of Independence

1. Roland Mortier, *Anacharsis Cloots ou l'utopie foudroyée* (Paris: Stock, 1995), 125–37.

2. Lynn Hunt, *Inventing Human Rights: A History* (New York: W. W. Norton, 2007).

3. Roger Dupuy, *La garde nationale, 1789–1792* (Paris: Folio.histoire/Gallimard, 2010), 85–96.

4. Arno Mayer showed how the revolutionary violence that broke out at the beginning of the process of change in 1789 is comprehensible only if understood in relation to another violence, that of the Counterrevolution. The Counterrevolution tried to present itself as a response, a riposte, a legitimate self-defense when the reality was that it preceded, gradually adapted to, and anticipated revolutionary violence. Arno Mayer, *The Furies: Violence and Terror in the French and Russian Revolutions* (Princeton, NJ: Princeton University Press, 2000).

5. Juan-Carlos Garavaglia and Jean-Frédéric Schaub, eds., *Lois, justice, coutumes: Amérique et Europe latines, 16e–19e siècle* (Paris: EHESS, 2005).

6. J.H. Elliott, *Empires of the Atlantic World: Britain and Spain in America, 1492–1830* (New Haven, CT: Yale University Press, 2006).

7. On the links between freedom and riches, see Bernard Cottret, *La Révolution américaine: La quête du bonheur, 1763–1787* (Paris: Perrin, 2003), chap. 1, 18–34.

8. Marcus Rediker, "Hydrarchy: Sailors, Pirates, and the Maritime State," in *The Many-Headed Hydra: Sailors, Slaves, Commoners, and the Secret History of the Revolutionary Atlantic*, ed. Marcus Rediker and Peter Linebaugh (Boston: Beacon Press, 2001), 143–73.

9. Robert Travers, "Imperial Revolutions and Global Repercussions: South Asia and the World (1750–1850)," in *The Age of Revolutions in Global Context, c. 1760–1840*, ed. David Armitage and Sanjay Subrahmanyam (New York: Palgrave Macmillan, 2010), 144–66.

10. Michel Vovelle, *La découverte de la politique: Géopolitique de la Révolution française* (Paris: La Découverte, 1992), especially "La Révolution vue d'en bas," 52–156. Viewed in this way, the counterrevolutionary crowds also participated in this politicization, a conclusion often rejected by despisers and advocates alike of the French Revolution. Roger Dupuy, *La politique du peuple: Racines, permanences et ambiguïtés du populisme* (Paris: Albin Michel, 2002).

11. Marc Belissa, *Fraternité universelle et intérêt national (1713–1795): Les cosmopolites du droit des gens* (Paris: Kimé, 1998), esp. 218–52.

12. Hannah Arendt, *Essai sur la Révolution* (Paris: Gallimard, 1967).

13. Patrice Higonnet, *Sisters Republics: The Origins of French and American Republicanism* (Cambridge, MA: Harvard University Press, 1988); and Pierre Serna, ed., *Républiques sœurs: Le Directoire et la Révolution atlantique* (Rennes: Presses Universitaires de Rennes, 2009), esp. 7–20.

14. Benjamin Stora, *La guerre des mémoires: La France face à son passé colonial* (La Tour d'Aigues: Éditions de l'Aube, 2007).

15. "La Révolution Batave: Péripéties d'une république-sœur (1795–1813)," special issue, *Annales historiques de la Révolution française* 326 (Oct.-Dec. 2001). Many of the articles evoke the memory of this glorious epoch of birth in revolt that was maintained in the Dutch Republic until the end of the eighteenth century.

16. Steven C. A. Pincus, *1688: The First Modern Revolution* (New Haven, CT: Yale University Press, 2009).

17. Gabrielle Randazzo, ed., *Guerre fratricide: Le guerre civili in età contemporanea* (Turin: Bollati Boringhieri, 1994).

18. Jacques Brissot remarked on this already in 1782 in his *Bibliothèque philosophique du législateur, du politique, du jurisconsulte* (Paris, 1782).

19. Voltaire, "Huitième lettre sur le Parlement," in *Les lettres philosophiques* (1734): "Ce qui devient une révolution en Angleterre n'est qu'une sédition dans les autres pays." He concludes that freedom was the goal of the English revolution, rather than the defense of privileges that motivated the revolts of elites in France. The quote can be found at http://www.voltaire-integral.com/Html/22/11_Lettre_08.html.

20. Gordon Wood, *The Creation of the American Republic, 1776–1787* (Chapel Hill: University of North Carolina Press, 1969).

21. Georges-Henri Dumont, *Histoire de la Belgique, des origines à 1830* (Brussels: Le Cri Édition, 1997).

22. Eric Golay, *Quand le peuple devint roi: Mouvement populaire, politique et Révolution à Genève, de 1789 à 1794* (Geneva: Edition Slatkine, 2001); and on later developments in the status of inhabitants of Switzerland, see Silvia Arlettaz, *Citoyens et étrangers sous la république helvétique, 1798–1803* (Geneva: Georg, 2005).

23. Michael Scott Christofferson, *French Intellectuals against the Left: The Antitotalitarian Moment of the 1970s* (New York: Berghahn Books, 2004).

24. Frédérique Leferme-Falguières, "Le fonctionnement de la cour de Versailles," *Hypothèses* 1 (1999): 207–18, http://www.cairn.info/revue-hypotheses-1999-1-page-207.htm.

25. On this possible coexistence, see Jean-François Chaney, *L'école républicaine et les petites patries* (Paris: Aubier, 1996).

26. Paul Cheney, *Revolutionary Commerce: Globalization and the French Monarchy* (Cambridge, MA: Harvard University Press, 2010).

27. Martyn Lyons, "Politics and Patois: The Linguistic Policy of The French Revolution," *Australian Journal of French Studies* 18, no. 3 (1981): 264.

28. Michel Antoine, *Louis XV* (Paris: Fayard 1989); and Patrice Gueniffey, *Le nombre et la raison: La Révolution française et les élections* (Paris: EHESS, 1993), 132–36.

29. Guy Saupin, *Histoire sociale du politique: Les villes de l'ouest atlantique français à l'époque moderne, XVIe–XVIIIe siècle* (Rennes: Presses Universitaires de Rennes, 2010).

30. Jean Nicolas, *La Rébellion française: Mouvements populaires et conscience sociale, 1661–1789* (Paris: Le Seuil, 2002), esp. 91–118.

31. Louis Sébastien Mercier, *Tableau de Paris* (Paris: Édition du Mercure de France, 1994), 2:260.

32. Ibid., 1:1273.

33. Sue Peabody, *"There are No Slaves in France": The Political Culture of Race and Slavery in the Ancien Régime* (New York: Oxford University Press, 1996); and Jean Ehrard, *Lumières et esclavage: L'esclavage colonial et l'opinion publique en France au xviii*e *siècle* (Brussels: André Versaille, 2008).

34. David A. Bell, *The Cult of the Nation in France: Inventing Nationalism, 1680–1820* (Cambridge, MA: Harvard University Press, 2001).

35. Keith Michael Baker, *Inventing the French Revolution: Essays on French Political Culture in the Eighteenth Century* (Cambridge: Cambridge University Press, 1990).

36. Pierre Serna, "Le noble," in *L'homme des Lumières*, ed. Michel Vovelle (Paris: Le Seuil, 1996), 39–93.

37. Camille Desmoulins, *Révolutions de France et de Brabant* (mid-November 1789).

38. Paolo Viola, *Il crollo del antico regime: Politica e antipolitica nella francia della rivoluzione* (Rome: Donzelli Editore, 1993), "Federazioni," 143–50.

39. Bronislaw Baczko, *Politiques de la Révolution française* (Paris: Folio/Gallimard, 2008), "Une passion thermidorienne: La revanche," 165–338.

40. Jacques Godechot, *Les institutions de la France sous la Révolution et l'Empire* (Paris: Presses Universitaires Françaises, 1968), 91–112.

41. *Mémoires de Monsieur le Comte de Montlosier sur la Révolution française: Le Consulat, l'Empire et la Restauration et les principaux événements qui l'ont suivie, 1755–1830* (Paris: Dufey, 1830), 348–50.

42. Marie-Vic Ozouf-Marignier, *La formation des départements: La représentation du territoire français à la fin du XVIIIe siècle* (Paris: EHESS, 1992), 79–105.

43. The American Federalists (not to be confused with the French federalists, since the Americans wanted a strong central state in order to contain the power of individual states) acted in the name of the country's defense and its good functioning to silence for two hundred years the popular democratic and anticentralizing movements opposed to the rewriting of the Constitution between 1787 and 1789. The situation was not the same, obviously, but the antidemocratic and unifying aspects are present in the United States, too.

Contributors

Rafe Blaufarb is Ben Weider Eminent Scholar and director of the Institute on Napoleon and the French Revolution at the Florida State University. He is the author of *The French Army, 1750-1820: Careers, Talent, Merit* (2002), *Bonapartists in the Borderlands: French Exiles and Refugees on the Gulf Coast, 1815–1835* (2005), and *The Politics of Fiscal Privilege in Provence, 1530s–1830s* (2012). He is currently writing a book on the naval dimension of the wars of Latin American independence.

Ian Coller is a lecturer in European history at La Trobe University. He is the author of *Arab France: Islam and the Making of Modern Europe, 1789–1831* (2010) as well as articles in the *Journal of World History* and *French Historical Studies*.

Denise Z. Davidson is associate professor of history at Georgia State University. She is the author of *France after Revolution: Urban Life, Gender, and the New Social Order* (2007) and with Anne Verjus, *Le roman conjugal: Chroniques de la vie familiale à l'époque de la Révolution et de l'Empire* (2011). She is currently writing a book that makes use of familial correspondence to discuss bourgeois families and their survival strategies during and after the French Revolution.

Suzanne Desan is the Vilas-Shinners Distinguished Achievement Professor of History at the University of Wisconsin-Madison. She is the author of *Reclaiming the Sacred: Lay Religion and Popular Politics in Revolutionary France* (1990) and *The Family on Trial in Revolutionary France* (2004), as well as editor with Jeffrey Merrick of *Family, Gender, and Law in Early Modern France* (2009). Currently, she is working on foreigners and foreign influences in revolutionary France.

Lynn Hunt is the Eugen Weber Professor of Modern European History at UCLA. She is the author most recently of *Inventing Human Rights* (2007), *Measuring Time, Making History* (2008), and with Margaret Jacob and Wijnand Mijnhardt, *The Book That Changed Europe* (2010).

Andrew Jainchill is associate professor of history at Queen's University. He is the author of *Reimagining Politics after the Terror: The Republican Origins of French Liberalism* (2008) as well as articles and essays in *French Historical Studies*, the *Journal of Modern History*, *Modern Intellectual History*, and *Annales Historiques de la Révolution Française*.

Michael Kwass is associate professor of history at Johns Hopkins University. He is author of *Privilege and the Politics of Taxation in Eighteenth-Century France: Liberté, Égalité, Fiscalité* (2000) as well as numerous articles on consumer culture in the age of the Enlightenment. He is currently completing a book on the legendary French smuggler Louis Mandrin.

William Max Nelson is assistant professor of history at the University of Toronto. He is the author of a book manuscript, *The Weapon of Time: Constructing the Future in France, 1750 to Year One*, and articles and essays that focus on the intellectual history of the Enlightenment in Europe and the Atlantic world, as well as the emergence of biopolitics and ideas of race in the eighteenth century.

Pierre Serna is professor at the Université Paris I Panthéon-Sorbonne and director of the Institut d'Histoire de la Révolution Française. He is the author of *Antonelle: Aristocrate révolutionnaire, 1747–1817* (1997), *La République des girouettes (1789–1815 et au-delà): Une anomalie politique; La France de l'extrême centre* (2005), and with Pascal Brioist and Hervé Drévillon, *Croiser le fer: Violence et culture de l'épée dans la France moderne, XVIe–XVIIIe siècle* (2002). Currently, he is working on the late eighteenth-century revolutions in a global context and the genesis of the republican phenomenon.

Miranda Spieler is associate professor of history at the University of Arizona and the author of *Empire and Underworld: Captivity in French Guiana* (2012). Her research focuses on the relationship between law and violence and the meaning of liberation in France and the colonies during the eighteenth and nineteenth centuries.

Charles Walton is associate professor of history at Yale University and associate scholar at the Institut d'Histoire de la Révolution Française at the

Université Paris I Panthéon-Sorbonne. His first book, *Policing Public Opinion in the French Revolution: The Culture of Calumny and the Problem of Free Speech* (2009), was awarded the Gaddis Smith International Book Prize by the MacMillan Center at Yale. He is the editor of *Into Print: Limits and Legacies of the Enlightenment*, a collection of essays in honor of Robert Darnton. He is currently writing a book about cultural reciprocity in the French Revolution.

Index

Abbema, Balthazar-Élie, 40
abolitionism
    asylum principle, 137–39, 142, 145–46
    Britain, 103–4
    feminism, connection with, 102, 104
    legislation, 106–7, 132, 134, 138, 142
    liberalism, effect of, 109–10
    London Society for the Abolition of the Slave
      Trade, 103
    Napoleon, role of, 109
    natural rights, concept of, 104, 106
    Revolutionary writers, 104–5, 109–10
    Society of the Friends of Blacks, 103–4
    United States, 103–4
    See also slavery
Account of Denmark, An, 62
Account of the Courts of Prussia and Hanover, An, 62
Adams, John, 61, 147
Adler, Jonathan, 157
Aelders, Etta Palm de, 105
agricultural production, 8, 25, 49–50, 79–84,
    142, 145
Alsace, 18–19, 80, 128, 166
Amar, Jean-Baptiste André, 106
American Revolution, 3, 33, 45, 47, 98, 147, 171–72
America's Advantage from Europe's Distress, 149
Amsterdam, 35, 41, 57, 60, 62, 119
Antoine, Michel, 176
Argenson, marquis de, 62–64, 67
Arnould, Ambroise-Marie, 52
Assembly of Notables, 32, 40, 42
Australia, 84
Austria, 34, 55, 88, 92, 100, 120, 173

Bahia, 143
Baker, Keith, 178
Balance of Trade Office, 52
Banco Nacional de San Carlos, 36–37, 40–41
Bank of England, 33–34
banking, 32–34, 36–42. *See also* fiscal crisis
bankruptcies, 32–33, 42, 49
Barére, Montagnard Bertrand de, 92
Barthélemy, François, marquis de, 47
Basczko, Bronislaw, 180
Basel, 119
Basire, Claude, 86, 93–94
Bastille, 28, 53, 115, 124
Batavian Republic, 119, 136–37, 158
Bayle, Pierre, 59, 69
Bayly, Christopher, 4, 117
Beccaria, Cesare, 26–27
Belgium, 3, 88, 98, 117, 119, 158
Belissa, Marc, 96, 118
Bemis, Samuel Flagg, 149
Bengal, 37
Benoist, Henri, 137
Benoist, Marie, 108
Bentham, Jeremy, 89, 92, 97, 99
Bergeron, Louis, 116
Bernard, Jacques, 59, 62
Bernard, Jean Frederic, 59–60
Bey, Ismael, 124
Bibliothèque britannique, 62
Bicêtre, 27
bills of exchange (*lettres de change*), 35–37
Blancard, Pierre, 37
Boislandry, François-Louis Legrand de, 54